Fantasies of the Other's Body in Middle English Oriental Romance

STUDIES IN ENGLISH MEDIEVAL LANGUAGE AND LITERATURE

Edited by Jacek Fisiak

Advisory Board:
John Anderson (Methoni, Greece), Ulrich Busse (Halle),
Olga Fischer (Amsterdam), Marcin Krygier (Poznań),
Roger Lass (Cape Town), Peter Lucas (Cambridge),
Donka Minkova (Los Angeles), Akio Oizumi (Kyoto),
Katherine O'Brien O'Keeffe (UC Berkeley, USA),
Matti Rissanen (Helsinki), Hans Sauer (Munich),
Liliana Sikorska (Poznań), Jeremy Smith (Glasgow),
Jerzy Wełna (Warsaw)

Vol. 40

Anna Czarnowus

Fantasies of the Other's Body in Middle English Oriental Romance

Bibliographic Information published by the Deutsche Nationalbibliothek
The Deutsche Nationalbibliothek lists this publication in the Deutsche Nationalbibliografie; detailed bibliographic data is available in the internet at http://dnb.d-nb.de.

This publication was financially supported
by the University of Silesia.

All publications in the series are peer reviewed.

Cover Design: © Olaf Glöckler, Atelier Platen, Friedberg

Library of Congress Cataloging-in-Publication Data
Czarnowus, Anna.
   Fantasies of the Other's Body in Middle English Oriental Romance / Anna Czarnowus.
      pages cm. — (Studies in English Medieval Language and Literature ; 40)
   Includes bibliographical references.
   ISBN 978-3-631-64446-1
   1. Romances, English—History and criticism. 2. English literature—Middle English, 1100-1500—History and criticism. 3. English philology—Middle English, 1100-1500. 4. Other (Philosophy) in literature. 5. Orientalism in literature. I. Title.
   PR321.C93 2013
   821'.109—dc23
                                                                  2013022668

ISSN 1436-7521
ISBN 978-3-631-64446-1 (Print)
E-ISBN 978-3-653-03119-5 (E-Book)
DOI 10.3726/978-3-653-03119-5

© Peter Lang GmbH
Internationaler Verlag der Wissenschaften
Frankfurt am Main 2013
All rights reserved.
Peter Lang Edition is an Imprint of Peter Lang GmbH.

Peter Lang – Frankfurt am Main · Bern · Bruxelles · New York · Oxford · Warszawa · Wien

All parts of this publication are protected by copyright. Any utilisation outside the strict limits of the copyright law, without the permission of the publisher, is forbidden and liable to prosecution. This applies in particular to reproductions, translations, microfilming, and storage and processing in electronic retrieval systems.

www.peterlang.de

Contents

Introduction 9

Chapter One
Ethnic difference and body marvellous:
the case of Chaucer's *Squire's tale* and *Sir Ferumbras* 37

Chapter Two
Community, *Richard le Coer de Lyon*, and chivalric anthropophagy 63

Chapter Three
Bodies enslaved in *Aucassin et Nicolete* and *Floris and Blancheflour* 95

Chapter Four
Black giantesses as communal flesh in the *Firumbras* romances 123

Chapter Five
Genealogy and desire in *King Horn* 153

Chapter Six
Transformation and regeneration in *Kyng Alisaunder*
and *The wars of Alexander* 177

Conclusion 207

References 211

*In memory of my father
Andrzej Majeranowski*

Introduction

> ". . . the history of a human body is not so much the history of its representations as of its modes of construction"
> (Michael Feher *Introduction* to *Fragments for a history of the human body*) (1989:11)

When investigating Middle English oriental romance, we need to remember that the Orient in the texts has to be separated from the real-life Orient as experienced in those times by some diplomatic envoys, travelers, merchants, and, obviously, crusaders. In the Middle English texts we are dealing with a uniform group of "Saracens", instead of a people who were diversified politically and also, to some extent, religiously (Beckett 2003:38). What is more, we must remember that at the time Europe itself was not entirely Christian and it did not uniformly belong to Christian culture. Here should be noted not only heathenism on such outskirts of Europe as Prussia or Lithuania, but also the existence of Arabic culture on the Iberian Peninsula and in Sicily, which, importantly, created a truly multicultural society, as it consisted of Berbers, Arabs, Mozarabs, neo-Muslims, and unconverted Christians and Jews (Beckett 2003:33). This society, speaking classical and colloquial Arabic, Latin, the four dialects of Romance Spanish (Castilian, Catalan, Galician, and Portuguese), Hebrew, and Mozarabic (*romance andalusi*), was highly diversified and relatively tolerant. Its representatives excelled in philosophy, science, translation, architecture, music, and literature, and their accomplishments influenced the Christian world.[1] The topic of the non-Christian identification of a considerable part of Europe, i.e. of a part of the Iberian Peninsula and of Sicily, has been noted by the scholars involved in the study of English literature at least in passing: one might mention the references to the crusades against pagans who also lived on the Iberian Peninsula in the *General prologue* to the *Canterbury tales* that the Knight participated in.[2] Fortunately, the state of

---

1 Lisa Lampert-Weissig names Ibn Gabirol, Ibn Hazm, Petrus Alfonso, Ibn Tufayl, Ibn Rushd (Averroës), Ghazzali, and Maimonides as the most notable representatives of those disciples in al-Andalus (2010:32).
2 Terry Jones included this historical context in his otherwise highly controversial ruminations on the Knight as a medieval mercenary who may have been modeled on the historical character of Sir John Hawkwood (1994:49-6).

research on, on the one hand, al-Andalus, which is what the Arabs called Muslim Spain, and its impact on the Christian European culture and, on the other, Sicily, is changing and shortly we will no longer be left with just María Rosa Menocal's fundamental study *The Arabic role in medieval literary history* and a few other titles which discuss the radiation of Arabic culture into the Christian one.[3] Even before Menocal's study, diverse historians noted the influence of al-Andalus on Christian culture, which resulted in the beginning of the idea called the age of Averroës, as Menocal notes (1987:2). Arabic learning, including both philosophy and what we might term proto-science, radiated into the Christian world (Menocal 1987:2), while literary texts by such authors as Provençal poets and Dante Alighieri bear marks of these writers having had access to, respectively, Arabic poetry and to *Kitāb al-mirāj*, the narrative about Allah's ascent to paradise (Menocal 1987:114-135). Even if the idea pronounced by Menocal, that "the Arab world has played a critical role in the making of the modern West" (1987:6), seems very powerful, it is not overstated. Even the deterioration of the Muslim culture due to historical conditioning did not make it insignificant in relations with the West. Importantly, medieval Christians misunderstood Islam, but not the culture of al-Andalus and the Arabic influences on European culture (Menocal 1987:37). Furthermore, the truth about the significance of al-Andalus should be acknowledged not only for the benefit of medieval studies, but for that of contemporary political discourse, as Lisa Lampert-Weissig argues (2010:14). After all, to quote Robert Bartlett, in the Middle Ages Muslims "were part of a wider world which easily matched the West in power, wealth and culture" (1993:296). It is a fact which cannot be underestimated these days.

In anticipation of our subsequent analyses, it has to be noted that the world discussed above, that of medieval Europe suffused with various cultural influences, shared little with the fictional world of Middle English oriental romance, a genre (or perhaps a mode, since the latter term is more all-inclusive) heavily laden with simplistic ideological messages. It cannot be argued, however, that only negative representations of the other may be found in those texts.[4] For example, the Emir's obsession with virginal slaves in *Floris and*

---

3 I refer, among other works, to the volume of articles edited by Suzanne Conklin Akbari and Karla Mallette, devoted to al-Andalus and to Sicily (forthcoming).
4 Unless indicated otherwise, the other will be primarily comprehended here as a construct whose existence has been established by Emmanuel Levinas in *Totality and infinity* (1969) and developed, among others, by Jacques Derrida (1991:11-48) rather than the narrower idea developed in various texts by Jacques Lacan (as the other and the Other), referring to the self and the feeling of lack this self experiences rather than to some entity

Blancheflour ends with his acknowledgement of the love between the two teenagers and his radical metamorphosis from a Muslim to a Christian able to wed them in church. Furthermore, Alexander the Great's proto-orientalism in Middle English romances occurs to be ultimately an attitude full of respect or even fascination. Perhaps then the rift that exists between those interpretations that focus on the negativity and those which emphasize the positive image of other cultures and their representatives should be healed. This study will attempt to remedy the situation by including some positive elements after the darker, prejudiced ones, because the latter are inevitable in a study devoted to the corporeality of cultural others. What is traceable in those texts, however, is that the mimetic principle is not followed in Middle English oriental romances, but the manner of representing others results from the writers' emotional attitude or the ideological import that they wanted to include in those literary texts. Furthermore, it needs to be emphasized that the negativity and positivity should not perhaps be seen as contrastive, but rather as two images mutually complementing each other, as it happens in the medieval Alexander romances. The tendencies of presenting the bodies of the others that were latent in the oriental romances should be analyzed in light of the above, but bearing in mind the intricacy of the image.[5] The crucial thing is to determine to what extent negativity or positivity were rules ordering the representations of the others' corporeality.

The eminent medievalist and historian of ideas Caroline Walker Bynum asks important questions about medieval corporeality in her article *Why all this fuss about the body? A medievalist perspective* (1995:1-33). The discussion of the topic starts with the questions posed by a friend of hers, a scholar who started to teach university courses in Central Europe in the early 1990s and suggested that her students should be given some food for thought about the idea of a pre-modern body. Bynum repeats after the anonymous friend that an idea originating long ago, such as that of a "medieval body", should not dissolve into language, but be investigated and explored as fairly material and the study should be made as concrete as possible. Our postulates here will be similar, but narrowed down to a specific idea: what is going to concern us here is the body of the other in Middle English texts, which likewise tends to dissolve into

---

representing cultural or ethnic differences; nevertheless, the idea of the Third that developed out of the Levinasian approach is not going to be dwelt on here.

5   Recently there has been published a collection of articles on the subject, *Contextualizing the Muslim Other in medieval Christian discourse* (Frakes 2011), which centred mostly on Muslims, or at least did not acknowledge the discussion of different cultural others in its title.

language, though it should be made more visible and studied in more detail. Bynum makes a number of noteworthy remarks about the functioning of the idea of a human body in the Middle Ages. She notes the Cartesian, hence relatively late, origin of the rigid boundary that supposedly separates the body from the soul,[6] questioning the allegedly perennial status of the dyad seen as two distinct phenomena and therefore undermining its applicability to medieval times (1995:6). She discards the theory that, unlike the modernity we live in, the Middle Ages had a fixed and immutable concept of the body or that human corporeality was despised then (1995:7). There existed diverse ideas of corporeality, including philosophical and theological ones which must have differed from the ones professed by the uneducated. As is argued by Michael Feher in the epigraph to the present introduction, we need to investigate how the body was constructed in the Middle Ages.

Multiple aspects of human corporeality, such as the post-ancient and medieval physiology, medieval *ars vivendi* and, more importantly, *ars moriendi*, the civilizing process and the function of deformity, the body as the microcosm and metaphors employing the image of the body have all been addressed by Jacques le Goff and Nicolas Trouong. In *Une histoire du corps au Moyen Âge* they argue that the history of the body should be studied in the light of two conflicting ideas of the Middle Ages, Gregory the Great's conviction that the soul needs a body, but bodies are disgusting in their sinfulness, and St Paul's concept that the body is the site of the Holy Spirit (2006:25). Furthermore, they contrast the ideas of the body as the outside (*foris*) and the soul as the inside (*intus*), with the former constantly inferior to the latter (2006:30). Here le Goff and Trouong impose on their readers the later dualist manner of thinking, since the matter was not so uncomplicated before the formation of dualism. Medieval thinkers did not have a dualist concept of the body, but in their discussions of human cognitive processes they employed a variety of terms concerned with knowing and seeing. Bynum indicates the threefold distinction into body (*corpus*), spirit (*animus* or *spiritus*), and soul (*anima*) and the consequent conviction that sense data, but also dreams and visions, are situated in *corpus* or in *spiritus*, not in *anima* (1995:13). If such was the idea, the body, including that of the other, must have been perceived as one consistent whole; it could not be expected to be seen in our modern manner, as a dichotomy of material corporeality and of the soul amalgamated with one's intellectual capabilities. Also the conversion process, so central to plots involving cultural others, must

---

6   Harry M. Bracken writes about the dualism that "the most fundamental reason Decartes radically distinguishes mind from body is that he finds no scientific way to explain mental phenomena" (1999:342).

have been understood differently, because it probably involved the body as well as *anima*, as the plots of such romances as the thirteenth-century *King of Tars* inform us, their modern readers.

The medieval idea of the body may seem to us rather inscrutable and disturbing in its otherness, especially if we adopt modern theories of writing about corporeality. Still, Bynum insists that it is "not only possible, it is imperative to use modern concepts when we confront the past" (1995:31). An adequate vehicle which could take us to the corpus of Middle English literature when the corporeality of the other appears and allow us to probe into it from our modern perspective could be a discipline called anthropology of the body. John Blacking describes it as a theory "concerned with the interface between the body and society, the ways in which physical organism constrains and inspires patterns of social interaction and the intervention of culture" (1977:v). Naturally, in medieval literature what may interact with the society is not a physical organism, but rather an imaginary construct labeled as the body of the other. The problem of whether that body interacts with the surrounding world and if it does, how the interaction takes place, needs to be addressed. Customarily anthropology of the body as a scholarly discipline involves also diverse types of psychoanalysis, because knowledge of the psyche is accessed in it through what happens to the body.[7] This type of anthropology assumes that the two are inextricably interrelated and one cannot be detached from the other. A partial application of the developments of psychoanalysis should not be found out of place in our investigation of bodies. As for the somehow limited interaction between the body and its surroundings, even if the interaction occurs, it might be limited to certain spheres, while other ones remain inaccessible. Then we should ask ourselves the question to what extent the physicality of others imposes constraints on the otherwise possible contacts between them and the world and how their corporeality interacts with the social world surrounding it, particularly the social world of the West in the oriental romances under scrutiny.[8]

The above cannot, however, be accomplished without historicizing the corporeality marked by alterity. In their introduction to *Thinking the limits of the*

---

[7] Other theoretical approaches which undoubtedly include at least elements of anthropology of the body are gender studies, disability studies, and the history of ideas.

[8] In the modern world interactions between the body and the world surrounding it and, more importantly, the idea of body consciousness have been explored in Richard Shusterman's study of somaesthetics, *Body consciousness: a philosophy of mindfulness and somaesthetics* (2008); in the *Preface to the Polish edition* he explains that he uses the term *soma* in order to escape from the term "body" with its dualistic soul and "flesh", associated with the Eucharist and with the fleshiness of the human (Shusterman 2010:7).

body, Jeffrey Jerome Cohen and Gail Weiss remark that human body wrongly appears to be an entity functioning on its own, "singular, atemporal, and therefore unmarked by history" (2009:1), detached from any historical and cultural contexts. Nevertheless, we should be well aware of the necessity of analyzing those contexts in any study of medieval romance, as the title of Rhiannon Purdie and Michael Cichon's recent collection of studies devoted to Middle English popular romances, *Medieval romance, medieval contexts*, suggests (2011). The body, including that of the other, is never entirely singular and therefore self-sufficient, atemporal, and unaffected by history. Especially historical romance, such as *Richard le Coer de Lyon*, calls for an investigation from the point of view of historical (or rather mainly pseudo-historical) events it represents. The body of the other becomes there a subject of colonizing policies and it is extensively controlled in order to keep it at a distance. It is purposefully externalized and the control extends to the manner in which we see it. In her study of the early modern scientific approaches to human body, *Muzeum ludzkich ciał [Museum of human bodies]*, Anna Wieczorkiewicz emphasizes not only the control to which a human body can be subjected in a Foucauldian way, but also the control of its image which is exercised by looking at it. She maintains that the act of looking at the body should be problematized (2000:6), which is supported by such scholars as Michael Camille, who discusses the medieval body as the object of public gaze (1994:73). Those various types of control demonstrate the complexity of strategies in which a body can be dealt with, especially in the case of the other's corporality.

Contrary to what has once been deemed to be true by sociologists, the human body is not only a natural and pre-social construct, but also a social one. Bryan S. Turner's sociology of the body put a stop to this thinking, employing sociology in order to understand the everyday life. In what he termed a "somatic society", a body becomes the site of political and cultural activities, which renders it important for the identity formation of an individual (2006:224). Modern Western societies tend to be Turner's somatic ones, where bodies are central and troubled, hence the problems issuing from the very fact of corporeality have to be solved. It remains highly questionable whether medieval societies were similarly body-oriented. Oriental romances imply that it could at least partly be true, since the bodies of others determine their identity and they are as much political and cultural constructs as they are material, biological ones. Still, romances remain merely texts and there might not be a direct connection between them and the external contemporary reality. As a result, it is safer to limit ourselves to investigating the functioning of the other's corporeality in those texts. Consequently, the societies depicted in oriental romances may be diagnosed as somatic: bodies become social and cultural agents there, often determining the identity of an individual, to name only the example of Saracen (and often black-skinned) giants from those romances whose plots originated from *chansons de geste* and which were often translations or travesties of that type of epic. There identification on the basis of the body and the psychological image appears fairly consistent. After all, if we argue after Sachi Shimomura that in the medieval world the body was a site of identity, this appears even truer in the case of bodies in literary texts (2006:76). In oriental romances the identity of the others is frequently constructed as a reverse image of the identity of Westerners characterized as representing "the same". The corporeality marked with cultural and ethnic alterity must by necessity connote those qualities which are completely different from those that "the same" attribute to themselves. Negativity may become the principle dominating the description, both physical and psychological, of the others. Both the body and the psychology of those others would therefore be predetermined by the ideological goal that the authors of oriental romances aimed at. As is shown by the example of the alleged Saracen idolatry evoked by, among others, by Akbari, the ideological purpose of downgrading the political enemy was continually stronger than any urge to present Islam and its believers as they really were. For instance, Akbari's textual sources prove that the theme of Saracen idolatry was almost omnipresent: she quotes from *Chanson de Roland, Jeu de saint Nicolas, Sowdone of Babylone*, and *Mary Magdalen* to show that the accusation of Muslim rulers and warriors praying to Mahoun, Terguant, and Apollo in the manner of polytheist idolatrers, was frequent (1998-99:9-27). Katharine Scarfe Beckett adds worship of Venus and/or stone-worship to the list of medieval convictions about Saracen religion (2003:212-217).

There has existed a widespread conviction that the body has to be viewed as an ideological construct. Diverse ideologies projected their systems of thought onto a human body, forcing the real-life physical bodies to adjust themselves to the expectations issued towards them. These have been the technologies of the self, as Michel Foucault named them, which require the body to adapt itself to the identity that it claims it is endowed with. The European Middle Ages, which was, after all, primarily a religion-dominated era, developed a wide range of Christian theories inextricably linked with human corporeality, among which we might mention only the doctrine of transubstantiation which gave rise to one of the decisive arguments in favour of the break with Rome in a later epoch, during the reformation. The various ideologies, pre-modern and modern, standing behind a representation of the body should therefore be inspected, as the author of the study *Religion and the body*, Sarah Coakley, highlights (1997:4). From the perspective of another French philosopher, Jean-Luc Nancy, it would be best to keep silent about the body, perhaps because there exist so many facets and images of it that the body as it is constantly eludes us (2002:52). Even in its religious dimension in the Middle Ages the wealth of texts and approaches is so considerable that no one uniform perspective on the body could ever emerge from them. Still, Nancy develops the paradox that it is impossible to discuss the human body, but it remains equally impossible to keep silent about it (2002:52). Using as a source French philosophy again, perhaps the primary question that has to be asked when referring to the human body could be Gilles Deleuze's "What can a body do?", denoting the power of action that he relates to Spinoza's theory of affections (1992:218). In the case of the cultural others of Middle English oriental romance the question is that about the body's potentialities and capabilities, as Judith Butler narrowed down the topic of Deleuze's scrutiny when she was interviewed about the human body in the film *Examined life* (Taylor 2008). In the oriental romances in question it is always arguable whether the bodies of the others may ever be deemed truly beautiful if they are culturally different and whether conversion to Christianity changes both that physicality and the Western perspective on it. It also becomes debatable in those texts to what extent slavery, an institution which in real life existed both in the East and in Western Europe, could mark the identity of a culturally different person, what position towards the Western self the other needs to adopt if those who are culturally different remain externalized, and what happens to desire once "the same" is exiled and turns into the other in a geographically different place. As well, it is controversial to what extent the self may change on contact with the other.

It definitely cannot, however, be argued that those numerous potentialities and capabilities of the other, or the lack thereof under some circumstances, reflect the realistic position of live people, the ethnic and cultural others who once stayed, even temporarily, in medieval Western Europe. What Derek Brewer elaborated on as the "mimetic fallacy", the attitude modern readers should be wary of when analyzing medieval romances, should be eliminated from our way of thinking. According to Brewer the assumption that actions, people and things can and should be closely imitated in words should be dropped, as it limits our correct understanding of the nature of medieval romance (1988:1). Brewer's thinking, which ultimately detaches medieval romance, including oriental, from the reality of the epoch, facilitates our cognition of the world of this fiction. Perhaps oriental romance cannot, after all, be interpreted as a direct reflection of some real position of Muslims and other culturally different peoples in medieval Europe. When reading those characters as purely fictional, we do not have to investigate the influence of Arabic culture and the historical relationships between Christians and representatives of other cultures. Nor is it necessary to argue to what extent Arabic literature projected its impact onto those Western texts, because the relation between Arabic literature and Middle English romance is very subtle. It is rather the influence on plots rather than on the manner in which characters or historical contexts are presented. Oriental romance that we will be dealing with here belongs, after all, to popular literature, which tends to simplify various ideas.

Obviously, there exist studies where the relationship between the culturally different literary characters and their historical equivalents is inspected. Vincent DiMarco writes about the Mongol world in Chaucer's times and before them, treating his *Squire's tale* as a point of departure (2002:56-65): various critics discussing *Richard le Coer de Lyon* mention the historical Saracens whom he confronted (Ambrisco 1999:499-528; Heng 2003:63-113; Akbari 2005:198-230; Yeager 2008:48-77); and Kathleen Coyne Kelly (1994:101-110) places Blancheflour's slavery in the context of medieval slave trade and thralldom. In *King Horn* the association between the Muslim invaders and the real Muslims has been dealt with by Dorothee Metlitzki (1977:120), Norman Daniel (1984:290), and W.R.J. Barron (1987:65), who all comment that the Saracens in this romance are disturbingly "real". Even if we note the purely fictional constituents of those representations, the literary images should be treated seriously, because their authors presented them in such a way. The opinion was expressed most famously by Metlitzki, who claimed that

> The Saracens are treated seriously in the *chansons de geste*. They are a crucial public theme – political, military, and religious – and what is fanciful in them is made deliberately so for purposes of patriotism, propaganda, and entertainment. In this there is no difference between medieval epic and romance (1977:119).

Oriental romances provide us with a perspective on Saracens as representatives of a well-developed culture, as a religious and political threat, and as people who are ethnically different from Europeans. Nevertheless, it could just as well be argued that Metlitzki's "foil and wonder" (1977:119) that Saracens supply to the Western audience in epic and romance dominates the message of most of those texts, making their historicity somewhat questionable. Wonder is included even more in romance than in epic, hence, quite unsurprisingly, romance transforms the historical others into the fictional ones with more subtlety and consequently it does it more definitely. After all, as Fredric Jameson importantly noted about the relationship between the reality and fiction in romance, "romance [is] a process of *transforming* ordinary reality" (1981:110). The transformation of confrontations and encounters with the others must have been an even more convoluted process, since the real confrontations were mostly military and only rarely diplomatic and the ordinary life encounters haphazard and already tinted with the negative perspective which was customarily adopted by Westerners. To exemplify the attitude with an idea concerning corporeality, in the Middle Ages the concept of an ethnically different body was such that corporeality was expected to reflect the inner otherness very clearly. According to Akbari, the physical bodies of Jews and Muslims were thought to be different by Westerners (2009:140-154). The inner difference was therefore expected to be ostensible: it was inscribed in the flesh and consequently very clearly visible in it. As Steven F. Kruger puts it,

> Appeals to the body's debility in the construction of otherness attempt to institute ontological differences among human beings at the level of "the natural"; they underpin the claims that such distinctions are not arbitrary but rather inscribed in the flesh, there for "anyone" to see and feel – especially as revulsion or disgust (1995:4).

The real-life contacts were then indelibly marked with the usually negative ideological approach adopted by Westerners, who could not savour the superiority of "Orientals" in various spheres of culture and science, such as philosophy, historiography, astronomy, or medicine, to mention only the disciplines discussed by Menocal (1987). This led to questioning the Eastern lifestyle and mental attitudes, but primarily to criticizing what was the easiest to criticize, physicality. The military, but mainly the cultural weakness of Europe produced negative images of Muslims, as David R. Blanks and Michael Frassetto argue (1999:3). Thomas Hahn insists that fictional Saracens had nothing in common with the historical ones (2001:35), confirming that there must have existed an ideological motivation for inventing that twisted image.

The oriental romances that will be of interest to us here cannot be put into one uniform category according to diverse previous divisions of Middle English romances. The first division of romances obviously comes from the twelfth-century cleric Jean Bodel, who discussed all romances as representing the famous three *matières*, "de France, et de Bretagne, et de Rome le grant". Metlitzki added "the matter of Araby" to the three "matters" above (1977), while Carol F. Heffernan enumerated, among others, "English and Germanic" and "Charlemagne" romances, treating such cyclical plots as the Constance-saga as separate (2003:4). The romances that will be the ground for our investigation here may usually be counted as either the "English and Germanic" or "Charlemagne" texts, apart from some of them indubitably being "of Araby", such as *Floire and Blancheflour*, while French *Aucassin et Nicolete*, whose interpretation here accompanies that of *Floire*, is not a romance at all, but introduces similar concerns within its plot as the Middle English romance and expands the issue of slavery to include the idea that also Muslims could be subjected to this institution in Europe. The famous category of "the matter of Araby" that Metlizki coined is, however, wider than the domain of romances about the Orient. She divided her study into to parts, "Scientific and Philosophical Learning" and the "Literary Heritage", and in the latter section discussed a selection of texts termed as "Arabian Source Books", "History and Romance", and *The travels of sir John de Mandeville*. The other literary texts are *The song of Roland*, the English Charlemagne romances, *Sir Beues of Hamtoun*, *King Horn*, *King of Tars*, *Digenes Acrites*, *The Man of Law's tale*, *Floris and Blancheflur*, Langland's *Piers Plowman*, and *The Land of Cockayne*. As can be seen from the selection, she does not discuss only romances, but rather searches for the influences of Arabic culture in a variety of genres. As a result, her "Matter of Araby" are various texts and their choice is not representative, but depends on the subject matter she intends to discuss. Here we are not going to provide the readers with a discussion of all Middle English texts about Saracens, Mongols, and Indians. We will limit ourselves only to romances, but this study will not cover all the Middle English romances with oriental elements. Since the body remains in the focus of our attention here, only certain texts will be analyzed here and not others, perhaps to the disadvantage of this discussion, but we cannot even aspire to all-inclusiveness here.

What will be called "oriental romances" here are texts that are set in the Orient or at least involve "oriental" characters whose ethnic identity is quite important for the plot. The romances do not necessarily have to be related to Arabic sources in any way. What is more crucial in them is the phenomenon of otherness and the treatment thereof by the author or what we, early twenty-first century readers, may read out of these texts in this matter. Unfortunately, the scope of this book did not allow me to include such examples of this subgenre as *Otuel and Roland* and *The sege of Melayne*. Nevertheless, they discuss externalization of the others and violence against them in a manner similar to what is analyzed below in other English Charlemagne romances. The plot of the penitential *Guy of Warwick* does not tie up with our discussion of corporeality of the other, so it is not included here, either. What further complicates our discussion is the multiplicity of Orients in Middle English literature. For instance, in *Guy of Warwick* the Orient which is more hostile and threatening is the Byzantine world of treachery and intrigues.[9] To sum up, the texts presented here have been chosen because they include some discussion of the other's corporeality and the lack of references to other romances does not mean that they cannot be classified as oriental ones. Oriental romances can be criticized for presenting a rather fixed image of the Orient instead of clearly distinguishing between the Muslim and the Christian one or accounting for the historical and cultural changes dynamically

---

9   See Wilcox's "Greeks and Saracens in *Guy of Warwick*" (2004:217-240).

happening in those parts of the world. As mostly popular texts they include stereotypes rather than try to reflect some aspects of the reality. It is controversial whether Eastern images of the West were equally biased. The sources where we can find them, such as Anna Comnena's *The Alexiad* or the Muslim accounts of Crusaders' activities, cannot be compared with the fictitious oriental romances produced by Westerners. Nevertheless, images of Franks that can be found there tend to be negative. Anna Comnena despises Latins (Sewter 1969:14) and describes at least some of them as "villainous characters" (Sewter 1969:311), since "the Latin race at all times is usually greedy for money" (Sewter 1969:312) and they conduct their conquests with "the usual Latin arrogance" (Sewter 1969:313). Muslims feared and loathed Franks as well, as Amin Maalouf consistently argues in *The crusades through Arab eyes* (1984).[10] Obviously, it can neither be stated that all Franks could be dangerous nor that crusaders were representatives of all Westerners, but such was the lasting vision that people in the East had.

The applicability of the word "romance" to what we will customarily call here "oriental romances" and not only their categorization is questionable. What Barry Windeatt claimed about romance in the context of *Troilus and Cresseide* tends to be repeated also in other sources which attempt to define the genre: the "medieval romance typically concerns itself with the idealized adventures of knights in chivalry and love, within a world open to the marvellous" (1988:129). The texts we will interpret here do not very frequently deal with love, or, if they do, the love interest remains rather marginal. Sometimes, like the unfinished *Squire's Tale*, they only suggest the topic of love very subtly. Yet for Windeatt the quest and supernatural elements appear to be more decisive in describing the genre than love or absence thereof, because he cites "romance of marvels and adventures which the Squire begins" (1988:130). Such previous attempts to define romance as a genre which were made by, for instance, Windeatt, were recently summarized by Raluca L. Radulescu, who evoked A.S.G. Edwards' judgment that the term "romance" is very elastic in Middle English literature (Edwards 1990:159, quoted in Radulescu 2009:33). As a result, the diagnosis that medieval generic categories tend to be elastic should perhaps be extended to Middle English oriental romance, and it could only be suggested that what

---

10 Maalouf's historiographic vision can be complemented by what Tariq Ali writes in his novel *The book of Saladin*, the second in a quintet of novels, where he mentions the crusaders as a primitive "Franj beast" (Ali 1998:202) which is difficult to tame when it desecrates Muslim holy places and murders the innocent; Richard the Lionheart is here called Richard the Lion-Arse and the lion, as the Muslim characters observe, "is not the most cultured amongst Allah's creations" (Ali 1998:352).

makes a romance "oriental" may be the characters involved in it, the setting, or even some subplots involving Orientals, such as the Saracen invasion in *King Horn*. In *Horn*, however, this subplot does not play a secondary role since it makes the text a discourse on sameness and otherness and on the desire incumbent on it. Nonetheless, even if the convenient label "oriental romance" may seem so ample that the use of the term is debatable in the case of some narratives discussed here, the term "popular romance" tends to be applied to almost all of them.

In studies of popular romance the question of the possible audience has often been raised. The serious argument over its readership entered scholarly discourse with Derek Pearsall's classic *Development of Middle English romance*, where he defined popular romance as ostensibly a low-culture genre aimed at a lower-class audience: "The audience of the Middle English romances is primarily a lower or lower-middle-class audience, a class of social aspirants who wish to be entertained with what they consider to be the same fare, but in English, as their social betters. It is a new class, an emergent bourgeoisie" (1988:12). Still, it cannot be argued that only those people who did not represent the upper or upper-middle class were the actual and not only the intended recipients of those texts. In contrast to what has been argued in Bakhtin's *Rabelais and his world*, it could be postulated after Richard M. Berrong that audiences belonging to higher social classes not only had access to popular literature and culture, but they also used this opportunity and participated in popular culture, as the difference between the lowly and the elitist was not so firm as it later became, in the early modern period. Berrong's example of the oncoming exclusion of popular culture is Rabelais' *Gargantua* (1986:21). Popular romance could therefore be popular only in terms of its form and content, but not in terms of the audience, who actually originated from various social spheres. The question of who the authors of popular romance were has been even more vehemently debated. In *A historical introduction* to *The spirit of medieval English popular romance*, Ad Putter insists that there exist two concurrent theories of authorship, which he calls the "romantic" and the "revisionist" ones. The romantic theory, originating in the epoch when philology was developing as a scholarly discipline, the eighteenth and nineteenth centuries, assumes that, as Putter summarizes it, "popular romances are the improvised compositions of minstrels. They are recited at feasts and festivals, intended for the ears of ordinary folk, for the 'people' (whence the designation of 'popular' romances)" (2000:3). The traditional idea of popular romance combines the belief in non-professional authorship with the conviction that those romances were "popular" because they were not only addressed to, but also listened to, by lower-class people. The alternative theory, which may sound more convincing to the modern ear, assumes the importance of hack-writers who not only gathered popular romances in such manuscripts as the Auchinleck MS, but also composed them before "anthologizing" them there. Writes Putter: "So-called popular romances were composed and copied for the amusement and edification of the newly literate classes – not the lower orders, but the gentry and the prosperous middle classes who formed the market for the trade in vernacular books in the later medieval period" (2000:3). "Popular romance" makes an equally convenient label for diverse texts as "romance" usually does. To simplify matters, perhaps we could argue after Lee C. Ramsey that a romance is always a popular romance due to both the contents, customarily involving the topics that could be engrossing for wide audiences, and, in the later Middle Ages, to the readership (1983:5). The thesis above was explained by Edmund Reiss, who argued: "Just as the audiences of these romances did not consist of common people alone, so it was not composed solely of courtiers . . . A successful romance would have had to appeal to many different kinds of people, including both 'the learned and the lewed'" (1986:110). This appears even truer if one understands the phenomenon of the previous centuries, i.e. the actual audiences of Anglo-Saxon literature, which was recited not only in front of the high-born, but also probably in the presence of such illiterate people as Caedmon, who participated in the drinking parties.[11]

All of the romances we are going to analyze here were successful in that they were preserved in many copies. There were concurrent versions of them, sometimes not only in other languages, but in Middle English as well, and some of them even entered the *imaginarium* of both medieval and modern culture, to take only the title characters of *Floris and Blancheflour* as a stock image of star-crossed lovers, hence the more fortunate predecessors of Romeo and Juliet. Naturally, according to rigid classificatory systems *Floris* could not be counted as a popular romance due to a possible difference between its intended audience and what the usual audiences of popular romances were. Argues Pearsall,

. . . romances [such as *Floris and Blancheflour*] are markedly more urbane and delicate than [such romances as *Richard le Coer de Lyon*] and were designed for a somewhat more sophisticated stratum of the audience, perhaps for women. They deal less in battle, more in love and the supernatural, and the narratives are shaped to a purpose (1988:22).

Neither of the two types, a courtly romance about love or a historical romance about warfare, needs to be read as dominating the category of romance. Reiss

---

11 Barbara Kowalik elaborates on those more realistic hypotheses of the circumstances in which *Caedmon's hymn* was composed in *Betwixt "Engelaunde" and" englene londe": dialogic poetics in early English religious lyric* (2010:99).

even argues that "romance" functioned as such an umbrella term that it combined romances "epic and historical, . . . exemplary, . . . saints' lives . . . , folktales, and ballads" (1986:109). What Reiss suggests is an expansion of the term or rather an acknowledgment of the medieval tendency "that a romance is a purposeful mix of these and other forms" (1986:109). No judgment about the quality of such a mongrel form is passed by Reiss; he rather treats the heterogeneity as typical of medieval literary texts, especially poetic ones.

In his 1988 article Pearsall discussed popular romance as a rather marginal form and argued that what made it non-noble were both the lower-class readership and the authorship. In his recent article *The pleasure of popular romance: a prefatory essay*, introducing the collection *Medieval romance, medieval contexts*, Pearsall at least partly withdraws those opinions, writing about popular romances as "not a special case", because "they are the hard core of medieval narrative poetry" (2011:11). The issue of who their audiences were proves to be for Pearsall not as important as the pleasure that they must have derived from those plots, which implies that the narrative could provoke pleasure in members of various social classes. What evoked that sensation could be the swift action almost without digressions, the simple division into black and white characters (which is, however, going to be complicated in our divagations on the double standards adopted in the treatment of ethnic others), and the easiness with which the anonymous authors introduced ideological messages into fairly simple plots. Even when conversion happens and the culturally different characters get politically involved on the side of the Westerners, they are continually extenalized, at least to a certain extent. The idea that the others cannot change their identification into "the same" once and for all seems to be the usual message of these romances.

In the popular romances which we will explore here we are rather going to concentrate on what Radulescu and Ashton defined as "disturbing images", which here involve the negativity with which cultural others tend to be treated (2009:3). Naturally, it cannot be said that all images of Orientals are constructed in this way in Middle English romances, but when probing into the question of how their bodies have been shown there, it appears that negativity is the predominating principle of their presentation. The images of the others' bodies tend to be really disturbing; if any of this difference starts to characterize Westerners, their bodies become equally disturbing. It appears that corporeality marked by alterity has to be visualized as a disquieting image in those narratives, or at least an image that raises questions as to what that different physicality denotes for Westerners. All those who are not Christian are represented as heathens who, even if righteous, pose interpretative problems since their existence needs to be accounted for as a part of some divine plan. In order to comprehend their imagined role in the Occident they were usually included in the unusually in the broad category of "Saracens". Metlitzki once argued that the group encompassed diverse identifications. Writes Metlitzki,

> The people who contributed to the formation of what, in the Middle Ages, was known as "Saracen" culture were of the most varied origin. They were Greeks, Persians, Indians, Copts, Nestorians, Zoroastrians, and Jews, whole populations living in a vast expanse of territories extending from the Indian Ocean to the Atlantic which the spread of Islam from the heart of the Arabian peninsula had engulfed with lightning speed (1977:3).

The label turned out to be so convenient that it became attached to various peoples not related to Islam, but associated with it in what we could term a variety of medieval orientalism, understood as a strategy of "orientalizing" those who were different both religiously, which appears to have counted the most, or culturally. For instance during encounters with Nestorians in Asia the hope was cherished that they were almost as Christian as Westerners; still, they could not be judged to be culturally the same.[12] Metlitzki's perspective thus goes beyond the purely linguistic and etymological aspects of the use of "Saracen". In his investigation of *chansons de geste* Daniel pinpoints the denotation of the term in academic and historical writing, which according to him was "Arab" or "Muslim", or both, depending on the context (1984:8). Such usage demonstrates that culture and religion were amalgamated in determining one's identity and even though religious identification must have played a considerable role in it, with time cultural identity began to be included as well. What ensued was a more specific ethnic identification: as Daniel insists, in the Renaissance "'Saracen' in the sense of 'Muslim' gave place to 'Turk' with the rise of the Ottoman" (1984:8). To specify those linguistic considerations, the etymology of the word could be evoked. According to the *Oxford English dictionary*, the term "Saracen" entered the vocabulary of medieval Europe from the discourse of the Roman Empire, where it had denoted the nomadic Arab peoples who sowed confusion in the Middle East. Phillipe Sénak finds the probable origin of the word in the Greek *sarakenos* (1983:14, quoted in Ramey 2001:8). In medieval times "Saracen" meant "Arab, Turk, Muslim, or simply non-Christian, heathen, or pagan, unbeliever or infidel", Elizabeth Fowler tells us in her study *The romance hypothetical: romance and the Saracens in "Sir Isumbras"* (2009:98).

---

12 Akbari notes that the premodern discourse on East Asia differed from the medieval attitudes to Islam (2009:11); nonetheless, despite the futile hope that Christianity flourished also in Asia and it could develop into allegiance to the Pope of Rome, alterity that stemmed from a different culture and religion dominated the literary images of Asians as well.

Beckett in turn argues that the etymology remains obscure and it probably arose from a Nabatean Arabic term for nomads living in the East, with its Arabic root meaning "east" or "marauder". It either originated from a tribal name or a place name (2003:93). The term *Saraceni* was firstly adopted from the Greek by Latin writers in the second century AD and referred to the nomads of northern Arabia (Beckett 2003:93). Importantly, settled Romans and Christian Arabs were also termed *Arabes* at the time.[13] Even the etymology of the word then implies its non-determinate designation.

The term "oriental", which we will apply to romances here if they involve Eastern setting, characters, or subplots, may be viewed as an equally convenient term as "Saracen". In medieval Europe the idea of the Orient was fairly specific, but it differed from the modern understanding of the word. In *The Orient in Chaucer and the oriental romance* Heffernan indicates North Africa and the Near and Middle East as its cultural location, making our discussion of race as a term having "oriental" associations highly relevant if Africans were included within the bounds of "medieval orientalism" (2003:2). It needs to be said that at times the texts in question are more "oriental" in nature than they are "romances". Both Metlitzki and Heffernan univocally term those narratives in verse "oriental romances", but the former emphasizes the fact that "the Middle English romances that depict the military confrontations of Christians and Saracens . . . barely fit the definition of romances" (1977:160). The rationale behind the terminology remains generic: if their plots directly derive from *chansons de geste*, the texts are closer to epic than to courtly romance. Nevertheless, even the romances which involve a lot of fighting between the two warring factions very often include a vision of Saracen identity and corporeality, so they need to concern us here. The topic of conversion in itself which emerges as a significant thematic strain there entails divagations about the possible changes to the other's body that result from baptism, which has been suggested by Siobhain Bly Calkin (2011:105-119).

One question which needs to be inspected in depth is whether oriental romances include what Edward Said termed "the reductive formulae", which according to him limit representations of the Orient in those texts to pure negativity, and to what extent we may rely here on what the critic is writing about orientalism (1994:xxiii). The negativity introduced by Said into analyses of the Western manner of thinking about the Orient has been thought by many to

---

13 Beckett also notes that the Christian etymology of the term *Saracen* came second and derived the group from Ishmael, the biblical son of Abraham by the slavewoman Hagar, who was cast out into the desert once Sarah bore Isaac (2003:94).

be the only principle ordering such images.[14] After all, as Said claims, "the Orient has helped to define Europe (and the West) as its contrasting image, idea, personality, experience" (1994:1) and advised his readers "to study Orientalism as a dynamic exchange between individual writers and large political concerns shaped by the three great empires – British, French, American" (1994:14). This line of thinking about representations of the Orient as negative is continued by various scholars, including those who probe into the medieval and early modern period. Introducing the subject, David R. Blanks and Michael Frassetto openly confront their readers with the thesis that the Western image of the Orient is "a photographic negative of the self-perception of an ideal Christian self" (1999:3). Lynn Tarte Ramey restates this concept in her discussion of *chansons de geste*, when she comments: "The Saracen is often (though not always) seen as the complete opposite of the Christian, Western, French self: to say 'Saracen' is in essence to say 'evil'" (2001:3). This appears to be a development of Said's idea, even if Blanks distances himself from such a simplistic perspective in an article published in the collection *Western views of Islam in medieval and early modern Europe*, where he states that "it is easy to overemphasize the role of such works as the *chansons de geste* or the anti-Turkish broadsides of the sixteenth century in the establishment of European public opinion" (1999:38), and he puts forward the suggestion that the image of Saracens was much more varied. Even though for Blanks *chansons de geste* involve a highly negative image of Eastern others, hence we may assume the same to be true in those oriental romances where plots from the French epic are translated, he distances himself from the idea that the negative image prevailed in the shaping of the image of the Orient in Western culture. He would rather see it as a multidimensional image, neither an entirely disparaging nor a fully affirmative one that would testify to openness towards and tolerance for the others. What is more, he argues that the image of Islam was not transferred into the modern era without any changes to it. Kathleen Biddick insists that Said viewed the Middle Ages as "the 'adolescent' stage preparatory to a fully mature, 'modern', imperialist Orientalism" (2000: 36). Jo Ann Hoeppner Moran Cruz supports the diagnosis of negativity as the main principle of representing alterity in *chansons de geste*, which stemmed from the wars against Saracens as the staple of that genre and from the general prejudice against cultural others (1999:71). Nevertheless, it remains debatable whether the image of corporeality marked by alterity is also multidimensional in

---

14 Currently it may be argued that Said's version orientalism is not the only possible one, since what Timothy Weiss termed "utopian orientalism", i.e. the tendency to idealize the Orient and treat it as either a liminal space or a space where the reality can be reimagined, has been traced in modern literature (2004:15).

oriental romance, or whether it rather embodies the principle of negativity representing the East in a reductionist manner. We lean here towards stating that in such wide corpuses as that of oriental romances a group of literary characters will never be uniformly negated, so this is true of Saracens as well.

Said himself was accused of reductionism, since he disregarded the fact that orientalist texts are heterogeneous, there exist alternative texts to the negativist ones, and there may exist among them "a textual dialogue . . . that would not codify knowledge and power relations", as Ashcroft and Ahluwalia assert (2009:72). The same authors criticize the very tenets that Said begins his considerations with: pinpointing Napoleon's invasion of Egypt rather than eighteenth-century philology as the beginning of the orientalist scholarly discourse, largely omitting Germany from a discussion of philological movement because it hardly possessed any colonies in the East, keeping silent over the philological doctrine that Eastern cultures could be superior to Western ones since in some aspects they could be models for the Occident, and stressing dominance and power rather than noticing cultural interaction (Ashcroft – Ahluwalia 2009:67). Other scholars who have criticized Said must be cited as well, beginning with Edward Alexander and the very harsh term "the professor of terror" that he attached to the author of *Orientalism* due to Said's political beliefs (1989:49-50). Dennis Porter wrote about the study as an ahistorical and discordant narrative, where the tension between knowledge and ideology was never resolved (1983:179-193), while Bernard Lewis attacked Said for "a disquieting lack of knowledge of what scholars do and what scholarship is all about" (1982a:46-48;1982b:49-56; quoted in Ashcroft and Ahluwalia 2009:70). Indeed, the problem Porter notes, namely whether the Orient is a real geographical area in this magisterial book or it is merely a textual construction, is highly controversial. Still, here we will limit ourselves to the textual Orient and the fictional Orientals from Middle English romances and will not try to establish possible relationships between the two, the real geographical land and the literary lands of oriental romances.

Another important accusation that has been made against Said refers to the degree to which the image of the East in orientalist discourse consists of representations or misrepresentations (1992:164). Nevertheless, if we were to admit after Brewer that his "mimetic fallacy" really exists, especially in romance, which is a purely fictional genre, then we could not find a truthful reflection of the reality in the texts: everything tends to be misrepresented in the arts, as Ashcroft and Ahluwalia emphasize (2009:74). It has also been argued that there is no escape from orientalism when writing about the Orient (Porter 1983:179-193; Young 1990:119-140) and that Said employs the very tools of that discourse in order to criticize it (Clifford 1988:255-276; Behdad 1994:1-

11). Mona Abaza and Georg Stauth (1988:343-364) and Michael Dutton and Peter Williams (1993:314-357) noted the methodological inconsistencies of Said's use of Foucault's theory tracing the relationship between knowledge and power. Lata Mani and Ruth Frankenberg rejected *Orientalism* as a study treating the Orient and the Occident as monolithic and disregarding the difference gender makes in representing Easterners (1985:174-192). Nonetheless, the reactions cited above testify to the range that Said's work has had and the influence it has exerted. The critiques of *Orientalism* are rather of secondary importance for us here, because our primary tasks, the investigation into how the themes of corporeality and alterity are interrelated in oriental romance, eliminates the problems that in Said ensue from the texts he cites and Foucault's theory he deploys. It will be neither postulated here that the oriental romances in question include only negativity, nor that the ones we analyze are the only significant romances of the type. What will interest us is not going to be Said's "*manifest* Orientalism", "the various stated views about Oriental society, languages, literatures, history, sociology" (1994:206), but "*latent* Orientalism", a style of thinking about the Orient, which according to Said is "almost unconscious" (1994:206).

Nevertheless, Beckett notes that there exists no latent orientalism that is not tinged with reverberations of the political situation (2003:11). The rest of her critique of Said's theory is also highly engrossing: she claims that his formulation is so general that it may be extended to the epochs earlier than the eighteenth and nineteenth centuries and that he refers to some medieval orientalism but does not exemplify it adequately. Furthermore, she insists that in the light of early medieval literature *Arabes* and *Saraceni* cannot be understood in the same manner as later and that Said attempts to hint at continuity between the "evil" Middle Ages and modernity (2003:10). Particularly the last argument is true if we return to the entangled issue of excessive negativity and very feeble positivity as two principles governing the images of the East in medieval literature. In turn, Akbari notes how subversive Said's strategy is when we consider his relation to Foucault and to modern philology. Said used Foucault's amalgam of power and knowledge, but instead of focusing on peripheral documents and texts, as Foucault recommended, he employed the canon of Western literature in order to illustrate the working of orientalism (Akbari 2009:7). Akbari explains the discord between enchantment with the Western culture and criticizing it by arguing that perhaps the Western literature that Said used to venerate betrayed him, hence the "undercurrent of anger that flows through *Orientalism*" (2009:8). Indeed, the relations between Said and the Western canon were very close, as he admits in *Out of place: a memoir* (2000), so the conclusion that the very same texts he cherished included an anti-oriental message must have come in as a shock to him. The negativity might then have been a natural psychological reaction to the growing realization that he was not only physically, but culturally "out of place" in the West despite his close links with its culture.

There exists a significant regularity associated with Middle English oriental romance that has to be mentioned. Oriental romances are always to a certain extent texts about cultural, religious, and ethnic otherness, but the theme of otherness as such is inextricably related to the Middle Ages in general. Oriental romances then explore otherness, while the Middle Ages as an epoch represent otherness. In *Medievalism and orientalism: three essays on literature, architecture and cultural identity* John M. Ganim calls the Middle Age's Europe's "Other", similarly to the Orient standing for various aspects of otherness (including corporeal) in European culture. Writes Ganim,

> The medieval past is also, often simultaneously, described as a result of foreign incursion, of alien influence, of disruption of what should be the natural movement in history . . . the most explicit expression of this hybrid identity [is] the twinned association of medievalism and Orientalism (2005:3).

Ganim insists that, similarly to the Orient, the Middle Ages can be perceived as "an imagined emptiness to which we may project our desires and fears" (2005:4) and it appears that medieval oriental romance is also prone to such projections. It should be remembered that the earliest studies of medieval romance viewed the genre as emblematic of the entire medieval literature and indicated the alleged Eastern origin of romances, not only oriental ones (Ganim 2005:5). The romance, and the entire medieval period with it, was perceived as outlandish, foreign, and exotic. The theory was first propagated in the eighteenth century by Thomas Warton, who described the similarity between chansons *de geste*, textual sources for many oriental romances, and the Arabic *sīrah*, also called the *sīrat*. The *sīrah*, a "biography, picture of life, reputation, history, story", developed side by side with sagas, epic poems, and *chansons de geste*, sharing with the latter warring as a topic and the love of realistic descriptions (Madeyska 2001: 9). *Sīrats* were only written down between the 14th and 16th centuries, but they could have been created as early as the 12th century. The epic poems have been classified as epic, epic poems, folk novels, folk sagas, folk books, folk romances, and chivalric romances, which shows that any classification of them has to remain a loose one even though Madeyska adopts the last term for her analysis (2001:10). The direct mutual interdependence between the two, *sīrats* and *chansons de geste* or the later chivalric romances, but they may have been inspired by similar plots and sources. For sure, the two traditions developed simultaneously.

The discourse on the Middle Ages as Europe's other is also developed by Catherine Brown in her *In the Middle* and by John Dagenais and Margaret R. Greer in *Decolonizing Middle Ages: introduction*. Brown states that the Middle Ages as we know them from a temporal and cultural distance have been "invented for us as a foreign country" (2000:547) and as such an invention the epoch has become "an other, perhaps even a foreign place, someplace, as the etymology indicates, beyond our own doors" (2000:548). The status of the Middle Ages as modern Western culture's other may be related to their existence as, as Dagenais and Greer claim, "a colonized space in the narrative of the West" (2000:444) and as such, again, it may be a focus of various fears and anxieties. The topic of negativity again must be mentioned, since the usual manner of describing others has been, as Jameson writes in reference to romance, negative:

> In the shrinking world of today, indeed, with its gradual leveling of class and national and racial differences, it is becoming increasingly clear that the concept of evil is at one with the category of Otherness itself: evil characterizes whatever is radically different from me, whatever by virtue of precisely that difference seems to constitute a very real and urgent threat to my existence . . . The point is not that . . . the Other is feared because he is evil; rather, he is evil *because* he is Other, alien, different, strange, unclean, and unfamiliar (1975:140).

The existence of Arabic and Middle Eastern analogues to many romances, which was already noticed by nineteenth-century scholars (Heffernan 2003:1), does not, however, indicate that those literatures influenced Middle English oriental romance in any manner other than by providing them with plots. Even if the first text we will be concentrating on here, Chaucer's *Squire's tale*, derives its plot from not only the French *Meliacin*, but also from the Arabic *The magic steed of brass* from *The hundred and one night* (DiMarco 2009:182-185), it should not alter our perspective on oriental romance as unrelated to the actual oriental cultures. Quite expectedly, perspective on the body of the other is usually Eurocentric in this romance, as the example of Chaucer's tale makes clear. Blanks and Frassetto maintain that the negative image of the others was more observable in *chansons de geste* than in other popular literature, probably for them including romance (1999:5). It may, however, be argued, that negativity is a phenomenon difficult to measure, hence there are diverse diagnoses as to which of the two, *chanson de geste* or romance, presents Saracens in a more hostile manner. It may seem that *chansons de geste* as a more military-oriented genre could develop the idea that the political enemy is culturally monstrous. Still, the Muslims of *chansons de geste* seem to be presented rather realistically, because they frequently display courage and a sense of honour similar to that of Westerners in these narratives. Despite being enemies, Saracens function as opponents who have a similar attitude to warring, since they also come from a culture to a large extent chivalric. Perhaps the historical import of *chansons de geste* was diminished once their plots became those of oriental romances, while arguably in those romances which were not translations of *chansons de geste* the depicton of Saracen honour and valour becomes vague and ultimately subservient to the ideological requirements of a given work. Not surprisingly, in *Richard le Coer de Lyon*, a narrative fairly detached from *chansons de geste* due to its lack of respect for Muslims, Saracens are represented as mere bodies that can be subjected to slaughter or digested if the monarch feels the urge to feast on them.

The choice of texts for discussing bodies marked by alterity is obviously very subjective here. What one should bear in mind, however, is that such texts have recently become central to the study of Middle English literature. What remains questionable is whether such texts may be read in an off-centre manner, that is, deploying the theoretical instruments that are otherwise reserved to modern literature. Homi Bhabha, one of the fathers and an important if controversial theoretician of postcolonial studies, writes that he has not been interested in canonical works at any point of his career (1994:xi). Argues Bhabha, "writers who were off-center; literary texts that had been passed by; themes and topics that had lain dormant or unread in great works of literature – these were the angles of vision and visibility that enchanted me" (1994:xi). The texts that provide subject matter for our discussion have been both central and till present fairly neglected, especially if we look at them from a different angle, that of psychoanalysis, postcolonial studies that situate themselves disturbingly close to psychoanalysis in the acknowledgment that the other functions in culture in a fairly unconscious manner, and gender studies, which explore the intricacies of roles people play in the society. A study which explores corporeality and alterity might seem to some as a text wandering on what Bhabha termed the "margins and peripheries" of culture (1994:xi). If such is the case, then our theme of corporeality and alterity is adjusted to the so far marginalized genre in question.

If Bhabha signals the importance of the *location* of culture, it is necessary here to see how the culture of the other is located in oriental romance and to what extent the culture of the other is materialized in those texts through the bodies marked by alterity. Ashcroft and Ahluwalia state that this was also Said's intention: to examine orientalism as "a way of defining and 'locating' Europe's others" (2009:48). In contrast to Said, Bhabha does not intend to characterize the images of ethnic others as positive or negative, but prefers to examine "the repertoire of positions of power and resistance, domination and dependence that constructs colonial identification subject (both colonizer and colonized)"

(1994:95). This study will avoid, as Bhabha does, analyses of misrepresentations to which cultural and religious others were subjected in oriental romance, but will rather reread the positions of power and domination in representing those others, even though the historical period we will be dealing with is not *sensu stricto* a colonial one. One argument in favour of reading those texts from a colonial perspective is the disconcerting similarity between our subject and the one Bhabha discusses when he refers to "the ambivalence of the object of colonial discourse – that 'otherness' which is at once an object of desire and derision, an articulation of difference contained within the fantasy of origins and identity" (1994:96). This is precisely the way in which cultural others functioned in the Middle Ages, even though colonization started in the early modern period and not earlier. Nevertheless, if we include the remarks of some critics writing about the position of Jews in medieval European societies, the idea that colonial discourse was unknown in the Middle Ages may change. Biddick maintains that "the periodization of colonialism. . . begins to look very different if one includes Jews" (1998:291). The negative perspective on this religious and ethnic group that was customarily adopted in the Middle Ages entailed a number of colonial strategies: downgrading those others, limiting their rights or even granting them null, if we assume that their expulsion from England in 1290 took away from them the basic right, the one to live where they were born. They were forced to convert even though it did not guarantee acceptance, especially later, when ethnicity started to be the main factor in identifying difference instead of the previously employed religious criterion, and spreading and various phobias were spread about them. Furthermore, colonial discourse has been adopted before the discovery of America, for instance during the exploration of Asia, when Prester John started to be sought due to the existence of the fictional twelfth-century *Letter of Prester John*, which signaled the possibility of conversion conducted in Asia on the grounds of the Nestorian communities living there. The fictional Prester John described the "Three Indies" as his kingdom, wealthy, full of magic, unusual animals, and monstrous races (Cruz 1999:63). What is more, the language that was applied in the discussions of the possibility of Christianization in the Orient, which ensued from the diplomatic missions sent by the Pope to the Mongols, was similar to the later discourse of conquest and colonization. So was the discourse of Franks when they crusaded in the East, as Bartlett argues (1993:254).[15]

---

15 The colonial discourse of Franks may be related to the colonial nature of crusading itself and the proto-colonial nature of the Kingdom of Jerusalem; after all, crusading only started as a pilgrimage, but it was continued as a military venture whose results created

It needs to be repeated that there has never existed one uniform Orient, as much as "the West" has never been a uniform category. Nevertheless, we will be dealing here with two literary images, that of the Orient and that of the Occident, and not with the real geographic parts of the world. This is why the use of what Said terms *latent* orientalism is not unsuitable here. "The Orient" appears to be a fairly consistent image in various literary texts even though some of them refer to Muslims, while others discuss Mongols or some mysterious black-skinned creatures, such as the giants helping the Saracens to combat Charlemagne's knights. It seems to me that the image of the body of the other is drawn in a similar manner in those diverse texts, so they have been analyzed side by side. Another critique of Said's theory, that he creates the illusion that the Orient is culturally uniform, is relevant, but only if we consider the real Orient and not its literary conceptualizations. Significantly, what Said did not include in his theory was the influence of the Orient, specifically the culture of al-Andalus on medieval Western Europe (Lampert-Weissig 2010:13), the cultural exchange between the East and the West in the crusader states (Georgopoulou 1999:289-321), and the division into Europe, Asia, Africa, with the concurrent conceptualization of the world as the East, the West, and the North, that Akbari notes (2000:19-34).

I have reserved mention of the most controversial aspect of this analysis for the end of this introduction, which by no means exhausts all the issues that could treat the topic of Middle English oriental romance as a point of departure. Postcolonial studies have become an important critical tool in my interpretation, but it is impossible to overlook the criticism that has been directed against the use of postcolonial critique in medieval studies (Freedman – Spiegel 1998; Freedman 2008). In contrast to those reservations, Bartlett's lengthy study, *The making of Europe: conquest, colonization and cultural change 950-1350*, centers on the argument that Europe would not have been consolidated but for the colonial expansion that took place inside it (1993). As a consequence, the boundaries between Europeans and non-Europeans were fixed through the expansion already before the Age of Exploration. Those non-European others could be interpreted from a postmodern perspective, if we understand postmodernity as the tendency to look to the margins and focus on them despite their non-centrality postulated by old canons. The existence of a discipline termed "the postcolonial Middle Ages" has been announced by Cohen (2000), but the studies of medieval literature and culture, such as, among others, Michelle R. Warren's *History on the edge: Excalibur and the borders of Britain*,

---

the need to administer the newly conquered territory in the way in which colonies had to be administered in the later centuries.

1100-1300 (2000), Patricia Claire Ingham's *Sovereign fantasies: Arthurian romance and the making of Britain* (2001), and David Wallace's *Pre-modern places: Calais to Surinam, Chaucer to Alphra Behn* (2004) have confirmed the fruitfulness of this approach in medieval studies. So even if someone should cringe at the combination of "postcolonial" and "Middle Ages", they could undoubtedly appreciate the connections between cultures and places that emerge from such studies and the sophisticated comparative structure of these critical texts. Importantly, they allow one to see a pan-European medieval culture rather than merely fragmentary "nationalistic" cultures, if the term "nationalism" can be used in this context at all. This study only attempts to follow the "trend away from Eurocentrism in medieval studies scholarship" (Lampert-Weissig 2010:10) and the postcolonial strategies prove to be at least partly useful for that.[16] Some of the modern tools of critical analysis appear, after all, to be very productive in reading old literature, even though this idea has often been criticized by the researchers studying older texts.[17]

Chapter One, "Ethnic difference and body marvellous: the case of Chaucer's *Squire's tale* and *Sir Ferumbras*", addresses the issue of the ethnic difference of Canace as the Lacanian *objet petit a*, while the magic object that is attached to her body increases the effect of attraction that could draw Westerners to her. She becomes potentially another enamoured princess of the oriental romance, similar to Floripas from the *Firumbras* group of romances, who remains to some extent out of reach of the Franks due to her ethnicity and to the betrayal of her own people that she commits. In the end, she cannot be fully integrated into the symbolic body of the Christian community. Instead, she repeats the pattern observable in *The Squire's tale*, but with a complication: not only does she embody the *objet petit a*, but it is Oliver who materializes the *objet a* for her. Significantly, in the *Firumbras* romances the communal body is, to say the least, as central as individual bodies.

What connects *The Squire's tale* and *Richard le Coer de Lyon* is the topic of cannibalism, in the fictional account of the Mongol court only hinted at, but fully developed in *Richard*, where no criticism is ever made of the Christian king as he feasts on the bodies of Saracens. In Chapter Two, "Community, *Richard le Coer de Lyon*, and chivalric anthropophagy", *communitas* is presented as a site of violence directed against the flesh of the others despite, or

---

16 Bruce Holsinger in turn acknowleged the indebtness of postcolonial studies to medieval scholarship when he noted that the latter allowed postcolonialism to develop (2002).

17 For instance, Teresa Bela argued that "deconstruction as a style of criticism applied to older literature does not seem to be a really valuable, trustworthy instrument" due to "its insistence on the a-historic nature of literary texts" (1994:7).

perhaps precisely because, this community is chivalric. This section of the book seeks to undermine Richard's consistently French identity, because the process of Anglicization, hence the spreading of the English culture, was occurring in his times.

While Chapter Three, "Bodies enslaved in *Aucassin et Nicolete* and *Floris and Blancheflour*", initially seems to depart from the topics of aggressiveness and communal life, as a matter of fact it continues them through the discussion of the ills of slavery. The identity of slaves in both of those narratives treating of youthful lovers deserves to be analyzed in terms of its hybrid quality. Conversion to Christianity remains in both the *chantefable* and the romance indispensable for the ultimate coining of a new self, even though the scene of baptism is not necessary to it, since characters such as Floris may have absorbed Christianity along with their wet nurses' milk. Desire is subjected to the will of the slave master in the two tales of love and loss, but the dire reality of slavery does not continue endlessly and desire is liberated upon freeing the slave.

The issue of communal life and the role of black-skinned giantesses as the flesh of the Franks' community are explored in Chapter Four, "Black giantesses as communal flesh in the *Firumbras* romances". The marginalized characters are studied from the perspective of the assumption that their bodies are made grotesque and very likely become carnivalized, but not in the entirely Bakhtinian sense, because the carnival order is, as always, only temporarily adopted. The giantesses' role in their own monstrous community also deserves investigation, while culturalism rather than racialism is observable in the romances deriving from the French *chansons de geste*.

In Chapter Five titled "Genealogy and desire in *King Horn*", the starting point for the interpretation of bodies, those of the same and those of the others, needs to be the genealogy of the ruler along with the position that a monarch occupies when the land is invaded by Saracens. The romance *Horne Childe and Maiden Rimnild* is cited here as well, since it shares various concerns with *King Horn* despite the invaders being Vikings in the former. The cultural others transfer Horn into the position of the other and he begins his exile with this status, which makes him abandon all individual desire in favour of the communal one. The Lacanian grid of the role of the Real and the barred and unbarred O is employed in this section in order to inspect Horn's intentions and the desire for death that motivates him more than erotic desire could.

The romances about Alexander the Great illustrate the ultimate concept of oriental romances as texts that feed on the fantastic rather than relying on the historical, as is discussed by Chapter Six. In *Kyng Alisaunder* and *Wars of Alexander* the ruler's cultured quality is not undermined by his supernatural origin. Instead, he breaks the link that connects him with the Egyptian magician

Anactenabus and confirms his identity as a European ruler through his conquests and the contacts with the cultural others in the course of his travels, sharing various elements with *The travels of sir John Mandeville*. The issue of Alexander's heathenism or his proto-Christianity is also debated, because the matter is not as uncomplicated as was once thought. The monstrous races of India not only evoke the sense of wonder in him, but also inspire the ruler to critically reflect on the transitory quality of his own victories. The traces of fascination that are observable in Alexander's attitude may signal the much later, eighteenth- and nineteenth-century infatuation with the Orient, in spite of the fact that the Romantic idea also propagated negative stereotypes of orientalism.

Apart from repeating the stereotypes of the earlier versions of orientalism, the Romantic infatuation with the East demonstrated itself in the belief that oriental travels could change a Westerner very deeply. The so-called orientalist renaissance involved the idea of deep metamorphosis of travellers to the East. As Marta Piwińska comments on it, in Romanticism "the East is something which may come from the outside, but it becomes the traveller's inner quality; it makes people 'lepers', 'Orientals', and 'sightseers'" (2005:307). The transformation from a Western rationalist to an "Oriental" becomes a positive change, since it means going back to the state of mind of a child, which was so much valued at the time. The late eighteenth- and early nineteenth-century fascination with childhood as the time of mental simplicity adopted the form of dreaming about being like Easterners, who are allegedly still childlike in their postulated innocence and in their postulated innocence and uncomplicated nature. The Orient became an object of dreaming and it was conceptualized as a state of mind rather than merely a place. As a place, to quote Piwińska again, it was visualized as yet another fragment of nature, but this time foreign and tempting (Piwińska 2005:61). Such medieval texts as the Alexander romances were probably one of the first texts that recorded the more positive attitude to the East, since they included the conviction that the Orient was both an attractive idea for the human mind and a fascinating place.

Chapter One
Ethnic difference and body marvellous: the case of Chaucer's *Squire's tale* and *Sir Ferumbras*

> Far from being a random component of a plausible narrative, the body "states" the problem of the individual vis-à-vis the community; it is a mode of apprehending the world, whether through the positive evaluation of the body or the rejection of ugliness and mortification of the flesh.
> (Danielle Régner-Bohler *Imagining the Self*) (1988:358)

In the epigraph given above, the evaluation of the body on which Régner-Bohler grounds her twofold diagnosis of the medieval culture and, more precisely, literature, entails a fairly prescriptive stance on the question of beauty and turpitude. Views on what beauty was deemed to be in the Middle Ages appear fairly consistent to us in various sources: Brewer summarizes one of the basic ones, Matthew of Vendôme's ideal of female comeliness in *Ars versificatoria* exemplified by Helen of Troy, as: "her hair is golden, forehead white as paper, eyebrows black and thin . . . Her face is rosy, her colouring white and red, like rose and snow" (1955:258). White skin appears also in Geoffrey of Vinsauf's description, and it may be inferred that such a complexion was needed for a favourable judgment of someone's appearance. Régner-Bohler sanctions the assumption that whiteness of skin was a medieval ideal, when in *The history of private life* she details the qualities of the romance heroines' appearance as "a creamy complexion enlivened by a touch of pink; blond hair; harmonious features; a long face; a high, regular nose; bright, happy eyes; and thin, red lips" (1988:358). Walter Clyde Curry, even though not commenting on the issue of ethnicity at all, claims that in the later Middle English texts, "the skin of beautiful women and children must be smooth, soft as silk, and above all shining white" (1916:80) and "the adjective *white* is very commonly used to describe beautiful women and children and handsome men as well"; it is synonymous with beauty and used alone referring to the skin in general (1916:80). All of those concepts entail a racially determined image of someone beautiful, not accounting for any possibility of ethnic difference in that person's physicality. Perhaps then an ethnically different body played a more complicated role in medieval culture, which could be analyzed by employing such psychoanalytical concepts as the Lacanian *objet petit a* and by examining the possible interactions of cultural others with the surrounding Westerners in oriental romances. In *The Squire's tale* there even appear colonial overtones in the characterization of the figure Douglas Gray calls "Canace(e)" and her ethnically different body is complemented by supernatural objects, becoming an example of the "body marvellous".[18] These elements of characterization appear also in the subplot of the *Firumbras* romances which treat of Floripas, another enamoured princess, who ultimately turns out to be treacherous and can never be fully incorporated into the *Corpus Christianorum* despite her conversion to Christianity.

It needs to be reaffirmed that ethnic difference was not included in the medieval descriptions of beauty at all, which must have given rise to ambiguity surrounding the category combining black, or at least coloured, and beautiful. This ambiguity had to influence the shape of works directed to a wide audience, such as the readers of oriental romance, due to the impossibility of combining colour with beauty. As Jacqueline de Weever insists in her introduction to the tangled issue of translating the blackness of Nicolete, a heroine of the Middle French *Aucassin et Nicolete*, in this medieval popular romance "'black' still cannot be applied to a beautiful woman" (1994:317). In the translations it led to the omission of the word "black" in reference to the Saracen heroine when she colours her face in order to meet Aucassin unrecognized by him as his beloved, which is a situation we will elaborate on in Chapter Three below. This observation led de Weever to conclude that even contemporary translators have difficulties in coming to terms with the fact that Nicolete, a Muslim, could have been dark-skinned. Obviously, her dark skin in the narrative remains merely a disguise, as is testified by the frequent employment of the word "faire" when describing or addressing her in other contexts (1994:317-325). On the other hand, however, Nicolete was not only whitened by the text's anonymous author, even though she could have been darker-skinned as a Saracen. She was made even whiter by the translators of the text, who spoiled the effect produced by her darkening of her own skin when they refused to employ the term "black", even when it was necessary in the description of her disguise.

As the case of Nicolete's "blackness" proves, in confrontation with ethnic alterity authors of popular texts resorted to simplifying the tangled issue of attractiveness and repulsiveness by whitening those characters or at least not focusing on their skin colour excessively. The superficial mental association of blackness with evil in the minds of the Europeans, visible even in the denotation

---

[18] Gray notes the double spelling of the Squire's "Canace(e)", which does not allow one to distinguish her once and for all from the "Canace(e)" mentioned in *The Man of Law's tale* (2003:69).

of the word "black" in English, as the oft-cited entry in the *Oxford English dictionary* reveals, led to the possibility of negative perception in confrontation with darker-skinned characters, which impinged on the sphere of visual representations: to put it briefly, when Muslim figures were to be judged as positive by the audience of an art piece, they were portrayed with a lighter skin colour than other characters of the same ethnicity (Strickland 2003:157-209). This suggests that both popular romance and visual arts relied on simple classifications and aimed at representing an artificially ordered world picture. Jean Devisse claims that the realm of visual representations with their easy labels did not affect real life that much: "blackness was associated with human beings only in a very abstract manner . . . [and] the view of the black and his color was considerably more ambiguous at the level of social life than it was at the ideological level" (1979:51). The black-skinned Christian saints, such as St. Maurice, appear to have been examples of avoiding the strategy of stereotyping ethnic others.[19] Still, Devisse has already argued that the legendary saint was granted the physicality not only of a knight in the ninth or early tenth century, but of an African before 1250, for political reasons (Devisse 1979:153). The Hohenstaufens dreamt about conquering the Mediterranean, but they had to abandon the dream later. The creation of the black St. Maurice was not a manifestation of their tolerance of ethnic diversity and the inadequacy of seeing blacks merely through the perspective of their skin colour, but a political strategy which aimed at acquiring the territories inhabited by dark-skinned people (Devisse 1979:204).[20] Hahn notes that "Maurice remains a stand-alone African, a single black face within a tableau of European, white countenances; his token presence is an appropriation of the Other that affirm the universality of the Same" (2001:5). So one ought to avoid hasty conclusions when comparing blacks in visual arts and in real life, since their situation in life was far more complex than it might seem. Also, more sophisticated literature problematized the ideological equal sign between blackness and evil, which in turn may have affected the sphere of visual arts. The legendary Queen of Sheba was not invariably portrayed as black-skinned in visual representations, as her biblical portrait required more reflection on the question of ethnicity, otherness and

---

19 A Christian saint whose skin was black through his physical otherness and cultural proximity may have complemented another type of the other in medieval culture, the "righteous heathen" that Frank Grady discussed, beginning the analysis with the story of Emperor Trajan from *The golden legend* (200:17-44).

20 This undermines Frederickson's thesis of "a definite tendency toward Negrophilia in the late Middle Ages" (2002:26), since St. Maurice was blackened and then politically used for practical reasons and not because of some highly positive image of blacks in that culture.

sameness. Furthermore, her story portrays the tangled links between Jewish and Muslim cultures, complicating the issue of her physicality and ethnicity (Lassner 1993:104). In some representations Sheba was exoticized through her skin being made dark, in others she was not, but what remained crucial was her identity as a potent ruler capable of rejecting the constraints of female gender rather than her whiteness or darkness. In the postbiblical Judaic account *The stories of Ben Sira*, her hairy legs suggest gender indeterminacy (Lassner 1993:18-24), while in the later Islamic versions her attitude towards King Solomon reveals that she did not resemble a stereotypical female in other respects, either (Lassner 1993:47-87). Those representations are going to be addressed here in Chapter Four. To sum up, whether St Maurice or the Queen of Sheba are portrayed as white- or dark-skinned may be both accidental and political, but it is by no means a decisive statement about them. Ethnic difference did not determine the judgment of characters in those cases.

The chief character in Part II of *The Squire's tale*, Khan Cambyuskan's daughter Canace, is endowed by the story-teller with a bodily frame which, though ethnically different, seems to conform to the precepts of feminine *physique* necessary for Western beauties. Yet so as to avoid a detailed description, the teller uses the rhetorical strategy of *occupatio* in the citation to which substantial critical space has already been devoted:[21]

> Bot for to telle yow al hir beautee,
> It lyth nat in my tonge, n'yn my konnyng;
> I dar nat undertake so heigh a thyng.
> My Englissh eek is insufficient.
> It moste been a rethor excellent
> That koude his colours longynge for that art,
> If he sholde hire discryven every part.
> I am noon swich, I moot speke as I kan.
> (V:34-41)[22]

The impression that the Squire intends to convey to his audience is the message that Canace mirrors Western ladies; the effect is achieved by the avoidance of supplying the listeners of the tale with any details of her physicality. Rather than being more beautiful than other romance heroines, she is made to be exactly like them, which does not need any description. Here Canace becomes a pure fantasy: even though she is introduced into the narrative as holding the position of a Tartar princess, she does not differ from the white-skinned heroines of other

---

21 See, for instance, Ambrisco's essay (2004:205-228).
22 The quotations from *The Canterbury tales* are taken, along with the line numbers, from Benson's edition (1987).

chivalric romances, which is not realistic, but propitious for fantasy. The exoticism of origin and background mingles with the conventional beauty of a courtly lady. Thus through her unrealistically treated physical appearance, not to mention her courtly comportment, she enters the Western chivalric culture and literature that Chaucer's tale appears to be firmly grounded in, as Stanley J. Kahrl and Jennifer R. Goodman have observed; that is precisely the culture populated by Régner-Bohler's blond-haired ladies.[23] The fragment referring to Canace's beauty may draw the reader's attention to her ethnic difference, even if the difference is not explicitly stated, and the difference may be the detail which sets desire in motion. She becomes an object of fantasy, unrealistically combining ethnic difference with similarity to Western ladies. On the one hand Chaucer depicts Tartary almost at a specific moment of its existence, as DiMarco remarks in *The historical basis of Chaucer's Squire's tale*: it is a time of increased political activity between the Russian Mongols and the Mamluks (2002:56-65). On the other hand, the teller, the Squire, fantasizes about the East and situates his Tartary against a background of magic interventions and outlandish mores set in an exotic location, significantly introducing there a Tartar princess who is as courtly as other romance ladies and thus a possible object of a Westerner's desire.

What is of importance for us here is that from the first half of the thirteenth century onwards, when papal missions were sent to Karakorum, Mongols were perceived as, at least in theory, culturally closer to Western Christianity than Muslims, since the latter were seen as totally separate in terms of both religion and culture and as a severe threat to Christianity. In contrast to Muslims, at the time Mongols tended to conform to the principles of Buddhism or Nestorianism, or even converted to Roman Christianity in single cases, because their religious syncretism allowed them to adopt the principles of religions other than the shamanism traditionally attributed to them and thus enter into desirable political alliances.[24] The naïve Squire might consequently see them as representing a

---

23 Kahrl traces in Chaucer's tale signs of Huizinga's "waning of the Middle Ages", the idea once thought to be present in all later medieval romances (1973:194-209), while Goodman sees the tale as one of late medieval "composite romances", the texts hailing the phenomenon of chivalry and doing it so extensively that Chaucer had to leave *The Squire's tale* unfinished so as not to disrupt the frame tale of the whole *Canterbury Tales* by inserting another elaborate structure inside it (1983:127-136); as for the finished or unfinished quality of the tale, before Goodman Joyce E. Peterson, for instance, argued that "it is not in the usual sense – as a story – complete, as a member of the family of the *Canterbury Tales* it is whole" (1970:62-74).

24 Literature reflected the occurrence of such conversions in, for example, the legendary conversion to Christianity of Mongol Khan Ghazzan, who was in reality a convert to

culture more proximate to Christianity and delude himself into thinking that they were not as "Eastern" as Muslims. Either the Squire remained ignorant of the frequent conversions to Islam which occurred in Tartary in the fourteenth century due to the conversion of khan Özbeg and his imposition of Islam on his people, or Chaucer himself created a vision of Tartary without Muslim influence so as to ideologically claim that Christianity could still find new believers there. It is arguable whether the poet could distinguish between Islam and heathenism. The customary identification of Muslims was that they were pagans, as is shown by the reference to the Knight in the General Prologue as one fighting against "heathen in Turkye" (I:66). Nevertheless, contacts with the world of Islam may have caused some type of Western awareness of the qualities distinguishing Muslim culture from other "pagan" cultures. After all, in political terms Islam and Tartary were distinguished from each other. In the thirteenth century Tartary functioned as the "third force" in Christian eyes, and only then could Europeans fantasize about uniting themselves with Mongols against Muslims. In the fourteenth century Islam had already gained such a high position in the Eastern world that the number of conversions to it rapidly grew in the Mongol empire. Perhaps, in order to deny this reality, Chaucer writes about Cambuskyan as a pagan ruler not interested in any conversion at all, since he clings to his pagan beliefs: "As of the secte of which that he was born,/ He kepte his lay, to which that he was sworn" (V:17-18). Thus *The Squire's tale* compounds facts with fiction, depending on what is convenient for Chaucer's vision of the Eastern world.

Returning to the issue of Canace's appearance, her beauty (even if it is not elaborated on) entails the topic of love because, as Brewer summarizes this connection, in romance "typical beauty is harnessed to the dominant emotion of the age, to love" (Brewer 1955:262). Beauty is the stimulus to love, usually being love at first sight, and then, once the relationship has begun, "love itself surrounds . . . beauty with a special radiance, gives it a special delight and power" (Brewer 1955:262). The statement about Canace's beauty (even if any possibility of description is negated) directly implies the later inclusion of love in the plot, which materializes in the subsequent story of a love-sick falcon. Still, Brewer disregards Canace's ethnic difference when he maintains that in *The Squire's tale* "Chaucer uses the rhetorical device of refusing to describe her, and indeed, we might say he has no need" (1955:268). Saying that the princess

---

Islam, and the legend very likely inspired the anonymous author of the thirteenth-century *King of Tars* to write about the whitening of the dark-skinned father of the "lump of flesh" once he decided to undergo baptism after the magic beautification of his son; for a discussion of Ghazzan's legend and his historical image see Perryman (1980: 44-47).

is the same as other romance heroines is inadequate, because in reality she cannot be like them. There exists a need for elaborating on her beauty, but any such bid to do it will always be impeded by the concurrent need to mention her ethnic otherness, and this is not how the Squire intends to see her. This non-realistic portrayal contrasts prominently with descriptions of Tartar women from proto-travelogues deriving from the actual experience of the Mongols, namely such relations as John Carpini's *Historia Mongalorum*, written in 1247 as a consequence of the papal mission to the Great Khan that the Franciscan friar undertook and successfully completed, or *Historia Tartarorum*, put down by the mysterious "C. de Bridia", but probably deriving from the lecture presented by another envoy in the same mission, Benedict Polonus.[25] In these works Tartar women, both common and those related to powerful rulers, are indiscriminately described as unattractive. Their greatest ugliness derives perhaps mostly from the fact that they dress like men and behave similarly. Gender indeterminacy becomes visible even in their clothing: "the clothes of both the men and the women are made in the same style" (Carpine 1955:7) and "it is hard to tell unmarried women and young girls from men, for they are dressed in every respect like them" (Carpine 1955:8). The author of *Historia Tartarorum* adds a similar comment to his relation when he writes: "As to their clothing, one needs to know that men and women wear the same kind of garments and *are therefore not easy to tell apart; and as these matters seem more curious than useful I have not troubled to write further about their clothing and adornment*" (Skelton – Marston – Painter 1965:86). Also Tartar men are affected by gender confusion, as Carpini writes: "On the top of the head they have a tonsure like clerics . . . Above the forehead also they likewise shave to two fingers' breadth, but the hair between this shaving and the tonsure they allow to grow until it reaches their eyebrows, and . . . they make the hair in the middle long; *the rest of their hair they allow to grow like women, and they make it into two braids which they bind, one behind each ear. They also have small feet* [the emphasis is mine– A.C.]" (Carpine 1955:6). In contrast to real Tartar women, fictional Canace is not such a challenge to Western eyes: she remains a paragon of Western femininity both in her looks and manners throughout the entire unfinished romance, without any hints of gender indeterminacy possibly resulting from her ethnic origin.

In order to extend the line of comparison relating Chaucer's princess to other romance heroines, Canace is in the Western mode portrayed as "ful

---

25 For details see Racheviltz's study of the historical documents referring to the papal missions (1971); for the controversy over the authorship of *Historia Tartarorum* see, for example, Plezia's article (1971:1967-72).

mesurable, as wommen be" (V:362) and thus placed in a row with other virtuous literary heroines from Christian culture, all of them being possible objects of a Westerner's desire. The passage where she is sketched as awakening, namely: "Up riseth fresshe Canace hireselve,/ As rody and bright as dooth the yonge sonne" (V:384-385), gives the readers the idea of how young, fresh, and delicate she should appear to the readers. According to Brewer, the freshness and sweetness of the morning was a trope frequently employed in the descriptions of feminine beauty and it was already such a cliché in medieval poetry that it had to be rejuvenated by elaborate comparisons, for example that in *The fair maid of Ribblesdale* from the Harley Manuscript, where the Maid's sides, "soft as silk", are likened not merely to "milk", but to "morenmylk" (Brewer 1955:261). Canace seems even more beautiful in the morning, as if the young son transferred some of its radiance onto her. Again, an allusion to the princess's skin colour appears here, as she is portrayed as ruddy and fair. Yet also this hint at her complexion is subtle; so is the remark that, prior to her awakening, "twenty tyme she changed hir colour" (V:370). The whitening of Canace becomes obvious: this is how the Squire wants to see the princess, regardless of what the actual physicality of Mongol women seemed to be in his times. This is perhaps the reason for which John M. Fyler described the entire tale as "certainly one in praise of exotic otherness" (1994:257).

Here the question of romanticization of Tartary that Brenda Deen Schildgen raised acquires adequate exemplification (2001:21). For the sake of contrast, the passage is preceded by the late nocturnal rest of other members of the court, since they succumb to the figure identified as Sleep after excessive eating and drinking and thank him for coming; they do it "galpynge, by two, by thre" (V:354), as the metaphorical image conveys it. There is nothing romantic in a late going to bed by drunken Mongols, which contrasts strongly with the subsequent early morning scene picturing Canace. The young Squire as the teller reveals his utter fascination with the Eastern princess and perhaps it is this enchantment that leads him to ignore the differences between East and West in the treatment of that character; this is how Schildgen diagnoses his notion of Tartary (2001:21). Nevertheless, the scene of Canace rising from bed subtly implies not just her own freshness and newness, but the newness of the world to which she wakes up. Surprisingly, the phrase "new world" appeared in accounts of Tartary in Chaucer's time and even before it. Europeans did not wait till the discovery of the Western hemisphere for the creation of descriptions of geographically remote regions as new and thus stimulating through their novelty. Scott D. Westrem observes that the "new world" image appeared in the Western thinking in the thirteenth and fourteenth centuries in the accounts of the missions to the Mongol empire (1991:x). Perhaps then for the Squire Canace is a part of this new world of Tartary and her aesthetically pleasing body both enhances the effect of the land's newness and freshness and derives a substantial amount of its rejuvenating quality from the associations with novelty that the land provoked. Reading audiences did not have to wait till the seventeenth-century imagery of John Donne's poetry to see a female body as part of the distant land, here not yet of "America", but of Tartary. The body of Canace is discursively colonized and she forms a fragment of the empire's opulence. She remains both exotic enough to be enticing and Western-like enough in her physicality and demeanour so as not to seem too menacing. She symbolizes the "new world" that presumably awaits Westerners in the East. The meaning of "world" should perhaps be surveyed here in more detail due to its equivocal quality. In *Second words*, C.S. Lewis distinguishes between what he terms the "*A*-sense" and "*B*-sense" of the word and his philological divagations lead him to pinpoint the idea in English as having either the temporal ("*A*-sense") or the spatial sense ("*B*-sense") (1990:214-230). If the character of Canace implies the possibility of newness, the new world she symbolically offers to a Westerner could be both additional time in his life and additional space. Lewis summarizes his considerations by stating that both *A* and *B* stand for "human life"; hence the Tartar princess as an inhabitant of the new world might denote the new life available to Westerners outside Europe (Lewis 1990:225).

Ethnically different women are tempting, as we infer from the tale, not only because their beauty is captivating, but also because their presence entails a promise. The very fact that they are Eastern suggests an invitation of sexual nature, as medieval orientalist stereotypes had it. Nevertheless, the erotic promise enveloping even such a virtuous princess as Canace also has a darker aspect: that of a possible seduction conducted by her. De Weever claims that in medieval oriental narratives the female characters portrayed as white-skinned symbolize all that Orient seems to offer a Westerner: they become alluring tokens and subjects of Christian desire, while they also stand for the dangerous seductiveness of the entire culture they belong to and of those who live in it.[26] The characterization of an Eastern woman as beautiful and of the land she lives in as promising in its novelty may be merely a lure for a gullible Christian; it is the lure of sexual nature which will lead to his subsequent enticement by the alien culture and abandonment of the one true faith in favour of other religions. Ultimately then the image of Canace might not be entirely positive, subtle as the indication is. The newness she

---

26 As de Weever emphatically argues, "Add the seductiveness of the East to the seductiveness of the women and the figure becomes doubly dangerous, containing two areas of damnation, the woman's body and the heretical East" (1998:34).

symbolizes in the morning scene may be illusory, because her apparent freshness can veil the reality of old heathen tricks aimed at drawing a Christian male away from his culture, if we remember that all non-Christian religions in the Middle Ages could be considered heathen. "This faire kynges doghter" (V:432) is probably pagan like her father, but if she were Muslim, like many Tartars in Chaucer's time, it would augur a danger not only of religious, but also of political nature. Sexual seduction may be a preliminary step to resultant cultural seduction.

Concurrently one might start wondering if Canace is "faire" because she is, after all, pale-skinned, like Chaucer's Constance among Muslims.[27] That would make her ethnicity a phenomenon not merely disregarded, but erased from the portrayal. Carolyn Dinshaw considers the pallor of Constance in more detail when writing about other references to paleness in Chaucer and concludes that the poet frequently drew the attention of his audience to skin colour when he emphasized the pallor of a given character (2001:19-41). While broaching the pallor of the *clergeon*'s mother in the anti-Judaic *Prioress's Tale*, Dinshaw claims that "paleness is both affective and racial/religious here, and indeed the relativity – the changeability, the transitoriness – of the affect suggests a certain fear of instability or infection of white Christian normalcy itself" (2001:22). In the Prioress's narrative the uncleanness of the Jews who cut a Christian boy's throat and dump his still singing body into a privy "where as thise Jewes purgen hire entraille" (VII:573) is visibly contrasted with the mother whose face is "pale of drede and bisy thoght" (VII:589). The contrast has to be racial, as the sacrilegious treatment of human body, which in Christianity remains a vessel for the Eucharist and for the word of God, is juxtaposed with maternal thoughtfulness and worry about one's offspring. The deeply unnatural deposition of the half-dead body in the privy contrasts with the natural love that Christians arguably have for one another. The effect produced by the whiteness of pallor is strengthened by the fainting that the mother experiences: "His mooder swownynge by his beere lay" (VII:625). Jewishness and generally racial difference may be infectious, as Dinshaw insists, but the effect of a threat to ethnic whiteness is decreased once this pallor ends with the swoon close to the *clergeon*'s body, singing *Alma*

---

27 Kim F. Hall (1998:64-83) argues that in early modern culture, in his article represented by Shakespeare's sonnets, "fairness" is a racial issue; further studies devoted to the idea of race in the Renaissance include Hendricks' *"Obscured by dreams": race, empire, and Shakespeare's "A midsummer night's dream"* (1996:37-60), while the colonial elements in *The tempest* have been famously examined by Francis Barker and Peter Hulme (1988:191-205).

Redemptoris Mater due to the grain deposited on his tongue by the Virgin. The whiteness of the mother's skin is a permanent quality, which distinguishes her from the Jews with their racial impurity. Consequently, the issue of Canace's "fairness" might also be a topic for such theorizing: was her skin colour a transitory feature, since she appeared "fair" to those who perceived her beauty rather than her different ethnicity, such as the young Squire, the teller of the tale whose Westernness is undeniable, as Heffernan argues (2003:63)? Or did Chaucer want to convince his readers that she was as white-skinned as them, erasing her true ethnic origin from the picture?

It has been argued by Metlitzki that the plot of *The Squire's tale* with its reference to the union of Algarsif and Theodora foreshadows a union between Christians and Muslims, which would mean that the question of ethnic origin was important in the narrative (1977:137). Still, the text evidently disguises Canace's ethnic difference along with its most discernible marker, skin colour. The two become hidden under the pretence of sameness allegedly detectable between the tale's heroine and the readers, as also occurred in the case of Josiane, the Saracen princess in *Beues of Hamtoun* (Metlitzki 1977:167). One may wonder about the real purpose of the concealment in the context of the East in Chaucer being a fantasy made flesh. When developing his theory of *jouissance*, Lacan identified the object of desire "framing reality", as Žižek called it (2008a:xvi), as the *objet a* (with *a* standing for *autre*, the Other functioning as the abstract system of the Law and the symbolic order), while the *objet petit a* would be "the object-cause of desire", that which is "in you more than you" (Žižek 2008a:xviii), "the object of fantasy" (Žižek 2008a:9). The other in Chaucer's tale, in contrast to "the big Other", distinguishes itself through the feature having the position of the *objet petit a*: "not what we desire, what we are after, but, rather, that which sets our desire in motion, in the sense of the formal frame which confers consistency on our desire" (Žižek 2008a:53). The disguised characteristics, here Canace's ethnicity, guarantee the experience of *plus-que-jouir*, surplus enjoyment, making the subject of desire even more alluring due to the secret it conceals. The *objet petit a* determines the identity of the other despite being only one of the factors contributing to the shape of this identity. According to Lacan, what remains hidden makes all the difference. The character of *jouissance*, functioning as "enjoyment" in Žižek's theorization of Lacan's ideas, conforms to the treatment of an ethnic other in oriental romance, because the other becomes there a potential factor of pleasure, but also one of coinciding unpleasure stimulated by the other's threatening nature.[28] The *objet petit a*, in Chaucer's tale being Canace's ethnicity, appears to Lacan also indispensable for the identity formation of the *I*: as Joseph Bristow puts it, "the subject must project a little object in the field of the other (*autre*) so that it can recognize itself" (1997:90). The ethnicity has to remain veiled so as to be a source of simultaneous pleasure and unpleasure, while Western readers may construct their own identity in relation to the experience of this secret. Canace's origin renders any concretization of desire impossible, hence it indeed stands for the *objet petit a*, according to Žižek "simultaneously the pure lack, the void around which the desire turns and which, as such, causes the desire, *and* the imaginary element which conceals this void, renders it invisible by filling it out" (2005:178).[29] The ascetic attitude towards the other, alluring as this other is, guarantees what Cohen also identifies as surplus enjoyment: renunciation of any pleasure on the part of the other gives one more than pure enjoyment, so a surplus of enjoyment is produced (2003:103), analogous to the way that surplus value is produced in the Marxist system of thought (Žižek 2008b:54).

Ethnicity becomes a visible subtext (also because skin colour is subjected to the criterion of visibility) in *The Squire's tale*: it is a subtext subtly indicated, but casting a long shadow on our modern (or rather postmodern) reception of the tale.[30] In Chaucer's tale ethnicity exhibits its true nature: that of a propitious ground for fantasy. Canace could become an object of verbalized fantasy if her different ethnic origin was conspicuous, but she might just as well become a Lacanian object of *jouissance*, or rather of *plus-que-jouir*, due to the concealment of her ethnicity. The term "ethnicity" should be employed here instead of "race", since the latter remained virtually unknown in the Middle Ages and was used in a different context even in the early modern period, the time of intensive confrontations with racial others during the colonial process.[31]

---

28 Fradenburg distinguishes between *jouissance* and enjoyment by maintaining that "*jouissance* is not full and absolute enjoyment, it must always be deferred, bought and paid for with the sacrifice *of* enjoyment" (2002:158).

29 "Fulfillment [has to be] forever deferred" in jouissance, as Fradenburg remarks in her illuminating psychoanalytic take on Chaucer's work (2002:6).

30 The validity of postmodern interpretations of medieval culture was considered by, for instance, Andrew Taylor, who in the essay *Chaucer, our Derridean contemporary* views the Middle English author as a writer commenting on the things preceding his age and adopting a "postmodern" attitude to them (1993:471-86).

31 It does not mean that "ethnicity" has been an ideologically neutral term; footnote 12 to Osborne and Sandford's "Introduction" to *Philosophies of Race and Ethnicity* includes a short discussion of "ethnicity" from the 1920s "cover[ing] over the forms of specifically

Margo Hendricks and Patricia Parker call *race* "a highly unstable term even in the early modern period" (1994:1) and explain that "*raza* in Spanish, *raca* in Portuguese or 'race' in French and English variously designated notions of lineage or genealogy, as in the sense of a noble (or biblical) 'race and stock'" (1994:2). It by no means indicates that no such notion existed then, because Jews and Saracens were permanently identified as not only culturally, but also physically different.[32] Significantly, no complication of the term "race" by the introduction of "ethnicity" was perspicuous in medieval culture.[33] Kwame Anthony Appiah summarizes the issue by stating that some scholars resist the use of the term race in medieval contexts, but avoiding the semantic controversy inherent in the term "would make a history of racism going back to the Middle Ages impossible" (2002, quoted in Lampert 2004:392). Also Akbari argues the same: she insists that there has been continuity between the medieval and modern ideas of alterity (2009:156).

Nevertheless, even theoreticians of race and ethnicity in the modern world stress the existence of, to quote Peter Osborne and Stella Sandford, "the widespread acknowledgement of its lack of objective validity as a principle for the classification of human differences", making the idea of race "an illusion" (2002:1). The illusive character of race derives from its entanglement with the somatic and with the act of perception, as Linda Martín Alcoff insists: "race is a particular, historically and culturally located form of human categorization involving visual determinants marked on the body through the interplay of perceptual practices and bodily appearance" (2002:17). As a result, there has never existed one unchanging idea of race: it "has not had one meaning or a single essential criterion, but its meanings have always been mediated through visual appearance, however complicated" (Alcoff 2002:18). Appiah undermines the category of race altogether when he argues that many people do not fit into any racial category at all and even if you manage to categorize someone on the basis of some characteristics, it "implies very little about most of their other

---

racial discrimination"; see Omi and Winant (1994:9-23), quoted in: Osborne and Sandford (2002:174).
32 Bartlett claims that as the time progressed, what he terms medieval racism grew (1993:236).
33 Osborne and Sandford thus explain the complication of the term "race" by introducing the idea of ethnicity: "'ethnicity' has not so much replaced 'race' as an object of conceptual analysis, genealogical construction and political critique, as supplemented and complicated it – displacing some dimensions of its meaning while reinforcing others" (2002:4); as a matter of fact, however, our usage of the word "ethnicity" is partly anachronistic since it entered English in the late fourteenth century only to acquire the meaning close to "nationality" in the fifteenth century.

biological characteristics" (1995:277). According to Appiah *belief* in races is deeply consequential to human life, whereas the existence of races *per se* is not (1995:277). As for "ethnicity", Werner Sollors claims that it is "typically based on a *contrast*", which distinguishes "us" from "them" defined by various categories (1995:288).[34]

Fantasizing about the implications of ethnic alterity in the case of Orientals led to psychologically grounded images of the enticing ethnic others in Western culture, as Cohen maintains, of oriental promiscuity and the pleasures it occasions for a Westerner traveling to the East. "Fantasies of Saracen bodily difference have always been inextricable from fantasies of the pleasures of Saracen bodies," as Cohen writes (2003:208). Ethnic difference, exposed rather than hidden, thus was a fantasy which entered oriental romance, perhaps due to not only the genre's openness to fantasies of all sorts, to mention only Ingham's "sovereign fantasies" of proto-colonial provenance in Arthurian romance, but also to the marvellous as an inseparable ingredient of oriental romance.[35] The body of an ethnic other, as *The Squire's tale* exemplifies it, is the unattainable object of fantasy: it is simultaneously wanted and rejected, and the schizophrenic reaction complicates the experience to such an extent that the other becomes an unattainable entity. The sexual fantasy becomes merely a point of departure for the fantasy of cultural difference, but the cultural fantasy is grounded in the conviction of the need to subjugate the other rather than the dream of being seduced by it.

Consequently, Saracen bodies become a fantasy object due to not only the sexual attraction and repulsion they simultaneously provoke in the phenomenon of *jouissance*, or rather the more complex *plus-que-jouir*, but also because they potentially belong to the category that could be named "the body marvellous"; it is the body whose human capabilities are enhanced or extended through magic objects and the marvellous capabilities the objects stimulate. Once the body of the other extended by such appendages is at hand, it calls for appropriation due to the practical dimension of the objects that enrich its capabilities. Ethnicity tends to signal the possibility of the marvellous in the case of a given literary figure, while Tartars were customarily identified as associated with the marvellous, as Debra Higgs Strickland says (2002:200-209). Magic is useful, as

---

[34] The difference between "race" and "ethnicity" that Sollors notes (that in current American usage "race" is more objective than ethnicity) (1995:289) is irrelevant to our considerations here, since etymologically the idea of "race" appeared after the medieval period.

[35] Ingham insists that Arthurian romances offer "a fantasy of insular union, an 'imagined community' of British sovereignty" (2001:2) and entail "the 'unending longing and loss' of late medieval colonial encounters" (2001:79).

romance writers appear to claim, so an ethnically different body may be desired also because of its potentially extra-human skills attained through access to the marvellous. The sexual fantasy is not enough: it has to be complemented by the fantasy of supernatural capabilities that ethnicity implies.

A medieval body seems to function as an amalgam of various factors, from which it cannot be stripped so as to be analyzed on its own. Ethnicity is one of those factors, possibly triggering desire, and gender is another. As a result, ethnicity cannot be detached from gender and other identity markers, such as religion and culture. As Lynda E. Boose puts it, in pre-modern European literatures ethnicity used to be a gender-marked issue. Ethnic origin connoted specific sexual behaviour in the Western eyes, with many stereotypes breeding sexual fantasies associated with the Orient: in medieval literature exotic lands tend to be inhabited by promiscuous ladies and effete men, a fantasy materialized in the Western vision of a harem (Boose 1994:37). A darker-skinned woman, or rather any representative of the East physically different from European women, becomes an (unattainable) object of desire. Only conversion to Christianity would transform her into someone not out of reach of a Westerner.

Canace's attractiveness derives both from the promising alterity of the ethnic other, veiled here as it is, and from the somatic indeterminacy grounded in the marvellous that allows the body to enter the realm of the supernatural: fantastically enough, Canace begins to understand the language of birds whenever she wears "of gold a ryng" (V:83), from the moment it is delivered to the court by a mysterious messenger. The magic object instantly acquires the label of "Canacees ryng" (V:247), as it is introduced to the court as such, which symbolically implies that it is inseparable from the princess's body. Yet the object remains a technological invention of a kind, since the power of technology lies, as Lee Patterson summarizes it, in "the capacity of human beings to transform the material conditions of their lives" (1993:51). The ring potentially allows Canace to become an interpreter of birds' words, especially if those words can be related, further on, to the Squire's (and Chaucer's) audience, which strengthens the princess's position in the romance as she becomes a go-between for the Eastern and Western cultures. The gift endows the Tartar princess with a new self, even more attractive to Westerners due to her newly acquired capabilities. It is an example of Patterson's "technology of the self", even though "the self" is here rather the Lacanian "other" against which Western selfhood may see itself. A new self is constructed for Canace by the narrator, materializing what Foucault termed "technologies of the self", which in our modern culture stand side by side "technologies of production", "technologies of sign systems", and "technologies of power" (1988:18).

"Technologies of the self," Foucault writes, "permit individuals to effect by their own means or with the help of others a certain number of operations on their own bodies and souls, thoughts, conduct, and a way of being, so as to transform themselves in order to attain a certain state of happiness, purity, wisdom, perfection, or immortality" (1988:18). In the case of Canace the operation is performed on her body by dint of magic and the magic object she wears undoubtedly makes her more perfect in the eyes of Chaucer's English audiences. A minor difference is that she does not transform herself fully consciously, but rather subjects herself to workings of the supernatural force, unaware of the outcome since she cannot control it.

The fantasies of an enticing ethnic identity and that of a somatic form enriched in its capabilities by magic objects, such as "the queynte ryng" (V:433), by no means exhaust the list of possible fantasies that the tale records. Alan S. Ambrisco indicates another illusion in Chaucer, namely that of effective communication transcending all languages and cultures. He writes that in Part II, where the narrative proper on Canace and her supernatural abilities start, "gone . . . are the Squire's inept paraphrases and his clumsy use of occupatio; in their place emerge a fantasy of linguistic competence and the dream of an immediate and unapologetic English translation" (2004:216). Canace, a dream-like princess from romance, becomes a medium through which the avian discourse is effortlessly transferred into human language. Frictionless translation from the birds' language to the human one entails an illusion that ideal translation is possible. The device of the magic ring alters Canace's bodily form to such an extent that her whole somatic frame becomes an instrument: her body transforms itself into a translating device functioning as a medium between languages, smoothly connecting that which would be kept separate but for the magic intervention. Her body thus exists on yet another level: it becomes a symbol of the illusion that there exists such a phenomenon as ideal translation, *verbatim* and artistic at the same time. Canace becomes the carrier of marvellous linguistic capabilities and hence an ideal wife for a Western Christian, symbolizing the illusion that ideal transfer between languages and cultures is possible. L.O.Aranye Fradenburg's statement about technology which is "not better than fantasy [since it is] the *realization* of fantasy" seems to summarize the situation well: owing to technology Canace becomes an even more attractive object of fantasy (2004:8). The body in *The Squire's tale* thus becomes a magical entity; John Finlayson's definition of magic is particularly relevant here, because he classifies it as "the marvellous controlled by man" (1999:364). It comes fairly close to technology, since it is a phenomenon deriving from human activity, so it remains symbolically close to the body from which it originates. Technology and magic do not necessarily have to be contrasted with the body, because they derive from the body (and intellect) of their creator and complement it, as *The Squire's tale* demonstrates with its display of marvels.

Fradenburg, however, maintains that we modern readers ought not to overestimate the importance of the marvellous in the Middle Ages. In real life people were not as uncritically fascinated with it as we usually deduce on the basis of literary works, especially romance (2004:3).[36] Fiction obviously stands on a different level than real life, a manifestation of which fact materializes in medieval people's indifference to the idea of the marvellous, as opposed to the preoccupation with the marvellous in romance, which a significant medieval genre, the one which currently symbolizes the Middle Ages.[37] Fradenburg insightfully associates the genre with the idea of wonder in her formulation that "medieval romance is fascinated *with* wonder. It seeks to provoke states of wonder in its various audiences and explores the nature of wonder in its narratives" (2004:5). Medieval authors were interested in portraying the psychology of wonder. Oriental romance in particular appears to be a fecund ground for the exploration of wonder: it is involved in the presentation of what we call here "the body marvellous" in oriental romance. Here the audience's wonder derives from at least two sources: the fascination with magical interventions and with the agent of those interventions, the body of the other, whose ethnic alterity may become only subtly marked, but such presentation not infrequently renders it more exciting. In that subgroup of romances the category of wonder resides in the material world, thus limiting the cultures of the other to the sphere of objects and other visible indices of difference. All the rich intellectual culture of the Eastern world is irretrievably lost for the romances' audience, flattening their cognition of the Orient.

Having Canace listen to a tale of love and betrayal, Chaucer makes her a figure that suggests affinity with the so-called "enamoured princess" type, for Metlitzki one of the "four stock figures of oriental romance", along with the converted Saracen, the defeated emir or sultan, and the giant defeated and killed by a Christian (1977:161). That may be another reason, aside from guaranteeing surplus-enjoyment to the audience, for concealing Canace's ethnic identity, since enamoured princesses in oriental romances also lack the markers of ethnic difference due to the conversion to Christianity they all undergo in the end. In

---

36 Fradenburg claims that "Medieval people were not enchanted by marvels *tout court* . . . [so] critique of the marvellous did not await the Age of Enlightenment" (2004:3).
37 Romance clearly symbolizes the medieval period for people living in the modern age, despite the genre's ancient provenance. Ganim describes the story of the study of romance as "the master narrative of the study of medieval literature and of medieval culture in general" (2005:17).

Middle English texts particularly the character of Floripas, appearing in *Sir Ferumbras*, *Firumbras*, and *The sowdone of Babylone*, remains a conspicuous illustration of the type. All of the texts mentioned are English versions of the French *Fierabras*, of whom two fourteenth-century manuscripts exist, but the romance, deriving from a *chanson de geste*, has to be dated much earlier because it belongs to the group of Charlemagne-romances (Herrtage 1879 [1966]:vi). *The sowdone of Babylone* embraces the content of the French original preceded by a translation of *Destruction of Rome*, though *Sir Ferumbras* is a modified version of the second part of the poem (Herrtage 1879 [1966]: xiii). *Firumbras* is very close to the substance of *Sir Ferumbras*, while the dating of the two remains a puzzle for the scholars; the first manuscript was mentioned by Guy de Beauchamp, Earl of Warwick, in the fourteenth century (Herrtage 1879 [1966]: xi). Mary O'Sullivan once identified *Firumbras* as more likely a pre- than a post-Chaucerian work (1935 [1987]: xx). *The sowdone of Babylone* is usually dated from around 1450 (Millar-Heggie 2004). Here I am going to analyze *Sir Ferumbras* as a text more focused on the characters of Ferumbras, Floripas, and their father Balam, rather than discuss the more elaborate *Sowdone of Babylone*, which has been addressed in more detail in the criticism (Metlitzki 1977; Lupack 1990; Millar-Heggie 2004).

Metlitzki stresses that for instance *The sowdone of Babylone*, as was stated earlier, "barely fit[s] a definition of romance" (1977:160), so perhaps we should call this bulk of translations from *chansons de geste* "oriental romances" only for the sake of convenience. At the same time, we should be aware of their "unromantic" nature, if we associate romance with "romantic" themes. Metlitzki insists that they are "essentially vehicles of fanatical propaganda in which the moral ideal of chivalry is subservient to the requirements of religion, politics, and ideology", citing mainly such figures as Floripas, "a Goneril virago", and Ferumbras, a converted Saracen (1977:160). Also the ethnicity of this romance character is hidden here by such phrases as the one that Floripas is a "maide fair & gent" (*SF* 1204), which implies that the "fairness" again eclipses the princess's real ethnic background.[38] It is a matter of contention whether the princess is whitened so as to make her marriageable for Christians or whether the favourable portrayal of physicality is meant to contrast with the character that needs to be judged negatively regardless of the anonymous author's intentions. Her comeliness, implied even by her flowery name, since it derives most likely from *passe-fleur*, the wood anemone (Herrtage 1879 [1966]:xviii), rather than from the *fleur de Paques* with all its religious connotations, confirms

---

38 All the quotations from *Sir Ferumbras* are preceded by the abbreviation *SF* and, along with subsequent line numbers, come from Herrtage's edition (1879 [1966]).

the intuition that she cannot be dark-skinned if she has a flowery, beautiful name. Her physicality, concealing her ethnicity, strongly contrasts with her gruesome acts, and this contrast illustrates the impossibility of directing real desire towards her by any of the Franks.

Floripas is introduced into the plot after the forcible conversion of her brother Ferumbras, carried out as an alternative to death. Vanquished, Ferumbras beseeches Oliver:

> "Haue mercy of me, iantail kny3t; for Marie sone þat mayde.
> & For his loue þat al may see; y pray þe, sle me no3t;
> Hit is my wille cristned to bee; certis þat is my þo3t.
> My godes þat y me affied on; buþ no3t to haue on mynde,
> þay mo3e no more to þan a ston; & þat y now auynde,
> 3if hit by-tideþ so þat y may; be y-wareschid of my wounde,
> y schal scaþye hem ni3t & day; þat bileueþ on Mahounde;
> Cristendom by me schal encressed be; sykerly if y may scape;
> & for payenye, so mot y þe; ful yuele wil y schape;
> þanne schulleþ peynymes cristned be; & hure lay for-sake.
> . . ."
>
> (*SF* 753-762)

Unsurprisingly, Ferumbras's zeal to convert other Muslims (in all likelihood also by force) cannot be justified merely by the prospect of death that he is facing. Furthermore, in the scenes to follow he will put his plans into practice, disillusioning those who thought that in terms of conversion he would limit himself to words uttered in order to save his life. On the other hand, the speech is made by a Muslim lying disembowelled in front of Oliver, a renowned Christian knight ready to slay him. The reaction to the promise that he will be christened is instantaneous: Oliver "pulte is bowels in ageyn" (*SF* 774) and took Ferumbras to Charlemagne's court. Another speech by the Saracen, this time delivered before the sacrament is bestowed on him, reveals that he agrees under duress, making "a grete sy3yng" (*SF* 1040), since he has "ynow of greuaunce" (*SF* 1043). He confesses motivation to become Christian in the following: "haue myn oþ y-swered/ þat y schal euere fro þys day; þe heþene lay for-sake,/ And beleue in cristene fay" (*SF* 1045-1047). Honour makes him do what he has sworn to do, though he must also realize the inevitable consequences of declining to be christened. His identity as an honourable man strongly contrasts with his subsequent actions: he ultimately betrays his Muslim folk, which leads to the downfall and death of his own father, sultan Balam. Still, he does it under the new baptismal name of "Florens", as if he had been given a new life during the sacrament, which allowed him to emotionally detach himself from the people he originated from. Notwithstanding his ignoble behaviour, Ferumbras's conversion has been enforced on him, while the change of sides by his sister Floripas has not been: she was not forced to take the side of Franks, so she did it out of her own accord.

Once Ferumbras has returned to his people as a baptized man, Floripas reacts with transitory sorrow: "for hure broþer sche gan to wepe; ac sone sche had ido" (*SF* 1214). She appears to act on the spur of the moment, because not much later she gets smitten with Oliver at first sight and is determined to free him and his people, regardless of the moral costs. The character just introduced to the audience as fair and sweet commits execrable acts of ruthless brutality. First, she sweeps the jailor Brytamon out of her way:

> She lefte þe dore & wend him ner & lifte vp the staf with mayne,
> & so on þe heued sche set him þer; þat out sterte al is brayne.
> "Rest," quaþ sche, "þow soty wy3t; god 3yue yuele chaunce!
> now schal y speke my fille ri3t; with þes kny3tes of fraunce."
> (*SF* 1250-1253)

The other murder, that of her own governess, is even more deplorable in its unscrupulousness. This one leaves no doubt as to how Floripas views her old kinship bonds; significantly, the governess begins her last dialogue with the words "doghtere", confirming the existence of those bonds between the two of them:

> "Do3tere," sche saide, "wat men buþ þeese; þat þou hast of prisoun
>   y-bro3t?
> þy fader loue þow schalt lese; for hymen as y ha þo3t.
> þe longe man wyþ þe pale fas; þat ys erld Olyuer
> þat ouercom þy brother Fyrumbras; ful wel y knowe hym þer:
> þat oþer wiþ þe crollid her; þat stent hym faste by,
> þat ys Berard of mountdisdier; & þe þridde ys Ausbery:
> þe ferthe þat stent hymen bytwyn; þat is Scot Gwylmere;
> þe fifthe ys Geffray Langeuyn; of france a doþþepere.
> ne schal y neuere ete no more; bi Mahoun, þat ys my lord,
> Or y ha told þy fader fore; þy doyngge euery word."
> (*SF* 1350-1359)

Again, the Franks' whiteness is set in opposition to the non-whiteness of the Saracens. Oliver is characterized as "þe longe man wiþ þe pale fas" (*SF* 1352), whose paleness unmistakably displays ethnic difference, which implies here also the difference in culture and frame of mind. The governess does not comprehend that the disparity is also noticeable between herself and Floripas: the latter will not scruple to shove her out of the window so as to release the Frankish knights from prison; when talking to the governess she probably has this new allegiance in mind.

It appears that, despite the romance's crude ideology and the fact that it can undeniably be classified as one of the "pulp fictions of medieval England" (McDonald 2004), the anonymous author plays with the audience by selling to them what could otherwise be morally reprehensible as acceptable behaviour. De Weever insists that the writer and his audience saw no wrong in the treachery of Floripas and other enamoured princesses betraying their folk. I would argue that Floripas is portrayed negatively so as to make her even more out of reach of the Western audience of the romance, who perhaps intuited that her behaviour was ignoble, regardless of whether Christians benefited from it or not. The possible ambivalence over her was produced on purpose so as guarantee even more surplus-enjoyment than her ethnicity did, which was concealed through negating her possible blackness. The audience was made to evaluate her behaviour as praiseworthy, so her immorality was concealed by the author's acceptance of the way she acted. Nevertheless, the audience could feel that she was unethical and repulsive, which made her the most interesting object of desire imaginable: the desire could not be realized, as Floripas both represented the other and ultimately turned out to be a traitor, that is, somebody who could also betray her new Christian folk. Desire, according to Lacan, can never be materialized; it stands for pure lack. The lack is here embodied in the oriental princess who will never be really marriageable for anyone due to the peril she represents; even if she should become the wife of one of the Christian characters in the end, it might end badly for them. Goodman supports this hypothesis when she insists that such enamoured princesses have to be slightly repellent even to their future husbands: they must not hold sway over a Christian through their beauty before they are baptized (1997:125). In this sense Floripas is no object of desire, but rather a figure that sets the desire in motion, while no termination or fulfilment is possible. As Bruce Fink comments on the Lacanian understanding of the idea,

> Desire, *strictly speaking, has no object*. In its essence, desire is a constant search for something else, and there is no specifiable object that is capable of satisfying it, in other words, extinguishing it. Desire is fundamentally caught up in the dialectical movement of one signifier to the next, and is diametrically opposed to fixation. It does not seek satisfaction, but rather its own continuation and furtherance: more desire, greater desire! It wishes merely to go on desiring (1995:90).

Floripas's ethnicity and the atmosphere of moral ambivalence that envelops her thus set the Westerner's desire in motion, but the process of desiring her does not expire once she is married to Oliver, but rather interminably continues, since the desire cannot be fulfilled regardless of her being married or not.

In the course of the princess's "adventures" while attempting to free the knights, she replicates the pattern observable in *The Squire's tale*: her body acquires the qualities of what was previously termed here, for the sake of convenience, "the body marvellous". The magic object complementing her corporeal frame proves to be imperative for the Franks starving during the siege: she owns a girdle, "þat gurdel fyn; no hunger ne may hem deere" (*SF* 2395), a talisman against hunger. The object becomes much coveted by the Saracens, too, because Maubyn attempts to steal it from the sleeping princess: "Slepyng was þat ladi softe; þe þef him bar ful stille,/ And to & fro wende he ofte; or he hauede ys wille:/ Ate laste þan gurdel he fond; liggyng at hure hede" (*SF* 2417-2419). Stripping Floripas of the most valuable object she owns does not suffice for the villain: "To lye be þat burder þoȝte he þo; & to don hure schame & schonde" (*SF* 2426); he intends to rape her, which will mean defiling her body and making it lose its attractiveness. Floripas awakes and cries for assistance, and Guy hears her, which leads to the instantaneous slaying of Maubyn. Nevertheless, the girdle is irretrievably lost once the Saracen's body is cast into the sea, as no one realized he was wearing the object after stealing it. Again, as in Chaucer, the bodily frame of the Eastern princess is not enough for her to remain a fantasy object interminably. Rather, she has to be endowed with some extra quality, which is here the ability to guarantee the flow of nourishment to the Westerners waging a war against Saracens. Her body becomes a result of employing of what Marcel Mauss termed "the bodily techniques": through them a bodily frame is ready to respond to the surrounding world in a way specific to it. As Feher says, Mauss' techniques "mingle physical capacities and mental mechanisms to form a body adapted to circumstances: the body of a charismatic citizen or of a visionary monk, a mirror image of the world or a reflection of a spirit" (1986:11). In *Sir Ferumbras* it is a body commenting on the world in which it lives: in this world the body of an ethnic other ultimately has to play a purely utilitarian role for Western Europeans. It is not enough for a Saracen princess to be sexually attractive to Franks; she also has to undertake the role of a nourisher through the talisman she wears. Clothed in a magic object which has the function of a talisman, her body becomes a talismanic entity itself: the magic quality of the girdle is extended to her whole person, perhaps attenuating her personal characteristics but in exchange of making her a desirable object during the hostilities. It may enrich the Christian community through its marvellous capabilities if it becomes a part of this social body.

If we ponder on the image of the social body in oriental romance, the late Middle Ages saw the popularity of *Corpus Christianorum* as the metaphor of the Christian Church. To quote Michael Uebel, "the body was the principal paradigm through which the sacral community was imagined" (1996:277). The bodily imagery had been employed in the Western Christian discourse before that stage: as Andrew Louth notes, prior to the twelfth century the term *corpus*

Christi designated either the historical body of Christ or the Church. The shift in terminology led to *corpus Christi mysticum* standing for the Church, while *corpus Christi* or *corpus verum* meant the Eucharist (1997:122). Nevertheless, the Church as the metaphorical body shared by all Christians was imagined to suffer interminably at the hands of infidels, regardless of whether they, like the fictional Jews from the anti-Judaic narratives, did real harm to the Eucharist, or they did not have any contacts with Christianity and its rituals. Once the Eucharist became central to the understanding of Christianity, the private contemplation of the sacrament gave leeway for mysticism as a phenomenon detached from the Church (Louth 1997:125). From then onwards the body was allowed to express private feeling. Perhaps the metaphors of the Christian body derived from this novel imagination: the body acquired an abstract life, abstracted from the lives of the actual believers, and it could symbolically be tormented by the very existence of people representing a different religion, particularly when that religion was culturally and politically threatening, even if real-life Christians were not affected by it at all. As Uebel notes, Robert the Monk and Guilbert of Nogent were explicit about the legendary Saracen cruelty to Westerners, which for these two authors materialized the symbolic torment that the "Christian body" underwent as a result of the confrontations between East and West. "The Saracens reduce the body to its utter materiality," as Uebel summarizes the reproaches, "stripping it of any religious signification and opening it up to the flux and chaos of the merely physical. Saracens make the Christian body into an object of manipulation and observation, converting the Christian from the position of subject to the status of object of knowledge" (1996:279). Attempting to appropriate the body of the other was a natural counter-reaction to the danger of scrutiny and incorporation that was posed by the Saracen culture.

The Franks in *Sir Ferumbras* must comprehend those mechanisms well if Floripas is wooed by their culture and incorporated by it. The individual body of the princess, equipped with the magic object that amazingly supplies one of the warring parties with nourishment, becomes an indispensable addition to that collective Christian body, as it can fortify it in its imperial enterprises. The potency of the metaphorical Christian body is thus enhanced, even if helping the Franks has to be viewed with considerable ambivalence as regards the morality of Floripas's attitude. The Christians' military power increases so significantly that they are able to defeat the sultan, so the question of morality does not have to become an issue at all. The victors are at all times morally right, it seems. Once Floripas enters the Christian community, she loses her individual qualities, including the disloyalty that led her to betrayal. The difference between right and wrong is blurred on purpose so as to situate the benefits for the collectivity above the detriment to private morality. The scene of Floripas's baptism is missing from the truncated Middle English manuscript, but in French *Fierabras* the moment is conveyed thus: Christians "ont donné la puciele sainte crestienté,/ Et par nom de bautesme ont son cors generé" [they gave the girl baptismal water,/ And they created her body through the baptismal name] (*SF* 5895-5896). Giving Floripas a new "body" is enough to make her trustworthy in the eyes of Christians: she becomes Guy's wife, while Spain is divided into the part assigned to her husband and that given to Fierabras/Ferumbras. Her physical beauty is underlined again when Charlemagne addresses her as "Bele" (*SF* 5923), as if no moral turpitude had ever characterized her. Furthermore, the scene in which she is stripped naked in order to be baptized has been termed by Metlitzki "sexual glamour in the unconscious" (1977:186).[39] After the sacrament as a symbolic incorporation of Floripas's body into *Corpus Christianorum* her identity becomes fragmented, as if the darker aspect of that character has never existed. Only a part of the princess is adopted by the Western culture, while its other, more treacherous, aspect is symbolically severed from her identity. All past betrayals become attenuated and forgotten. If in *chansons de geste*, the genre which inspired the type of oriental romance in question, the enemies' bodies were literarily fragmented, here the Saracen princess's body is metaphorically severed from the body of Islam. Furthermore, her identity has to be dissected if she is to become the wife of a Christian knight. Obviously, the act of forgetting her real role in the events is artificial, but it well illustrates the policy of Westerners towards the East. If her fairness was superficial, because it disguised her actual ethnicity, so is her new virtue.

As for the betrayal in the romance, it appears that it may result from the situation in which Oliver becomes the *objet a* for Floripas, whose disguised ethnicity in turn has the function of the *objet petit a*. The *objet a* "subtracted from reality . . . gives it consistency", but it cannot be included in the reality (Žižek 2008a:xvi). Oliver is Floripas's object of desire, but he remains situated outside the reality in which she lives. The love which leads to causing death and destruction in one's original community suggests a mechanism in which Oliver would be, to cite Fradenburg's words referring to the Gawain-Poet's *Pearl*, "the epitome of the *objet a* – the object of love so powerful that it can rival and replace the love of the self or the group"(2002:108). Incorporation of Floripas's literal and symbolic body into the Christian community could then only be a natural consequence of the "big Other" coming into play and emerging as a representative of the Real. The horror would be natural in confrontation with Floripas's act representing the unspeakable. Had she loved herself more, she

---

39 Akbari also discusses the scene of Floripas's baptism in the French version (2009:178).

would not have sentenced her own father to death at the hands of Christians. Yet the love for the fair-skinned Oliver proved to be an imperative for her, which drove her to enter *Corpus Christianorum*, despite the aura of otherness surrounding her and reactions of revulsion that she would always inspire in the Christians of the romance.

In conclusion, the theory of the *objet petit a* allows us to see the function of ethnically marked female bodies in oriental romances in a different light and to inspect the workings of fantasy in those texts. The ambiguity stemming from the inadequacy of equating "ethnically different" with "beautiful" results in the formation of a very complex image, especially if we add the idea of the "body marvellous" to our interpretation of Canace as an enamoured princess type and of Floripas from the *Firumbras* romances. Terminology concerning "race" and "ethnicity" does not matter as much as the fact that the enamoured princesses should remain out of reach for the Westerners who surround them. The new world they initially promise appears to be a false track for all Christians, because the women cannot be made fully Christian themselves. Furthermore, in those texts our discussion always needs to go beyond the concept of an individual body, because the communal body of all Christians and the metaphorical tainted body of Islam should be included in this image.

Chapter Two
Community, *Richard le Coer de Lyon*, and chivalric anthropophagy

> "The history of its modes of construction can . . . turn the body into a thoroughly historicized and completely problematic issue"
> (Michael Feher *Introduction* to *Fragments for a history of the human body*) (1989:11)

In *Communitas: the origin and destiny of the community*, Roberto Esposito delineates the community as both a gift which has to be accepted (2010:4) and an obligation of its members towards one another, "benefit and service rendered, joining and threat" (2010:13). Modern individualism proved to be conducive to attempts to be released from that twofold relationship, which would eliminate "possible conflict with [one's] neighbor" and "the contagion of the relation with others" (2010:13). The medieval idea of *communitas* must have been structured on what Thomas Hobbes defined later as fear that perpetrated the social life within it.[40] The fear increased violence and, as Esposito argues after René Girard's theory of scapegoating, "the community can survive the violence that traverses it only by shifting violence onto an enemy that is able to attract it" (2010:33). For the English *communitas* in the Middle English romance *Richard le Coer de Lyon* the enemies able to draw this negative attention are ostensibly Saracens in the far-off lands to which the king crusades. The communal violence culminates there when the flesh of the other undergoes ingestion and digestion so that the community in England can be reaffirmed. Nevertheless, the benefit proves to be dubious once we consider what Esposito characterizes as "an absolute exteriorization that subtracts community from itself", resulting from "that power, which is founded precisely on the impossibility of suppressing the enemy, [and which] can keep the community united only by dividing it, eliminating it as a community" (2010:33). The violence against others then

---

40 The idea of *communitas* employed here refers to Esposito's recent concept rather than the oft criticized idea of Victor and Edith Turner (1995), who described the alleged uniformity of medieval groups of pilgrims and disregarded the social diversification observable during the pilgrimages; their idea has frequently been undermined.

simultaneously unites the community and leads to its dissolution, as the Muslim threat can never be ultimately eliminated. The bodies of the others, always potentially dead as they are subjected to continuing violence, stand in the way of communal life and paradoxically keep it operating.

The bodies of those materializing cultural alterity are oftentimes presented as prone to what Freud identified as taboo in his study of "primitive" cultures, *Totem and taboo* (1946). As a matter of fact, this is a text which Esposito sees as continuing Hobbes' pessimistic account of human "natural aggressivity" (2010:35). In this magisterial but still not adequately appreciated work, the founding father of psychoanalysis starts with an interpretation of what he considered to be the first taboo phenomenon in those cultures, incest. Anthropological investigation into native cultures is for him but a point of departure for arguing that incest remains within the range of taboo issues in all cultures, including ours (1946:3-25). Another taboo mentioned by Freud has been cannibalism. The question of whether cannibalism was a customary practice, as was imagined by the medieval European visitors to Asia and the early modern Western conquerors of America, and whether it existed at all, gave rise to many controversies. Cannibalism was usually discussed as a literary image that became a part of numerous ancient and medieval panoramas of the remote lands whose reality was hardly known. Anthropophagy either occasionally ceased to be taboo in those cultures and it existed there then or, as William Arens implies, was a myth narrated by the European explorers but hardly ever experienced by them, because they usually discussed it in their ethnographic writing as a thing of the past (1998:41). Arens claims that ethnic others were subjected to exoticization so that they conformed to the discourse interpreting alterity from the perspective of colonial fictions (1998:41), even though he does not explore the question whether people have ever eaten each other; consequently, he does not undermine the idea of the very existence of the phenomenon, but rather inspects it as something operating in all cultures, including ours (1979:9).

The term "anthropophagy" could be more adequate in our discussion of medieval man-eating practices, since the word "cannibal" derives from the Arawak *caniba*, a corruption of *cariba* ("bold") that the Caribbean Indians of the Lesser Antilles gave to themselves. Arawaks were the peace-loving Native Americans of Cuba, who were often attacked by another tribe, Caribs (Lestringant 1997:15). The antagonism between the Arawaks and the Caribs gave rise to the image of *canibs* as bloodthirsty and highly uncivilized. It is no wonder that European explorers, who arrived in America with many preconceptions about man-eating natives, readily adopted the Arawak vision of their ferocious neighbours. European culture had long sustained the legend of the man-eating cynocephali; hence Columbus and his companions combined the mythical monstrous race with the real-life natives notorious for their fierceness. In one of his letters Dr. Diego Alvarez Chanca, who sailed with Columbus during the second voyage to the Caribbean, discusses their suspicion that the islands where a few human bones had been discovered were "those islands of Caribe, which are inhabited by people who eat human flesh" (Hulme – Whitehead 1992, quoted in Hulme 1998:16). These two terms, *canib* and *carib*, were later reworked by Shakespeare into *calib*, which appears in the name of the island's disempowered ruler in *The tempest*. The association between the monstrous race and *canibs* intensified also through a sound similarity: Frank Lestrigant points out that *canis* and *caniba* seem so close to each other that a false etymological link was created. Nevertheless, anthropophagy remained a set of different culinary habits rather than a strategy of aggression. Only later, and according to Frank Lestringant for the first time in André Thevet's *Singularités de la France antarctique*,[41] could cannibalism be portrayed as a strategy of taking revenge on the enemy rather than a peculiar manner of sating one's appetite (1997:62). The cannibalism of Richard le Coer de Lyon should arguably be seen both against the background of mythical savages eating human flesh out of hunger and against the medieval idea of revenge as part of chivalric culture. Revenge as something chivalric was, after all, a concept that predated the later association with anthropophagy as an act of vengeance. The romance was consequently a text combining a discussion of the king's chivalry with the portrayal of his vengefulness, culminating in these two acts of consuming the Saracen others, the first unwitting and the second entirely conscious.[42]

The literary tradition of writing about anthropophagy entered the European cultural imagination with Pliny's *Natural History* and then with the *Mirabilia* texts which treated of the monstrous races dwelling in the East. Columbus was familiar with it as well, because he repeated the myth and its association with Mongols when he erroneously took America for India: "I therefore repeat what I have said several times already: that the Caniba are none other than the people

---

41 Thevet's ethnography became one of the objects of scrutiny in Mary Baine Campbell's *Wonder and science: imagining worlds in early modern Europe* (1999:30-50).

42 Jacek Mydla stresses an important difference between discussions of anthropophagy from the Anglo-Saxon, predominantly Protestant, perspective, which are symbolic and metaphorical, and the Catholic view, concentrating on the deeply ambiguous idea of the Eucharist as close to literal anthropophagy (2003:5); this is supported by Merrall Llewelyn Price, who discusses the Eucharist in the context of Corpus Christi (2003:25-42), and by Heather Blurton, who writes that in the Middle Ages "the image of anthropophagy becomes an extended metaphor for the positively charged creation of religious and social identity" (2007:5).

of the Great Khan, who must be neighbours to these. They have ships, they come and capture these people, and as those who are taken never return, the others believe that they have been eaten" (Janes 1930, quoted in Lestringant 1997:17). Cynocephali were man-eating creatures and the myth of their shape and mores entered medieval scholarship so firmly that eradicating the conviction of their existence in the Orient proved difficult even upon the first real-life contacts with the actual peoples inhabiting the territories. Again, John Carpini's *Historia Mongalorum* and de Bridia's (or Benedict Polonus') *Historia Tartarorum* prove to be invaluable as points of comparison.

The myth of Tartar cannibalism originated from the ancient Wonders of the East (*Mirabilia*) tradition, where dog-heads represented in one image a man-eating monstrous race and ethnic others, incomprehensible in their "barbaric" speech as if they barked like dogs. The medieval *Mirabilia* sources began to identify Saracens with people with the heads of dogs, as visual representations make clear (Strickland 2003:159-160). The well-known legend of *cynocephali* combined with accounts of Tartar culinary habits on first contact with the Mongol world. The envoys from the Pope expected to find a profusion of monstrous races in the East and any hint that the *Mirabilia* sources accurately identified the oriental races of monsters was welcomed by the friars. The *Tartar relation* informs its readers that Tartars indeed ate what was deemed inedible for Europeans; for example, placenta was a possible food for them, as de Bridia or Benedict Polonus claimed. Nonetheless, the writer ends his Mongol "menu" with human flesh as one of the foodstuffs inedible for civilized people, as if he had succumbed to the fiction of the Tartars' relationship with *cynocephali*: "they eat immoderately all forms of unclean food, wolves, foxes, dogs, *carrion*, afterbirths of animals, mice, and, when necessary, human flesh. *Similarly, they reject no species of bird, but eat clean and unclean alike*" (Painter 1965:96). The friars do not take into account the starvation that steppe peoples must have suffered from owing to severe weather conditions; famine in all likelihood made them resort to unusual dietary practices. Yet the Christian writers emphasize the inadequate amounts of food that Mongols have at their disposal. Consequently, as Carpini writes, "they consider it a great sin if any food or drink is allowed to be wasted in any way; consequently they do not allow bones to be given to dogs until the marrow has been extracted" (Carpine 1955:17).

Having witnessed Tartar omnivorousness ensuing from their frequent starvation, John Carpini and Benedict Polonus gullibly trusted everything they heard from their hosts, particularly if it referred to the topic of dogs mating with women. George D. Painter insists that Tartars poked fun at the Westerners by telling them stories of their having encountered unusual hybrids when engaged in conquest under the leadership of Genghis Khan. The following narrative must have come to Carpini's ears through the Russian clerics who acted as interpreters. They spoke Russian to Benedict, the only envoy who knew the language and very likely joined the expedition because of that skill:

> On their return journey through the desert they came to a land where – so we were definitely told at the Emperor's court by Russian clerics and others who had been living among them for a long time – they found monsters who had the likeness of women. When they asked them by means of many interpreters where the men-folk of that country were, they replied that every female born there had a human form, but every male had the shape of a dog (Carpine 1955:23).

Painter jokingly calls such narratives "evidently one of the earliest occurrences of a shaggy dog story", emphasizing the speakers' jocular intentions (1965:72). Tartars were, after all, a jesting folk, almost indecent in the discourse used in order to entertain themselves and provoke laughter. Carpini noted that jocularity and verbal indecency, but could not associate it with the stories that were narrated to him by the Tartars (1955:15). The jokes appear to have provided a fruitful ground for what Benedict described as his personal experience of the monstrous races in Tartary. He approached the realm of fantasy even further when he discussed the unions of "dog's women" and Tartars:

> ... and Friar Benedict believes beyond doubt that he saw one of the dog's women with the Tartars, and says she had even borne male children from them, but the boys were monsters. The aforesaid dogs are exceptionally shaggy, and understand every word the women say, while the women understand the dogs' sign language (Painter 1965:72).

If Mongols were cannibalistic in their resorting even to human placenta as food, perhaps Benedict expected at least some of them to represent the monstrous race of dog-heads. This indicates the fear that belief in the *Mirabilia* entailed. *Cynecephali* were thought to be threatening creatures and perilous sinners through the mixing of kinds that they resulted from and further spread in the world. The negative emotional attitude to them caused Benedict to adjust what he saw to fit his expectations, which had been formed by the lore he had had access to in studying about the Wonders of the East.

Both in Carpini (1955:30-31) and in Benedict (Painter 1965:74) the list of monstrous races includes the Samoyeds, the ox-feet, and "the Parossits",

> *tall in stature but thin and frail*, with a tiny *round* belly *like a little cup. These people eat nothing at all but live on steam, for instead of a mouth they have a minute orifice*, and obtain nourishment by inhaling the steam of meat stewed in a pot *through a small opening; and as they have no regard for the flesh they throw it to their dogs* (Painter 1965:74).

Again, fiction mingles with facts, as the Permiaks, a Finnish tribe, indeed offered the steam of cooked meat to the souls of the dead and this idea was combined with Pliny's legend of an Indian tribe living on the scent of apples (Painter 1965:74). The myth of Mongol anthropophagy was thus maintained through the eyewitness accounts of the dog-heads living among them.

This may cast a different light on the description of Tartars feasting in Chaucer's *Squire's tale*. Thus the tableau-like image of Canace's father, the khan, having the food served to his guests may be interpreted as both an exemplification of Eastern opulence and of eating what should remain inedible, which implies possible cannibalism:

> This Cambyuskan, of which I have yow
>   toold,
> In roial vestiment sit on his deys,
> With diademe, ful heighe in his paleys,
> And halt his feeste so solempne and so ryche
> That in this world ne was ther noon it lyche;
> Of which if I shal tellen al th'array,
> Thanne wolde it occupie a someres day,
> And eek it nedeth nat for to devyse
> At every cours the ordre of hire servyse.
> I wol nat tellen of hir strange sewes,
> Ne of hir swannes, ne of hisr heronsewes.
> Eek in that lond, as tellen knyghtes olde,
> Ther is som mete that is ful deynte holde
> That in this lond men recche of it but smal;
> Ther nys no man that may reporten al.
>   (V:58-72)

On the one hand, the feast introducing Cambuskyan's court to the audience provides them with a commentary on the legendary opulence of the Orient. Akbari insists that the East has existed in the Western culture as a representation of not only sexual, but also economic surplus (2000:19), which could be materialized in alimentation. On the other, the Tartars in Chaucer seem to relish food which would be deemed inedible in the Western world. The Tartar "body marvellous", here on the point of being complemented with magic objects, ingests and digests types of meat considered at best quaint in Western culture: swans and heron chicks. The implication that Tartars might sate their hunger with food which is not only inedible but is also a taboo, because eating it means committing anthropophagy, is palpably present here. After all, the association of Mongols with cannibalistic practices in Matthew Paris's *Chronica maiora* may have been of relevance for Chaucer's vision. In his myth-disseminating text Matthew writes:

The Tartar chiefs, with the houndish cannibals their followers, fed upon the flesh of their carcasses, as if they had been bread, and nothing but bones for the vultures. But, wonderful to tell, the vultures, hungry and ravenous, would not condescend to eat the remnants of flesh, if any by chance were left. The old and ugly women were given to their dog-headed cannibals – anthropophagi as they are called – to be their daily food; but those who were beautiful were saved alive, to be stifled and overwhelmed by the number of their ravishers, in spite of all their cries and lamentations. Virgins were deflowered until they died of exhaustion; then their breasts were cut off to be kept as dainties for their chiefs, and their bodies furnished a jovial banquet to the savages (Paris 1877, quoted in Guzman 1991:38).

According to Matthew, the cannibals accompanying Tartars in their military ventures did not limit themselves to devouring Christians, but raped their virgins, sating not only culinary appetites, but also sexual ones. The state of disorder affected both the cuisine of the savages and their morality. To be fair, in his discussion of Tartar savagery Chaucer does not go to such lengths as to portray them as sexually insatiable, but perhaps his allusions to possible incest on the part of Mongols derive from the black legend grounded in Matthew Paris's pseudo-ethnography. Eating the inedible does not suffice for the uncivilized people: their followers are free to wreak chaos in Christian society by making sexual attacks on the Christians' young and beautiful women.

In the description of the feast in *The Squire's tale*, the symbolic Eastern body, clad in sumptuous clothes indicating political authority, emerges as an organism ingesting meat which is utterly unacceptable in Western Europe; *occupatio* here implies rather that the foodstuffs are too repellent to be elaborated on by a narrator from the Occident. The symbolism of clothes and adornment of the life at court, which suggests political and military power resulting from the opulence displayed, starkly contrasts with a diet that degrades for the eaters. Their alimentary mores, if interpreted only as bizarre, metaphorize the oddness of the oriental way of life. If not interpreted that leniently, the practices imply that a body eating the uneatable deliberately fouls itself, displaying the superficiality of its outward splendor and showing that it is not omnipotent, but rather weakened by the excess of nourishing itself on what should be avoided rather than relished. This association of eating with political authority will be important in our discussion of *Richard le Coer de Lyon*: also in that medieval romance it is not only significant what the circumstances of feasting are, including the apparel, but also what is actually ingested. The role of what (or rather who) is eaten for the English community will also be stressed.

If the preliminary part of *The Squire's tale* does not exclude the possibility of cannibalism, its ultimate lines imply another taboo: a possible incestuous relationship between Canace and her brother, Cambalo. As the Squire announces, "And after wol I speke of Cambalo,/ That faught in lystes with the bretheren two/ For Canacee er that he myghte hire wynne" (V:667-669). Again, the medieval lore about the Tartars may have included verifiable information about the frequency of relationships which in our culture would verge on incest: marrying one's cousins was common there. There also occurred situations when a relationship did not merely suggest incest, but was undoubtedly incestuous to the Western eyes: in Chaucer's times the almost legendary ruler Özbeg even married his own daughter.[43] The image of Tartars' unnatural behaviour would thus have probably been complete in Chaucer, since he alluded to the union between a brother and a sister, but for the Franklin, who interrupted the Squire and cut the narrative short. Perhaps then the distinction the poet introduced, between the Canace "that loved hir owene brother synfully" (II:79) from *The Man of Law's prologue*, and the virtuous Canace(e) from *The Squire's tale*, was artificial and formulated only for the sake of omitting all "unkynde abhomynacions" (II:88) from the *Canterbury Tales*. This would make Canace even more inaccessible to a Western audience, as the plot would entail two types of taboo, cannibalism and incest.[44]

Nevertheless, cannibalism was not taboo in all circumstances. The association with cannibalism and with incest that put Canace, the Tartar princess discussed at length in the previous chapter, out of reach of the young Squire and his like, did not make Western literary characters repulsive to medieval audiences. Richard the Lionheart, the central character of the text written around 1300 but which was in all likelihood a translation of an earlier Anglo-Norman or French narrative (Ambrisco 1999:500), commits cannibalism twice in the course of this narrative and one of the current interpretations of his act, put forward by Geraldine Heng, even characterizes it as a nationalistic joke comprehensible to medieval audiences (2003:75). On a first reading of the text, the combination of cannibalistic acts with the idea that Richard represented chivalric culture could be unpalatable to a modern audience. Nevertheless, perhaps chivalry itself entailed the possibility of cannibalistic treatment of the Saracen enemy, even though it may at first be difficult to imagine, given the medieval knights' postulated courtesy, valour, and honourable comportment. Indeed, there exists a theory relating chivalric code to the question of corporeality, that of the self and

---

43 Keiko Hamaguchi addresses the issue in her study on postcolonial women in Chaucer; she analyses it in the chapter "Canace's Problematic Marriage in *The Squire's tale*" (2006:47-62).
44 Later travel literature includes a straightforward association between these two types of taboo: in Alberico Vespucci's 1507 *Mondo Novo e Paesi movamente ritrovati da Alberico Vespuzio fiorentino [New World and Countries discovered recently by Alberico Vespuzio of Florence]*, the "incestuous cannibal" is constructed as a type (Lestringant 1997:27-31).

that of the other. As John Gillingham puts it, the chivalric code entered the culture of the British Isles after the Norman Conquest (2000a:209), diversifying the treatment of the body on the grounds of social rank, religion, and ethnicity. The history in *Richard* portrays this new idea in a striking way, emphasizing the king's cannibalistic acts directed against his Saracen foes as acceptable if not praiseworthy and simultaneously hailing his chivalric virtues visible on the battlefields of the Middle East during his crusading venture, which shows that these two attitudes were not deemed incompatible. On the contrary, the combination of the two may have led to the community in England being strengthened through externalization of the other.

The stereotype of Richard as a "French" king, more historically grounded than his romanticized portrait in the much later Robin Hood legend, where he appears as a truly English ruler deeply involved in the affairs of his island territories despite being preoccupied with the duty of Christianization by means of the crusades, proves to be exaggerated.[45] Gillingham questions the oft-repeated statement that "Richard 'neglected' England" (2000a:60), pointing rather towards the ideological message of the king's reign and disregarding the question of the language he spoke, French, since according to R.R. Davies at the time language did not determine national identity to the extent it did later.[46] Richard's reign was marked by the continuing Anglicization of the Isles, which was consciously conducted by the king himself, or at least he did not impede its progress. Writes Davies, "in the process of colonization and settlement it was the English who were the numerically dominant and critical group, regardless of the role played by non-English personnel in the leadership, momentum, and documentation of the movement" (2000:144). The anonymous author of *Richard le Coer de Lyon* abandons the issue of the king's Norman origins altogether, consistently emphasizing his Englishness (the phrase "He was Ynglysch" appears very early in the text) (*RCL* 677) and the postulated Englishness of his people which matched that of the king very well.[47] On the other hand, the romance addresses Richard's adventures in the Middle East whither he departs on a crusade, rather than with English setting, where his own "civilized" quality would not be as conspicuous as in the Orient, where he could construct his Englishness more efficiently. The pilgrims to the Holy Land

---

45 Gillingham demonstrates how the negative image of Richard as a French crusading-crazed monarch was created, starting with seventeenth-century historiography (2000b:12-14).
46 As Davies claims, the fourteenth century was the time when use of the English language started to determine people's national identity in the British Isles (2000:181).
47 All the quotations from *Richard le Coer de Lyon* come from Karl Brunner's edition (1913); the line numbers, preceded by the abbreviation *RCL*, are taken from it as well.

emphasize the strangeness of the foreign territory he is bound for by talking to Richard about: ". . . auentures that may betyde/ In straunge londes where thou ryde" (*RCL* 731-732). The Anglo-Norman king is made more familiar to the Western (and possibly English) readers through his identification with all that is neither strange nor perilous. The question of his Frenchness continues to be avoided in this dialectic of sameness and otherness. After all, this romance belongs to the Matter of England group of romances, as has been noted by Pearsall (1988:17).

Richard's historically grounded French origin is only hinted at by the romance's anonymous author when he reports the story of Richard's birth and the subsequent disappearance of his mother. In reality the historical Richard jokingly referred to himself as a son of the devil, alluding to the Angevin legend, a version of the Mélusine story (Gillingham 2000b:24). This is how Heffernan describes the historical association between Richard's real genealogy and the legend:

> The legend of Cassodorien and her strange revulsion at the holy sacrament and her magical disappearance through the roof has its origins in a legend about King Richard's ancestor, Fulk of Anjou, who (according to the legend) married a woman of unknown origin who, like Richard's mother in the romance, is unable to sit through the eucharistic part of the mass. She, also detained, is said to have taken flight through the church roof, carrying off her children. While the romance's incorporation of the legend of Richard's ancestor, Fulk of Anjou, recognizes the king's Angevin ancestors, it suppresses his actual mother, Eleanor of Aquitaine (2003:14).

As for its version recorded in the fourteenth-century romance, the legend of Mélusine started its existence in English culture for good around 1300, as is known from the existence of a fragment of Walter Map's *De nugis curialium* (written between 1181 and 1193) and of Gervase of Tilbury's *Otia imperialia* (1209-1214). In *De nugis curialium* "Large-toothed Henno" (*Henno cum dentibus*) marries "a most lovely girl", whom he met "in a shady wood at noonday near the brink of the shore of Normandy" (Map 1983:363). She speaks to him "in such innocent and dovelike voice that you might think a lady angel was speaking – one who could deceive at will any angel" (Map 1983:383). The deceitful lady instigates their marriage and conceals her supernatural leanings: "In order to bring her evil desire to the wished-for end, she fulfilled every comely duty in the sight of men, except that she shunned the sprinkling of holy water, and by a wary retirement (making the crowd or some business an excuse) anticipated the moment of the consecration of the Lord's blood and body" (Map 1983:349). Since she neither participated in the Eucharist nor even ever witnessed the sprinkling of holy water in church, she was furtively observed in her bath by her mother-in-law, who discovered the young mother's real physical form, that of a dragon: ". . . after a short time she saw her leap out of the bath onto a new cloak which her maid had spread for her, tear it into tiny shreds with her teeth, then return to her proper form and thereafter minister in the same way in every point to her maid" (Map 1983:349). The suspicion over the lady's body appears more natural if we analyze the parallelism between the Eucharistic body and the virginal one that Ruth Evans analyzed. She inspected the legends of female virgin saints whose bodies were subjected to violence, and the anti-Judaic narratives of Jews torturing the Eucharist and discovered that "the virgin's body is metonymically both Church and eucharist" (2003:169). Then perhaps Mélusine's revulsion towards the Eucharist may have questioned her virginity when she married the count of Lusignan. Forcibly sprinkled with holy water in church, Mélusine flies away through the roof. In the *Otia imperialia*, the mother's real nature as a serpent is revealed and she disappears in the bathwater. Later French texts, Jean d'Arras' *The noble history of Lusignan* (also known by alternative titles, *The book of Mélusina in prose* and *The romance of Mélusina in prose*), written between 1387 and 1394, and Couldrette's *The romance of Lusignan of Parthnay*, written in 1401-1405, tell similar stories of a supernatural wife, here called "Melusigne", which probably derived from "Mère Lusigne", as she enters the Lusignan family on marriage and has children by her husband.

In *Richard le Coer de Lyon*, a romance preceding the later and more popular versions of the supernatural motherhood narratives of d'Arras and Couldrette, the figure of the mother is also based on the "Mélusine" tales, which, as le Goff argues, later entered folklore, including that of Poland and Ukraine.[48] In *Richard* the mother is the princess of Antioch, Cassodorien, who encounters King Henry miraculously at sea while sailing to England with her father Corbarans owing to a vision he has had. The father's very name evokes oriental associations, since Corbarans was the historical Kerbogha, a convert to Christianity fighting on the side of the crusaders, immortalized in the thirteenth-century continuation of the Jerusalem cycle *Chrétienté Corbaran* (Akbari 2005:201). Even prior to marrying Henry, Corbarans' daughter Cassodorien declares: "I dar neuere see þe sacrement" (*RCL* 194) and when she gives birth to two sons and a daughter, she firmly maintains the resolve. In contrast to Mélusine, she is "oriental" by origin, but Frenchness, possibly signaled by the origin of the character in the French tale, could make her equally exotic. When the children have grown a little, "an

---

48 Jacques le Goff argues that the Polish translation of the German version, published in 1569 by Siennik, entered Polish and Ukrainian folklore and gave rise to numerous manifestations of "Melusina" in the seventeenth century (1980:215).

earl" [priest] (*RCL* 208) prevents Cassodorien from leaving the church so that she witnesses the sacrament at last. Forced to flee, she flies through the roof, taking with her one of her sons, John, who, however, falls onto the ground and breaks his thigh. She manages thereupon to abduct her daughter, who disappears with her forever:

> Sche took here douȝtyr in here hond,
> And Johan her sone she wolde not wonde;
> Out of the rofe she gan her dyght.
> Openly before all theyr syght.
> Johan fell frome her in that stounde.
> And brak his thygh on the grounde.
> And with her doughter she fled her waye,
> That never after she was isey.
> (*RCL* 227-234)

Still, the supernatural nature of the mother is not dwelled on at all, but rather presented very briefly, either in order to obscure Richard's real descent from the French Queen Eleanor of Aquitaine, as Ambrisco remarks (1999:505), or so as not to unduly stress his supernatural origin, as that could eclipse Richard's postulated Englishness, which in the discourse of the romance is presented as an identity without supernatural qualities.

The negative identification of Eleanor may stem not only from her origin, but from her authoritarian nature, at least by medieval standards. The anonymous author of the romance dismisses the possibility of Richard taking after his supernatural mother in any way. Instead, he stresses Richard's similarity to his English people and their loyalty and devotion to him. Yet once we reflect on it, the supernatural origin of Richard may contribute to our understanding of his predilection for bestiality and cannibalism. Ramsey insists that Richard's supernatural origin, emblematically identified by her as belonging to the "devil birth" type frequent in romances, "indicates that Richard comes from a combination of nobility with beauty and of God's power with the devil's, this strange and unholy mixture being necessary to a leader of this sort" (1983:79). This identification indeed appears later in the text, as when Saladin refers to Richard as a devil or a saint:

> Saladyn meruayled than,
> And sayde it was none erthly man:
> "He is a deuyll or a saynt,
> His myght founde j neuer faynt."
> (*RCL* 6949-6952)

To be exact, Richard's partial identification with the devil is grounded in historical sources, where there appears Archbishop Baldwin's anathema at the punishment meted out by Richard to the perpetrators of the Jewish pogroms in London and York. The chroniclers noted how during the events following the slaughter Baldwin claimed that the young king should become the devil's servant if he did not wish to be God's (Runciman 1987:7). So the idea about Richard's supernatural origin and not entirely human identity followed the real-life accusations resulting from his fair judgment of the anti-Jewish incidents in England and his condemnation of the perpetrators.

The topic around which both of the two, Cassodorien's and Richard's, revolve is on the one hand the question of the Eucharist as possible theophagy which the queen will not commit, and on the other the issue of anthropophagy, which the young king willingly indulges in.[49] Christian theological teaching about the sacrament involving the actual ingestion and digestion of Christ's flesh and blood verged on man-eating, because devouring the body was treated literally as the effect of transubstantiation and not symbolically, as Protestant theologians saw it later. Lestringant sees the transfer from a Catholic literal approach onto the level of pure symbolism as yet another example of the Protestant rejection of human corporeality (1997:142). The Protestant denial of theophagy was followed by the later rejection of cannibalism as not sharing any characteristics with the secularized European Enlightenment culture. "Anthropophagy, bereft of its religious overdetermination, had no further excuses," writes Lestringant (1997:11). The romance describes a much earlier epoch when cannibalism had its direct Christian equivalent and justification. Richard's mother was repelled by the Eucharist, which could be seen as a refusal to commit cannibalism inherent in the sacrament, while later Richard himself practised not only the Eucharistic theophagy, but also anthropophagy directed against cultural others. Through his Christian theophagy and through his anthropophagy of Saracens he got involved in eating the other, while his mother as an infidel flinched from accepting the sacrament. Obviously, if one inspects the matter further, the Eucharist is not the same as eating the other, since the Church is the mystical body of Christ and believers are parts of that body as well. As a result, the sacrament of the Eucharist is more an example of autophagy, eating oneself, than of eating the other. In this ideologically laden romance, the author is able to reconcile Richard's Christianity and his regular sharing in the Eucharist with the aggression he displays by eating cultural others and his negative attitude to Islam, which is different from the more tolerant views that Muslims initially had about Christians.

---

49 Perhaps it could be argued that participation in the Eucharist goes poorly with Richard's aggressiveness, but the anonymous author of this popular, and indeed very crude, romance probably would not mind his audience making this association.

Later versions of the Mélusine narrative, such as Jean d'Arras's *The noble history of Lusignan*, portrayed the fairy as both supernatural and Christian, with the Christianity of saintly motherhood as a dominating element of her characterization (Taylor 1996:165-182), even though her monstrosity also played a crucial role in it (Spiegel 1996:100-124).[50] In d'Arras's romance the question of the Eucharist does not occur, because Mélusine does not even maintain her human form on Sundays, not to mention subjecting herself to any Christian ritual practices, but she paradoxically remains Christian through her emulation of the Virgin Mary, a nurturing and caring mother. That gives her an air of someone who fits the culture in which she lives. In *Richard*, however, Richard's mother is otherness embodied, as she abandons her children when she flies away from the Christian sacrament. If sacraments are signs, her refusal to take the Eucharist also signifies cultural difference and dissent. When forced to abandon the position of the other, she prefers to abandon one of her three children, Richard. Through the situation his mother put him in Richard enters the stock of abandoned children of romance, which perhaps partly accounts for his later status as an outstanding hero, who distinguishes himself from others through his courage and valour. As a character abandoned by his mother in childhood, he repeatedly attempts to assert his value, so what could be seen as superhuman efforts may just as well be the king's bid to establish his superiority.

If we set Richard against his parents, it appears that the king is supposed to be primarily interpreted as a continuator of his father's lineage and of the chivalric code Henry established in England, rather than as a supernatural hero taking after his oriental (but in reality French) mother, notwithstanding Richard's cannibalistic practices. The view of Richard as his father's loyal follower is obviously false from the historical point of view, since he remained in constant conflict with Henry before he acceded to the throne himself. Nor did he quarrel with his mother at any stage; he remained a loyal son and carried out what was thought to be Eleanor's political schemes. Another historical inaccuracy concerns Henry: in the romance manipulated by his nobles, in reality he was as determined a ruler as Richard later was. Gillingham writes that on marrying Eleanor Henry, a twenty-four-year-old, "was to be a great king, for thirty-five years the master politician of Western Christendom, able to overwhelm or outmanoeuvre his rivals" (2000b:27). Weakened by illness, he

---

50 Tania Colwell balances those two arguments by claiming that Mélusine's exemplary motherhood and her monstrosity do not clash, but rather form a unified identity (2003:181-203).

was defeated by Richard in his old age. Nevertheless, Richard's rebellion against his father did not enter the subject matter of *Richard Coer de Lyon*.

To call *Richard* a historical text works only if we cease to criticize the narrative's fictional subplots, possible anachronisms, and its involvement in the staple of romance, a quest, amorous relationships with a courtly lady, and other typical chivalric preoccupations, including supernatural occurrences. "Romance", with its overtones of chivalric culture, is an equally suitable label for *Richard* as "historical text" is. "Romance" obviously remains the text's customary designation in the criticism, even though Finlayson points out that *Richard* is "usually discussed as an unsuccessful example of it" (1990:158). Nicola McDonald incorporates it in a group of "pulp fictions of medieval England" and lists it among such "composite romances" as Chaucer's *Squire's Tale* due to the combination of fact and fiction in *Richard* (2004:128). The text involves a crusading venture whose very nature could be termed "colonial", which here means intended to subjugate an ethnically different enemy in a far-off land. Romance as a genre itself, as Sara Suleri postulates in her seminal study, is colonial (1992:10)[51] and illustrates a quest for national origins (1992:7). In this sense the romance designation of *Richard* is appropriate, because the text begins with the king's (half supernatural) origin only to construct an idea of his Englishness which matches that of his people. His participation in the Third Crusade acquires the nature of a quest for self-identification. The romance elements there are indubitable, but the text has to be read as a mixture of romance fiction and medieval historical writing.[52] In his essay on the text's genre, Finlayson demonstrates that in Thornton manuscript "Richard appears in contexts which suggest that it was viewed as 'historical and heroic', not 'romantic' and fantastic, both in the B and A version" (1990:165).[53]

The medieval audiences probably did not mind the incorporation of romance elements into a text they wanted to see as historical. On the other hand, the realism of Richard's depredations during the crusade did not impede the development of the chivalric and "romantic" idea of the king. Finlayson writes:

---

51 Suleri writes as follows about the transmutation of the genre in the Victorian era: "When the nineteenth-century Anglo-Indian writer transmuted the convention of romance in order to make desire take on the lineaments of an unreadable exoticism, he or she produced an unreadable text psychically dependent on an estranged intimacy though which the metaphor of adultery could be raised to the power of culture" (1992:12).
52 Ramsey groups it in the category of "History and Politics" romances (1987:69-96).
53 Brunner's edition which is the source of the quotations here is based on the longer version, known as Version A, which includes fabulous romance-like material (McDonald 2004:146).

The critical error lies in the view that the "chivalric" concept of Richard is marred by the massacre and cannibalism, since it assumes that the author intended to present a *chevalier errant* of the Lancelot or Perceval type, whereas it seems clear that his intention was to present a portrait of a Christian warrior-prince of the old, heroic and *more realistic* cast (1990:175).

The code of chivalry did not eliminate violence and brutality altogether, but directed it against people from lower social classes and different religious, ethnic, or even, as here, national backgrounds. In the text Richard, who in his adulthood gradually gains the reputation of a ruler living up to the chivalric ideal, manifests a singular treatment of matters of the body in confrontations with his enemies. Gillingham throws some light on the question when he discusses chivalry as

> a secular code of values, and – more precisely – a code in which a key element was the attempt to limit the brutality of conflict by treating prisoners, at any rate when they were of "gentle" birth, in a relatively humane fashion . . . the compassionate treatment of defeated high-status enemies is a defining characteristic of chivalry – and entirely compatible with very different treatment meted out to people regarded as low-status (2000a:209).

Nevertheless, a humane attitude to the enemy did not extend to people who were religiously and ethnically different, as the romance shows. Consequently, the text may be seen as a commentary on a culture which combined a "reluctance to kill or mutilate each other . . . suggest[ing] that nobles were beginning to value their bodies in new ways" (Gillingham 2000a:210) with unscrupulous treatment of such cultural others as Saracens. The bodies that appear in *Richard le Coer de Lyon* thus need to be historicized during the course of interpretation, because the historical context demonstrates both the transformation of practices concerning the body and also the transformation of attitudes towards it. The context is vital to what Marcel Mauss calls "bodily techniques", since the manners in which bodies act are closely linked to the circumstances in which people live. Consequently, viewing the bodily practices of cannibalism in the light of the chivalric culture to which the Western ruler belonged may not be inappropriate. In fact, Richard's anthropophagy could be seen as twofold: he was metaphorically cannibalistic in the sense of being a cruel exterminator of Saracens and he practiced cannibalism on them.

Richard's adventures in the East begin with his confrontation with a king's son in "Almayne" (Germany) on his return from a preliminary pilgrimage to the Holy Land. Richard is held captive there, which reflects the historical event when the English ransomed their king who had been imprisoned by the prince of Austria. In the romance the German king's son is certainly "other" from the cultural perspective adopted by the author, despite his objectively being as

Western as Richard; therefore, as could be expected of the "other" in a chivalric romance, he challenges Richard and gives him food, only to test his strength in a more equal fight afterwards. Perhaps then the one who captured the truly Western king Richard had to be described as barbaric, even if "German" did not necessarily denote "uncivilized" in other contexts. The event is constructed by the author against the historical fact that Richard was held captive by the humiliated Austrian prince Leopold and released only after the huge ransom of 100,000 marks had been paid and hostages for 50,000 given (Gillingham 2000b:248), because this happened on Richard's return from the crusade. From the historical perspective, Richard ruined his kingdom: one hundred thousand marks was more than twice Richard's annual income from England (Gillingham 2000b:252). This is how the entirely ahistorical part of the romance treats of the captivity:

> The kynges sone with good wyll
> Badde they sholde haue theyr fyll,
> Bothe of drynke, and eke of mete,
> Of the best that they wolde ete,
> That he myght not awyte
> For feblenes his dente to smyte;
> And into bedde be brought to reste,
> To quyte his that he be preste.
> The kynges sone was curtese,
> That nyghte he made hym well at ease.
> (*RCL* 765-774)

The German prince's encounter with the English king ends in death for the former, as he challenges Richard to strike him in order to test his own strength. Unaware of Richard's extra-human strength and the ruse he uses, that is, the candle wax that he covers his hand with, the prince dies instantly upon being struck, which naturally rouses his father's outrage at the aristocratic prisoner. Richard tears the body of the heir to the throne into pieces, demonstrating not just his physical strength, but also bestiality and his bloodthirsty appetites:

> He that it sawe the sothe sayd,
> Flesshe and skynne awaye he droughe,
> That he fell downe in a dede swoughe.
> In twoo he brak hys cheke-bon
> He fel doun ded as ony ston.
> (*RCL* 794-798)

This scene perhaps provides us with a case in point when arguing about different treatment of cultural others by a knight who otherwise is an emblem of chivalry. Even though the Austrian king's son is not an inhabitant of the "strange lands", yet as the king's "national other" he is confronted with ruthless physical force and unscrupulousness. The idea of "nation" in the English context, where Anglo-Norman and more "Anglo-Saxon" influences were interspersed, not to mention other identifications, would mean cultural belonging or the feudal allegiance to one's lord rather than actual ethnicity.[54] Richard's "Englishness" contrasts here with the attitude which condones stooping to capture another king for profit. Such a stance distances Austrians from the culture represented by Richard and arguably entitles him to use brute force when fighting against the prince. The slaying of the prince testifies to Richard's vengefulness: it becomes an act of revenge for his captivity. The victory over the German heir to the throne appears to be but a practice of military skill prior to the actual stage of destroying the infidels during the crusade. Characteristically, no remorse ever appears in Richard. The English king sits in gaol passively, not pondering on the sorrow he caused and awaiting a fortuitous reversal of fortune instead, which comes with the visit of Margery, the king's daughter. In a manner typical of the enamoured princesses already discussed here, Canace and Floripas, she compels the jailor to grant her permission to see Richard, as if she expected to become infatuated with him even before she met him:

> "Jayler, sche sayde, let me see
> þy prisouns now hastyly!"
> Bleþely he sayde: "Sykyrly."
>   (*RCL* 888-890)

Granted permission to visit Richard, enamoured Margery is manipulated by him into bringing him food and drink (". . . þis is the thyrde day jgon/ þat meete ne drink ne hadde j non!") (*RCL* 903-904), and she brings on herself disgrace and punishment by her kinsfolk when she spends a night with him. Nevertheless, Richard reveals the qualities of an outstanding warrior to the king once he is sentenced to death by being devoured by a lion, for he tears out the animal's heart, lungs, and liver through its mouth, himself remaining unscathed. Pearsall comments that the romance is precisely "most remarkable for the streak of crude physical brutality which it displays . . . in the lion-heart episode" (1988:20), showing that a good display of violence may impress even modern critics.

Enamoured Margery remains a helpmate for Richard because she provides him with a bandage that he can wrap around his arm so as not be hurt by the fierce beast:

---

54 Susan Crane lists *Richard le Coer de Lyon* among what she calls "insular romances", which were both Anglo-Norman and Middle English, since they treated of similar topics and were a part of the culture of medieval England; she analyses them as different from French romances written at about the same time (1986:6).

Rente out þe herte wiþ hys hand,
Lungges, and lyvere, and al þat he fand,
þe lyoun fel ded to þe grounde,
Rychard hadde neyþer wemme ne wounde.
He knelyd doun in þat place,
And thankyd Jhesu off hys grace,
þat hym kepte fro schame and harme.
He took þe herte, al so warme,
And brouȝte it into þe halle,
Before þe kyng and hys men alle.
  (*RCL* 1093-1102)

Slaying the beast shows his strength and if he is capable of slaying a lion and devouring its heart in a manifestation of victory, he may just as well have inadvertently murdered the heir to the throne. He transcends the borders between the human and the bestial, demonstrating to the audience that the lion-like strike directed against the prince was more natural for him than any more chivalric comportment would have been. When among cultural others, he behaves in a more beastly manner than when surrounded with those belonging to the English culture and of his own rank. The historical context situating Richard in the light of the chivalric culture, of which he was certainly a part, allows us to view his unscrupulous treatment of the king's son in a proper light: care for his own body and the bodies of other English knights did not prevent utterly different treatment of all bodies subjectively identified as "other". The subplot in question presents the issue more drastically than the scenes of slaying Saracens in battle that follow, even though those scenes make the text more historical, because, in contrast to the supernatural confrontation with the lion, they are closer to the facts. The story of Richard pulling out a lion's heart "had always been recognised as a tall one," Gillingham writes, but it "did not stop it being told and retold" (2000b: commentary under plate 4). The nickname of Richard was first used by Ambroise, the author of *L'Estoire de la Guerre Sainte*, a historian of the Third Crusade, and it did not refer to any historical event even vaguely reminiscent of that above (Gillingham 2000b:3).

Characteristically, upon his stay in the Holy Land it is firstly Richard's severe illness that accounts for his cannibalism, which is committed unwittingly. Thus his own bodily weakness leads to his consumption of the other's body. We may ask whether anthropophagy committed unbeknownst has to be treated in the same way as the conscious cannibalism; still, to eat a human body when one is unaware of it is to break the taboo. Richard's all too strongly emphasized Englishness leads him to crave pork, available in Europe but not in the Holy Land dominated by Muslims ("But afftyr pork he was alongyd") (*RCL* 3071).

Disease and fever justify the craving, or perhaps rather the need of any Western body, as the poet insists:

> Why Kyng Richard so syke lay,
> þe resoun j ȝou telle may:
> Ffor þe trauaylle off þe see.
> And strong eyr off þat cuntree,
> And vnkynde cold and hete,
> And mete and drynk þat is nouȝt sete
> To hys body, þat he þere ffonde,
> As he dede here in Yngelonde.
> (*RCL* 3041-3048)

The cook invents a means of preparing similar meat for the king, and his culinary efforts are portrayed in detail. He prepares the broth that will restore the king's stamina, which is described in a manner reminiscent of a recipe, and the flesh of the other is objectified as that which will be used for the cooking. The English community in the British Isles is contrasted with the culturally diverse communities in the crusading territory; consequently, the communal body on the crusade rejects the flesh of the other, reinstituting its own ostensibly monocultural Western identity by devouring the body of a Saracen. The status of the other renders the Saracen both abjected, to use Julia Kristeva's term, and desired, if we only consider his indispensability for the existence of the uniform community centered around those who represent "the same":

> Takes a Sarezyn ȝonge and ffat;
> Jn haste þat þe þeff be slayn,
> Openyd, and hys hyde off ff'layn,
> And soden fful hastyly.
> Wiþ powdyr, and wiþ spysory,
> And wiþ saffron off good colour.
> (*RCL* 3088-3093)

The intricacies of sophisticated man-eating make the act perilously civilized in our eyes. This is not a procedure indispensable for survival but a complex practice of slaying, disemboweling, and vilifying the earthly remains of one's enemy. The young Saracen's existence becomes justifiable once his body can be put to good use by feeding the fevered king. A human body becomes nothing but flesh, and the flesh can be relished if there is no other flesh of animal origin. The scene in which "þe kyng eet þe fflesch, and gnew þe bones" (*RCL* 3111) obviously illustrates the king's strategy towards all the Saracens whom he encounters while crusading. His unwitting digestion of the enemy emblematizes the entire plan of annihilating the other on account of the difference he represents and the political power he yields or aspires to. Thus the body of the other will be literally displaced, as it will enter the Westerner's entrails, and be turned into waste (but not annihilated altogether).[55] The less symbolic context for Richard's cannibalism was the historical reality of the starvation that the crusaders suffered from due to strategies adopted by Saracens: Gillingham records 1190 as the year when winter marked the onset of severe food shortages in the Christian army. "They had to contend not only with Muslim attacks," he writes, "but also with the threat of starvation and the diseases associated with malnutrition" (Gillingham 2000b:139), even though hunger did not afflict the ruler himself. Yet real-life cannibalism became possible under such circumstances. The anonymous author of *Gesta Francorum et aliorum Hiersolimitanorum*, Raymond d'Aguiliers, and Fulcher of Chartres all testify to the cannibalism of the dead that Christian knights committed in the Syrian desert during the First Crusade (Blurton 2007:114).

The crusades, which formed the context for the cannibalistic acts in the romance, meant displacement for the crusading Westerners; it was a displacement from the space they usually occupied, but also from the culture they originated in. Diane Speed highlights the status of a quest as a form of displacement and exile (1994:146) and such interpretation is relevant to the quest of Richard, in reality a non-English king for whom perhaps residing in England was a form of relative exile if compared to dwelling in France, the historical domain of Plantagenets. Richard both becomes an exile voluntarily, when he sets off for the Orient, and accepts his position of an exile that is imposed on him in England because he is French. The role of this romance in the ideological project of nation formation is clear, following Speed's analysis of the general role of the romance and subsequently the novel in nation formation. "The nation is defined and asserted essentially as a response to the challenge of the unknown," Speed insists (1994:146). Richard needs to be viewed as a character searching for his place in the English imaginary community, regardless of whether his origin was partly "oriental" or French, and he finds that place through confrontations with the other. The popularity of the text only illustrates how vital the project of nation construction was for Anglophone audiences (Heng 2003:110).[56] Paradoxically, eating the other

---

55 The relationship between Mahommad as a representative of Saracens and the topic of waste has been discussed by, for instance, Susan Signe Morrison; she interprets the illustration for Book XXVIII of Dante's *Inferno* in the manuscript originating from northern Italy and dating from the third quarter of the fourteenth century (Oxford, Bodleian Library, Holkham misc. from Bodleian Roll 389.1, canto 28, page 42, frame 43), where "some matter, possibly excrement, is on the ground" (2008:30).
56 Heng enumerates the later, printed, versions of the romance, such as Wynkyn de Worde's between 1509 and 1528, John Purfoot's of 1568-69, or that owned by James Haword in

contributes to the process of building civilization in England, if we consider a nation as an ideological construct situated higher on the ladder of what Norbert Elias called "the civilizing process" (1939 [2000]). The English community becomes partly displaced, as some of its members go on a crusade and abandon their place in the world, and it is reinstituted through the interminable violence that escalates in the East.

The role of vengeance within chivalric culture may be broached here. Vengeance was a strategy well established within English culture before the Norman Conquest, in Anglo-Saxon times when blood feuds were frequent, but not at all understood as sinful. Quite the reverse, since earlier Germanic and later chivalric culture included the conviction that taking revenge on the family of one's enemies was an honourable idea. Otto Brunner and Howard Kaminsky write about feud and vengeance as "inseparable concepts of Right", comprehended as justice, order, equity, or stability (1992:23-24, quoted in: Fletcher 2003:10). Slaying one's enemies and also their family members functioned in those cultures as a noble act, illustrating the warrior's and later the knight's integrity, the steadfastness of his intentions, and his will to protect his own kin and his lord. The bodies of enemies and their family members were attacked for a reason which implied guarding one's honour and the practice was continued in the times when Norman culture mingled with Anglo-Saxon. Dieter Mehl compares Richard with Charlemagne and his peers for a reason. He detects the same "unusual militant Christian spirit and a brutal hatred of all unbelievers" in the Charlemagne narratives and in *Richard*, which corroborates our thinking about revenge as an entirely chivalric idea according to the ideology of the romance (1968:244).

Richard le Coer de Lyon also illustrates the symbolic dimension of the king's body and the bodies of his enemies. As Sarah Kay and Miri Rubin have noted, the metaphor of the king's corporeality represented the idea of good government, but it simultaneously remained "a privileged site, vehicle, and metaphor of political struggle" (1994:5). The image was employed in order to impose and stabilize the social order and it justified political power as it was exercised in practice (Kay – Rubin 1994:5). The idealized vision separated the king's literal body and his symbolic one, guaranteeing the stability of the country due to the latter's mystical nature. As Ernst Kantorowicz claims in his classic *The king's two bodies*, the medieval version of the political myth consisted in the theory of *gemina persona* (1997:87), the double nature of the ruler's corporeality. The mystical body of the king represented his people, who were as subjected to him as limbs and organs are to the head, as we read in John

---

1562, which shows that the text's popularity continued beyond the Middle Ages (2003:110).

of Salisbury's *Policraticus*, written in 1159.[57] The order of the state modeled on John's theory was visualized by artists in the ensuing centuries in the image of the body politic.[58] In the Middle English romance not only does the literal body of king Richard devour and digest the young Saracen's body, which symbolizes the struggle for power in the East, but also the symbolic body of the English nation devours a representative of Muslims in the Holy Land. It becomes a seemingly civilized action performed by the cultured monarch, who commits symbolic incorporation by performing the literal one.

Nonetheless, if we inspect the question of whether Richard is civilized or uncivilized, we find that his cannibalism may be interpreted as displacing the king from the civilized world and situating him closer to the legendary barbarity and primeval instincts allegedly found in all non-Westerners. Indeed, if the first act of anthropophagy occurred unbeknown, the other happens at the king's behest and it shares with the mythical cannibalism of natives the idea of eating the enemy as an act of vengeance, even if the interpretation of anthropophagy as revenge was secondary to the more basic vision of the practice. As Gillingham argues, on the other hand, vengeance also occurred in chivalric societies, even though Gillingham excludes both blood feud and rebellion from the circumstances in which Westerners acted in a chivalric manner (2000a:210). It appears that Richard does not apply chivalric practices in confrontations with Muslims at all. "If you lived in a chivalrous society . . . it was no longer thought decent to kill or mutilate aristocratic enemies openly," as Gillingham writes, but the rule was apparently not observed in contacts with Eastern nobles (2000a:229). As a result, Richard's uncivilized treatment of his enemies did not render him less chivalric in other contexts. In order to affect the enemy emotionally, Richard devises a feast at which the heads of the Saracen rulers' scions will be eaten. The idea might have come to him when he learned the truth about the broth which helped him to recover. Forced to reveal what kind of flesh was so delicious to Richard, because the king craves more, the cook fetches the bearded head of the young Saracen:

"Loo here þe hed! my lord, mercy!"
Hys swarte vys whenne þe kyng seeþ,
Hys blacke berd, and hys whyte teeþ,
Hon hys lyppys grennyd wyde:
"What deuyl is þis?" þe kyng cryde,

---

57 See John of Salisbury's *Policraticus* (Nederman 2000).
58 Over time, controversy entered the theory of the head's superiority once the primacy of the heart over the head started to be considered, because medieval artists needed to account for the existence of the soul and its superiority over each body, which connoted the heart rather than the head as central (Camille 1994:70).

And gan to lauȝe as hee were wood.
"What, is Sarezynys flesch þus good?
And neuere erst j nouȝt wyste?
By Goddys deþ and hys vpryste,
Schole we neuere dye for defawte,
Whyl we may in any assawte
Slee Sarezynys, þe flesch mowe take,
Seþew, and roste hem, and doo hem bake,
Gnawen here fflesch to þe bones.
. . ."

(*RCL* 3210-3224)

The bearded grinning head seen as a joke leads Richard to the conscious repetition of his first act of cannibalism, and now it is plainly amusing for him. He employs the dialectic of laughter and sorrow as he laughs over the grinning head: what is a source of joy for him will be tragic to the Saracens who will immensely grieve over the death of their kin. When Richard discusses the plan with his marshal, he describes another act of eating the other in minute detail:

Kyng Rychard callyd hys marchall stylle,
And in counsayl took hym alone:
"I schal þe telle what þou schalt don.
Priuely goo to þe prison,
þe Sarezynys off most renoun,
þat be comen off þe ryhcheste kynne,
Priuyly slee hem therin;
And ar þe hedes be of smyten,
Looke euery name be wryten
Vpon a scrowe off parchemyn;
And bere þe hedes to þe kechyn,
And in a cawdroun þou hem caste,
And bydde þe cook seþe kem ffaste;
And loke þat he þe her off stryppe,
Off hed, off berd, and eke off lyppe.
Whenne we schole sytte and eete,
Loke þat ȝe nouȝt fforgete
To serue hem herewiþ in þis manere:
Lay euery hed on a platere,
Bryng it hoot forþ al in þyn hand,
Vpward hys vys, þe teeþ grennand;
And loke þey be nothynge rowe!
Hys name faste aboue hys browe,
What he hyȝte, and off what kyn born(e).
. . ."

(*RCL* 3410-3434)

Civilized comportment and allegedly barbaric rudeness clash in this scene. Serving the heads on platters, with the grinning faces upwards, is a sophisticated way of torturing the victims' fathers, the ambassadors; the murders' gruesome nature seems even more abominable due to the splendor of the feast. The mythical provenance of the torture inflicted on the victims' fathers, who will be afflicted with intolerable grief, is evident. Thyestes' grief at having devoured the flesh of his own children, which resulted from Atreus' trick, leads to an outbreak of rage, as Anne L. Klinck emphasizes (2010:16). Thyestes was made to commit what Lestringant termed "alimentary incest", matching like with like (1997:82). Richard's dinner of young Saracens' heads severed from their bodies also aims to cause immense sorrow in his enemies in order to weaken their spirits and enhance their rage at the crusaders, perhaps so as to lead them to abandon rational behaviour and demonstrate vulnerability in later military confrontations. The inscriptions on the foreheads will leave the Saracens in no doubt as to whose flesh they are served at what would otherwise seem a diplomatic bid at reconciliation. The inscriptions will "speak" to them about the torture to which their children were subjected and the children's heads are going to become a text to be read as a warning issued by the Western adversaries. Furthermore, the moral victory needs a written record, which is also materialized in the inscriptions on the heads turned face upwards:

> What þey were whenne þey seyen,
> þe teres ran out off here eyen;
> And whenne þey þe lettre redde,
> To be slayn fful sore þey dredde.
> (*RCL* 3465-3468)

Horror and despair, naturally observable in the fathers of the slain, contrast with Richard's complacency; the king apparently demonstrates his peculiar sense of humour as a manifestation of superiority over the grieving ones. What was suggested by Richard's exhilaration at the young Saracen's head being shown to him is confirmed here in all its shocking brutality. He eats heartily and relishes the food enormously, emphasizing a lack of any sense of regret. Kantorowicz traces the idea of the head as central to the *corpus mysticum* to the medieval period, so to interpret feasting on the heads of Saracens as symbolic is not incongruous, especially if the heads are served to the victims' fathers. Serving the heads at the feast materializes the superiority of Richard over the enemy, because the very centre of their symbolic community is affected (1957:32).[59]

---

59 Developing his theory of the king's two bodies, Kantorowicz thus writes about Shakespeare's *Richard II*: "No longer does Richard impersonate the mystic body of his subjects and the nation" (1997:32).

The *corpus verum*, the literal body of Richard, devours the bodies of the other in the way that the English *corpus fictum* intends to combat the Saracen rulers. If in the Eucharistic theology a part, *pars*, not only stands *pro toto*, but is *totum* itself, as Bynum writes (1995:24), the severed head is also *totum* in the sense of illustrating Richard's authority and provoking grief and rage in the Saracen ambassadors. The remaining part of the body no longer serves any ideological function. The analogy shows that Richard remains a Christian even here, in the gruesome scene of causing emotional torment in the ambassadors. This displays Richard's double standards, since Christianity entails having charity for others, but religious, ethnic, and cultural others are obviously excluded from it according to the romance's devious ideology.

Cannibalism emerges as the king's strategy for terrorizing the enemies in order to make them surrender to the English. Richard issues the following address to the Sultan through an envoy, the father of one of the slain ones:

> Say hym, it schal hym nou3t avayle,
> þou3 he forbarre oure vytayle,
> Fflesch and ffysch, samoun and cungir.
> We schal neuer dye ffor hungyr,
> Whyl that we may wendeu to ffy3t,
> And slee þe Sarezynes dounry3t,
> Wassche þe fllesch, and roste þe hede;
> Wiþ oo Sarezyn j may wel ffede
> Wei a nyne, or a ten
> Off my goode Crystene-men.
> (*RCL* 3537-3546)

Superficial courtesy is replaced with outright daring and Richard unscrupulously announces a threat to all Muslims. His perspective on Saladin does not place the two of them, the English ruler and the Muslim one, on an equal footing. If the Sultan's subjects emerge from this message as flesh to be devoured in order to satisfy Western appetites, the Muslim ruler's powerlessness is clear. The cultural difference is illustrated by the disrespectful treatment of even the highest member of the Arabic society, whom the historical Richard never met, perhaps due to the etiquette which did not allow Saladin to participate in such meetings.

Nevertheless, cannibalism here means not merely demonstrating hostility, but also the paradoxical closeness that results from eating the other. What Maggie Kilgour elaborated on in her study of the metaphor of incorporation is relevant here: the other becomes incorporated into the self, thus becoming an intimate part of that self (1995:215). In Lacanian terms, the other ceases to be merely repulsive, but adopts the status of a desirable entity, readily incorporated into the self due to the difference it represents. The difference of the other, here not only ethnic but also, on a larger scale, cultural, acquires the position of the *objet petit a*, "that which is in you more than you", as was noted in the previous chapter; a part missing from myself that I desire to be integrated in myself. The self and the other may mutually attract each other. Writes Fradenburg:

> I fascinate the other by appearing to be "one", the other can see a wholeness in me, and need not look elsewhere. But "I" am founded on the image of the other. And the stranger, the *jouissance*, inside me is also inside the other. It is no wonder we cannot tell ourselves apart; yet the image has sufficient power of generalization to suspend that confusion in a solution of oneness (2002:103).

If Westerners as "one" are alluring to Orientals, Richard may equally be longing for the Eastern culture with its material splendour, so he craves the symbolic incorporation of the difference the East represents. Still, literally to follow in the footsteps of the Saracens remains impossible for the monarch of mixed origin, who according to the romance writer intends to manifest his Englishness so that his authority over England was not questioned. So he forms oneness with the Saracen other symbolically.

The alterity of Saracens has the ambiguous status of difference that is both radically remote from what one is familiar with and that is more intimately close. Terry Eagleton observes this paradox in his suggestion that the other becomes closer to the self through the difference he represents, because the difference is what the self leans over. The perusal of the difference makes the other strangely intimate to ourselves: "Perhaps what is outside is also somehow inside, what is alien also intimate – so that man needs to police the absolute frontier between these two realms as vigilantly as he does just because it may at all times be transgressed, has always been transgressed already, and is much less absolute than it appears" (Eagleton 1989:133). Richard attempts to distance himself from the enemy by threatening him with gradual extinction, which will occur if more and more Westerners come to the Holy Land and feed on Saracen bodies, but both the king's cannibalism and his close inspection of Muslim culture make him resemble the cultural other. He materializes the stereotype or rather the myth of anthropophagic Orientals, placing himself at the intersection of the Western and Eastern cultures. Kilgour maintains that cannibalism involves both hatred and love, as the self appropriates the other through cannibalism: incapable of communing with the other, the self incorporates him to make the contact as close as possible (1990:215). The medieval body is more collective than individual, Kilgour notes, evoking Bakhtin's theorization of corporeality (1990:119); hence the collective body of the English symbolized by Richard intends to annihilate the Saracens through ingestion. The individual feasting on Saracen flesh materializes the desires of the collectivity.

Nonetheless, perhaps the individual body of Richard longs for integration of the other with himself, so as to abolish the distinction into the one who eats and the one who is eaten. Cannibalizing others may result from desiring them and the concomitant inability to commune with them in any other manner but anthropophagy.

The difference between chivalric Christians and savage infidels has arguably been grounded in false assumptions, because neither did chivalry exclude cannibalism of the other, as *Richard le Coer de Lyon* illustrates, nor did cannibalism render the other culture less "civilized" according to the medieval way of thinking. In regard to the relationship between aristocratic lineage and cannibalism, Peter Hulme remarks that

> The commonest explanation for cannibalism – vengeance – could associate cannibals with the aristocratic code of honour that passed as a social relationship under feudalism, facilitating the analogy between conspicuous consumption and savage cannibalism (1998:35).

Richard not only approaches the others' savagery, but also situates himself even more firmly in his own chivalric culture, in which taking revenge on the foe was a customary reaction to the wrongs done by him. Arguably it is Christ who is avenged here: occupation of the Holy Land meant for Christians a symbolic appropriation of the space which had been occupied by Jesus and in which his body had reposed only to rise from the dead later. The Holy Sepulchre was imperiled by the Muslim appropriation of the Holy Land, the site of the Holy Sepulchre, and the land was expected to return to the Christian hands. During the crusades, God supports the noble plan of regaining the land so strongly related to Christ's body, so Westerners should be praised for all their victories over the infidels. Consequently, Christian chivalry ought to be rewarded by God whenever the crusaders achieve victory over the Saracens. "þus Kyng Richard wan Acrys,/ God graunte hys soule moche blys!" (*RCL* 3755-3756), as the anonymous author of the romance expresses it.

Cannibalism both establishes difference, as Kilgour says (1998:240) and annuls it, as it appears both among exotic people and, as the romance shows, in the midst of Western feudal culture. Richard's treachery towards the Saracens he invites for a feast is not emphasized by the author of the romance. Neither is his cannibalism censured in any way, since anything done by Richard has to be seen as praiseworthy. His partly supernatural origin may account for his bestiality in contacts with Muslims. It becomes a convenient excuse for cruelty and sating bloodthirsty appetites. Mary Douglas's idea of purity and taboo also sheds light on the different perspective on these acts of Western cannibalism: the other's corporeality remains impure, so feasting on his flesh may be an efficient method of eliminating the impurity. Hardly anything remains of the other's unclean body after the cannibalistic feast; consequently, anthropophagy of the other introduces more order and discipline in to the surrounding world. As Douglas remarks, "Dirt offends against order. Eliminating it is not a negative movement, but a positive effort to organize the environment" (2009:2). Disorder betokens both danger and power, Douglas says (2009:117), so eliminating the disorder introduced by the other's body is important for those who aspire to absolute authority over the other. Cannibalizing the cultural others minimizes the danger that they represent, so it is vital for the English nation, represented by the king's physical body, to consume Saracens in the Holy Land. Richard paradoxically becomes more "oriental" and simultaneously places himself even more on the side of the civilized ones when committing the act of devouring the other. Still, the boundary between the civilized ones, bent on eradicating impurity, and the unclean uncivilized ones is again established; the king is simply not subjected to such brazenly straightforward classifications.

In Richard's time and later, the dialectic of culture and barbarity was employed as an interpretative key not only overseas, in crusading ventures or other confrontations with ethnic otherness abroad, but also in the British Isles, where "civility and rudeness" were allegedly juxtaposed during the gradual Anglicization of Wales and Scotland (Davies 2000:113-141). The "civilizing process" of the non-English territories occurred not solely through military confrontation and ensuing exploitation of the subjugated lands: its main strategy was of an ideological nature, as the "barbarians" were to adopt the belief in the cultural superiority of the conquerors (Davies 2000:169). The cannibalism performed by Richard in the romance could metaphorize not only his political relations with Saracens, but also the strategy he adopted towards the Welsh and the Scots. In Richard's time Anglicization, comprehended by Davies as "the penetration of English peoples, institutions, norms, and culture . . . into the outer, non-English parts of the British Isles" (2000:143), was well underway, instilling a sense of English superiority in ethnic groups who were becoming more and more subjugated to the conquerors in the psychological sense. The uniform English identity started to be formed then, when, as Davies writes, "the sense of a separate Norman or French identity wilted" (2000:145). Richard continued the process of erecting castles, which became "the instruments of power and lordship" (Davies 2000:147) and fostered aggressive settlement in Wales and Southern and Eastern Ireland (Davies 2000:156).[60] Englishness exceeded what is nowadays seen as the English state (Davies 2000:155),

---

60 Furthermore, he was very much interested in administering the country well and controlling the Church in England (Gillingham 2000b:276).

metaphorically cannibalizing other cultures and civilizations in places that otherwise still remained "elsewhere". The process advanced regardless of political allegiances and alliances, forming a ground for future political acts of inner colonization and for complete appropriation. Richard's support of the process or at least the fact that he did not impede it meant that "Anglicization" must have been influenced by the Norman elements within the English culture at the time. It is arguable to what extent the cultural belonging overlapped with the political allegiance, because such may have been the mechanisms of self-identification under feudalism. Still, probably in Richard's times identifying oneself with a monarch of French origin who supported Anglicization and one's waking Englishness were not in conflict. The English community underwent continual strengthening through Anglicization, but its Englishness was simultaneously subjected to fragmentation due to the incorporation of ethnic others into the *communitas*. The Welsh and the Scots as "barbarians" both extended the range of Englishness and imperiled it through the difference they represented. Paradoxically, the historical Angevins consistently viewed the English over whom they ruled as uncivilized in comparison with the French from whom they themselves derived. The "civilizing mission" undertaken by them in Scotland and Ireland entailed spreading their own civilized quality to those lands, since the English still lacked these virtues.

Characteristically, even though his political plans in the British Isles demonstrated that he related his own identity to the idea of a new, more civilized, "Englishness", Richard never returned to England from his mission. He was not allowed to metamorphose into an ever more English ruler, because he died on the continent, in France. The historical truth, transmitted also in the romance, is that an archer from the insurgent viscount's castle at Chalus-Chabrol, close to Limoges, killed Richard accidentally. "Syþþe he was schot, allas," (*RCL* 7207), as the narrator concludes his account of the king's deeds. The incorporation of Richard into the postulated Englishness remains an incomplete project in the romance, making him even closer to his Saracen enemies, whose bodies he willingly cannibalized. The historical Richard was accidentally shot on the left shoulder in the evening and died of gangrene, forgiving the man who shot him on his deathbed and receiving extreme unction at confession (Gillingham 2000b:324). His five-year stay in France was never rounded off with a return to England, but his Frenchness did not impede the Anglicization of the British Isles that was progressing at his time.

To sum up, neither Richard's chivalry nor his historical French origin marred the projection of his anthropophagy as praiseworthy and beneficial for the English community. This makes the text different from the criticism of cannibalism included in, for instance, *The alliterative Morte Arthure*, or from its ambiguous treatment in *The sege of Jerusalem* (Price 2003:65-82). In the romance we analyzed above, Richard is granted the right to eat the other whatever the circumstances, since it is a way of vanquishing Saracens. The cannibalism acquires a symbolic dimension, because it epitomizes his quest for political authority in the East, but arguably also in the Angevin land and in the British Isles. Devouring the body of the other is both uncivilized and civilized, similarly to Richard's double identity as a devil and a "holy" crusader. The uncanny combination seen in this demonic holiness carries over onto his anthropophagy. Through it, he both sates his beastly lion-like appetite and performs revenge which is inherent to the aristocratic code of honour. As Gaye Poole argues, in various cultures "food . . . is an important analogue of the self; it 'places' and defines individuals as certainly as does their clothing" (2003:12). Richard sends a contradictory message: he eats what is otherwise a taboo, but his strategy is Christian and chivalric. Chivalry, it appears, does not exclude anthropophagy once it does not denote eating those of the same social standing and religious and ethnic background. The identity as the English king is identifiable through his unusual diet: he is paradoxically a civilized savage through his cannibalism. Richard's double nature remains justifiable in a culture which does not respect the corporeality of the other in any manner and does not object to its physical elimination and symbolic annihilation. Nevertheless, full physical destruction will never be possible, so in the romance the English community is both united and continuously disintegrated through Richard's man-eating practices. The paradox displays the unreachable nature of a true *communitas*: according to Esposito, in the light of Rousseau's and Kant's theories the community "needs to remain only an idea of reason, an utterly unreachable destination" (2010:71). As a fictional entity, it is both continually reinvigorated and demolished due to the impossibility of materializing the design.

Chapter Three
Bodies enslaved in *Aucassin et Nicolete* and *Floris and Blancheflour*

> He startled her; but soon she knew his face,
> And grasp'd his fingers in her palsied hand,
> Saying, "Mercy, Porphyro! hie thee from this place;
> They are all here to-night, the whole blood-thirsty race!
> (John Keats *The eve of St. Agnes*)

When delving into the medievalist imagery of John Keats' *The eve of St. Agnes*, it is easy to treat it as a fantasy on love, spiritual and sensual, set against the fantastic backcloth of the Middle Ages. *Flores et Blanchefleur*, a medieval story about young lovers separated and then reunited, provided Keats' subject matter along with *Cléomades et Claremonde* and *Pierre de Provence et la Belle Maguelone*, all of them collected and written by M. de Tressan and published in Paris in 1777 in the ninth volume of the *Bibliothèque Universelle des Dames: Romans*. Keats owned this collection and was familiar with its subject matter (Gittings 1971:89). In Keats' poem Porphyro, like Floris, visits his beloved in the castle, and he persuades Madeline's nurse, Angela to let him observe his beloved while she undresses and falls asleep. The narrative poem, which employs Spenserian stanza, concludes with love, here also sexual, triumphing over the constraints of the outside world and over the virginal coyness of the lady:

> Thus whispering, his warm, unnerved arm
> Sank in her pillow. Shaded was her dream
> By the dusk curtains: 'twas a midnight charm
> Impossible to melt as iced stream:
> The lustrous salvers in the moonlight gleam;
> Broad golden fringe upon the carpet lies:
> It seem'd he never, never could redeem
> From such a stedfast spell his lady's eyes;
> So mused awhile, entoil'd in woofed phantasies.
> (*ESA* 198)[61]

---

61 The page numbers, preceded by the abbreviation *ESA*, come from Bullett's edition (1992).

Passive contemplation metamorphoses into desire in "young Porphyro, with heart on fire" (*ESA* 193), who turns into "burning Porphyro" (*ESA* 195), and real love emerges from the scene as a combination of the two. Characteristically, Madeline does not subject herself to Porphyro's desire entirely consciously, as she dreams of him on the Eve of St. Agnes in the manner she has anticipated and reciprocates the lover's amorous intentions while half-asleep. Kelvin Everest expounds as follows on the superstition related to the Christian holiday which sets the events in motion: "If a young virgin maintains throughout the day a steadfast downward gaze, looking neither forwards nor to the other side, but simply down at the ground, refrains from food, and goes to sleep having resolutely persisted in this ritual", she will dream of her future husband (2002:74). Nevertheless, once Madeline fully awakens, she sees Porphyro as a diminished version of the perfect masculine body she had observed in her dream (Everest 2002:76), a creature "pallid, chill, and drear" (*ESA* 199). Love in the material world does not involve perfect bodies, because all perfection, corporeal and other, remains inaccessible in human relationships. Love occurs somewhere between dream and wakefulness and attempts to overcome all limitations imposed on it. Such is also the love between the characters in the medieval romance *Floris and Blancheflour*. Nevertheless, Keats' poem differs from its medieval predecessor in that it does not account for one of the central impediments in the plot: the dire reality of slavery. Furthermore, *The eve of St. Agnes* is not, despite its inspirations, overtly orientalist, while the incontestably oriental plot of the medieval romance entails the issue of hybrid identity, which is absent from Keats' uniform vision.

In the Middle English thirteenth-century version of *Floris et Blancheflour*, slavery figures as a prominent obstacle to the burgeoning love between these two lovers. Their love even became "a proverbial example of faithful and intense love" when the text was written (Price 1982:12). Still, even if their love does not change, what does alter is the characters' social and cultural status. The status of a slave, after all, often leads to curious metamorphoses in terms of gender, religion, and even ethnicity, since the slave's body has to adapt itself to the circumstances in which it has been placed, while the reality of religious conversion frequently becomes also the reality of a slave's life. In a medieval romance slaves may also experience various changes of fortune which reveal their actual identity, liberating them from previous social constraints. The fact that a slave's body in romance changes so considerably well illustrates what Bynum recognized as the medieval fascination with change, hybridity, and metamorphosis (2001:31). Furthermore, the slave's body, like all bodies, interacts with the society which surrounds it. Slavery is a state conducive to hybridity, comprehended both as juxtapositions of various elements of identity and the (later colonial) situation of oppression exerted on identity, including ocular oppression, because being subservient means subjecting oneself to the gaze of one's master, and implies the slave's possible violent reaction to this situation. Cohen takes this idea even further, arguing that by being "never synthetic in the sense of homogenizing, hybridity is a fusion *and* a disjunction, a conjoining of differences that cannot simply harmonize" (2006:2). This definition is appropriate in the case of the combination of Saracen and Christian elements that can be found in the texts we will interpret here, even though Cohen notes that hybridity at the time meant dual identity, the options one could choose from, which were, however, not conjoined (2006:80).

Medieval French literature includes yet another text about slavery as a constraint that restrains young love, *Aucassin et Nicolete*.[62] It deserves to be mentioned in a study of Middle English oriental romance, because *Aucassin et Nicolete* and *Floris et Blanchefleur* (with the latter's translations into other languages, including Middle English) may be interrelated.[63] The theory of *Floris et Blanchefleur* as a romance originating in the Byzantine tradition, in particular, links the text with *Aucassin et Nicolete*, a narrative of more obviously Byzantine provenance (Grieve 1997:16).[64] Both the French *chantefable* and the Middle English version of the romance portray the institution of slavery as being oppressive to the body and detrimental to the self, even though once slaves change into free people, nothing remains of the misery once suffered by them.[65]

A study of the slave's hybrid identity and the transformations to which he or she may be subjected should cover the historical context of a given narrative. Slavery constituted, after all, one of the cornerstones of ancient cultures, the primary source of labour in the Middle Ages if we include serfdom (since it was a modified version of slavery), and then a system indispensable for the development and maintenance of colonialism around the world and of the agrarian system in such places as the Southern part of the United States before

---

62 Ramey mentions the thirteenth-century *Fille du comte de Ponthieu* and the fourteenth-century *Lion de Bourges* as texts following the tradition of writing about Christian and Muslim intermarriage (2001:68).
63 Other translations, apart from the Middle English, were made in Germany, Iceland, Sweden, Italy, Spain, and the Netherlands (Sands 1986:279).
64 Other theories of the origin of *Floris et Blanchefleur* give either French or Hispano-Arabic sources for the story (Grieve 1997:16-20).
65 After various generic categorizations of the text (romance, tale, novella, and fabliau), sung-story, *chantefable*, became the usual label for *Aucassin et Nicolete* (Roques 1969:iv); Menocal stresses that it is the only known French example of the genre (1989:497).

the Civil War. The institution of slavery is so multi-faceted that Pierre Dockès' legal definition might be valuable:

> To the question What is slavery? we may first give an answer based on law, on the right of property in another human being, comprising three elements: *usus, fructus, abusus*. Consequent upon the legal definition of the property right is the purchase or sale of *slave commodity* [the latter emphasis is mine-A.C.] (1982:4)

Instrumental treatment of one's slaves and the resulting *abusus* they suffered was a natural effect of the legal status that bondage entailed. Still, the management of slaves varied not only individually, but also from one culture to another. Domination, however, remained the key to operating the system. Moses I. Finlay cites the Roman definition, which emphasized the question of the natural order which is not respected within the limits designated by that institution: "In classical Roman law, slavery was defined as an institution 'whereby someone is subject to the *dominion* of another contrary to nature'" (1972:3). In the two medieval narratives we will examine here, *Aucassin et Nicolete* and *Floris and Blancheflour*, natural youthful love clashes against the unnatural system that allows people to be subjugated and possessed by others.

The conflict between love (primarily parental) and slavery as a matter of fact was a recurrent element of the system, as Dockès maintains:

> The *paterfamilias* can kill because he has given life; and it is because he can kill his children that he can also sell them: historically, this has been one of the most deeply rooted sources of slavery (1982:5).

Here slavery confirms its status as a symbolic, social death. If parents selling their own offspring were a lasting constituent of the system, then other people benefitting from the slave trade simply followed in the footsteps of people earning money by selling their own children into bondage. Ancient slavery and the antebellum system in the United States are the most frequent images of bondage in our culture, but the Middle Ages also had its own system of thralldom. At the time "slave" was employed in English merely as a derogatory term, whereas the actual forms of bondage varied (Handlin – Handlin 1972:41).[66] Medieval slaves had the same legal status as livestock (Dockès 1982:8), demonstrated the master's wealth because they were a luxurious commodity (Dockès 1982:9), and became a rather common sight particularly in some regions of Europe as a result of historical conditions. England after the Norman Conquest was a particularly propitious ground for the flourishing of the system due to the ethnic divisions between the Norman masters and the Anglo-

---

[66] Carl N. Degler notes that even though the use of the word "slave" before the seventeenth century was rare, the institution of slavery was very much in existence (1972:71).

Saxon serfs, so this form of slavery "gathered strength" in England, as Dockès writes, from the latter half of the twelfth century throughout the thirteenth (1982:238). A slave trade developed which led to the emergence of a practical attitude to it in the English society: in the centuries to come the merchants trading in slaves were thought to be people on the road to gentility (Finlay 1972:8). The acceptance of the occupation as natural and even proper, as it led to the enrichment of individuals and to an increase in the overall wealth of the community, further stressed the status a slave already had: that of the other. Finlay stresses the idea that in any culture "the slave is an outsider: that alone permits not only his uprooting but also his reduction from a person to a thing which can be owned" (1972:5). The relatively high social status of slave traders exacerbated the already low position of a slave, because the institution seldom received condemnation. On the contrary, it was understood then that slavery constituted one of the cornerstones of the medieval economy, as Bartlett has said (1993:305). The institution of bondage undoubtedly affected entire communities, but such individual factors as ethnicity, gender, age, and even wealth all proved to be important in the situation of a slave, as I mean to demonstrate. What will be analyzed is the trajectory of those factors in the position of a slave in the two texts under view, along with transformations, metamorphoses, and hybrid states.

The association that has been made between racism and slavery even in the historical epochs to follow the Middle Ages proves to be too simplified, as Robert W. Winks demonstrates: he writes that the two were not the same problem, even though they were interrelated (1972:xiii). Eric Williams emphasizes that in the US antebellum slave system racism was secondary to the institution of slavery and instrumental to it (1972:26). George M. Frederickson in turn maintains that black skin could be identified with slave status only beginning in the fifteenth century, when Portuguese merchants began to trade in Africans, but the identification remained a loose one at that time (2002:29). Particularly in the Middle Ages earlier than the fifteenth century ethnic difference does not seem to have been important for enslaving a person. Furthermore, as has been noted above, perhaps we should cease discussing medieval "race" altogether, since otherness at the time usually consisted of a combination of diverse "othering" factors, such as religion, ethnicity, culture, gender, and social position co-related with economic rank. As William Chester Jordan claims, medieval race "encompass[ed] change and independent biological markers", making diverse examples of exteriorization cultural rather than based on a purely ethnic distinction (2001:169). The medieval examples of "othering" a slave were usually undertaken on cultural and social grounds rather than "racial", understood as "ethnic" in the biological sense.

Susan Crane describes slavery as an unnatural obstacle to the naturally developing love in *Floris and Blancheflour*, but the remark equally pertains to *Aucassin et Nicolete* (1986:196). In this *chantefable*, Count Garin de Biaucaire fathers a son christened Aucassin, whose name could connote that of an Arabic ruler (Menocal 1989:497).[67] The son's appearance is described in a manner which is laden with diverse cultural meanings emphasizing his European ethnicity:

> Aucasins avoit a non li damoisiax. Biax estoit et gens et grans et bien tailliés de ganbes et de piés et de cors et de bras ; il avoit les caviax blons et menus recercelés et les ex vairs et rians et le face clere et traitice et le nes haut et bien assis: et si estoit enteciés de bones teces qu'en lui n'en avoit nule mauvaise se bone non. (*AN* 119)

> [Aucassin was the youth's name. He was handsome and noble and tall and his legs, feet, body, and arms were well formed. He had blond hair with little curls and sparkling, laughing eyes, a fair, oval face with a high, well-positioned nose; he was endowed with so many good qualities that he had no bad qualities, only good ones] (*AN* 120)[68]

Despite his possibly oriental name, no foreign elements may be observed in his identity. He is fair-skinned and handsome. Even his hair is fair, while his entire body is shapely. According to the mainstream medieval discourse on sameness and otherness, Aucassin's fairness had to imply kindness and greatness. In contrast, Nicolete is first introduced to the narrative as a heathen captive bought by a viscount from Saracens and christened:

> ... ce est une caitive qui fu amenee d'estrange terre, si l'acata li visquens de ceste vile as Sarasins, si l'amena en ceste vile, si l'a levee et bautisie et faite sa fillole, si li donra un de ces jors un baceler qui du pain li gaaignera par honor ... (*AN* 119)

> [... she is a slave girl who was brought from a foreign land, and the viscount of this town purchased her from the Saracens, brought her from a foreign land, and the viscount of this town raised her at the font, baptized her and made her his godchild, and one of these days he will give her a young man who will earn bread for her honourably ...] (*AN* 120)

The situation reflects the historical fact of European merchants selling Christian slaves to Muslims, which was not, as Metlitzki claims, recorded in the chronicles of the time because the clerics writing those texts "were not interested in recording the activities of merchants in the sinful pursuit of worldly goods" (1977:127). In *Aucassin et Nicolete* the status of a slave itself is not

---

67 Nevertheless, Menocal says that the issue whether Aucassin's name is Arabic or not is a "pseudo-question" (1989:497).

68 Both the original text and the English translation are taken from Cobby and Burgess's edition (1988) and are followed by the abbreviation *AN* and page numbers in brackets.

honorable, whereas marriage improves the position of a female slave in that she will be provided for by her husband. As a result, her legal position is complex: she will only be granted more liberty if she is married to the one who is her like and has been chosen for her by her godfather. She represents pecuniary value not only as a slave, but also as a marriageable woman, the one who can be married well in the sense of her husband generating revenue. Her chances for such marriage increase once we consider her unusual, European-like, appearance. Nicolete is consistently referred to as "fair", as de Weever points out (1994:317-325) and she is very much like Aucassin in this respect:

> Ele avoit les caviaus blons et menus recercelés, et les ex vairs et rians, et le face traitice, et le nes haut et bien assis, et lé levretes vremelletes plus que n'est cerisse ne rose el tans d'esté, et les dens blans et menus, et avoit les mameletes dures qui li souslevoient sa vesteure ausi con ce fuisent .ii. nois gauges ; et estoit graille par mi les flans qu'en vos dex mains le peusciés enclorre, et les flors des margerites qu'ele ronpoit as ortex de ses piés, qui li gissoient sor le menuisse du pié par deseure, estoient droites noires avers ses piés et ses ganbes, tant par estoit blance la mescinete (*AN* 135).

> [She had blond hair with little curls and sparkling, laughing eyes, and an oval face with a high, well-positioned nose, and tiny lips which were redder than a cherry or a rose in summer. Her teeth were white and close fitting, and her small, hard breasts pushed out her dress as if they were two large walnuts; and around her waist she was so slim that one could encircle her with two hands, and the daisies which she crushed with her toes, as they came up over her insteps, were quite black in comparison with her feet and legs, so white was the young girl] (*AN* 136).

Her consistently stressed "poil blont" (*AN* 139) [hair so blond (*AN* 140)] appears as important for her ultimate union with Aucassin as her Christianity. The "whitening" of Nicolete emerges from the narrative as an invisible subtext which yet seemed possible according to the logic of medieval romance. Perhaps what is not mentioned is the girl's magic beautification through baptism, a supernatural event depicted in other texts, for instance in the thirteenth-century *King of Tars*, where the sultan of Damascus transmogrifies into someone whose skin is patched black and white. In medieval romance christening has the potential for whitening dark skins: it purges the body of blackness as radically as it purifies the soul. Nicolete may have become fair and golden-haired once she was baptized and given the French "viscount of the town" as a godfather. Biological paternity, marking her body with ethnic difference, becomes temporarily supplanted by symbolic fatherhood resulting from baptism. It could be read as the first example of transformation in the narrative, with the girl physically metamorphosing into a European, rather than visibly becoming a hybrid in the manner the two-tone sultan in *The king of Tars* is. If blackness was erased from her body, there remained no traces of her origin apart from her status as a slave. Only at the end does she display her hybrid identity. Luckily for her and Aucassin, the baptism did not provoke a full metamorphosis and total oblivion, because the recovered memories cause an improvement in the situation of the young lovers. She first lives in the Christian culture, only to resort to her previous cultural identification once it proves to be propitious. This turns her identity into a hybrid: she inhabits simultaneously at least two, if not more, cultures. In accordance with the modern understanding of hybridity, Nicolete's identification as either a Christian or a Saracen continued to be renegotiated, with no fixed relationship established between these two elements.

The question of the other's body as a *tabula rasa* becomes pertinent here. Perhaps christening does not erase a different religion, culture, and ethnicity from such a body, but inscribes its own text on it, producing the effect of a specific hybridity: one layer covers the other so that the previous one seems to be erased, but it actually remains dormant underneath. Nicolete acquires what Bhabha terms a double identity, a self that is different from other forms of identity characterizing ethnic and cultural others. The process of hybridization operates "where the trace of the disavowed is not repressed, but repeated as something *different* – a mutation, a hybrid" (1985:96). Naturally, Bhabha is discussing hybridity in its chronologically later, more obviously colonial context; yet the identity type experienced by a slave shares with it specific qualities, since the situation of slaves may be interpreted as colonial. After all, it involves domination, oppression, and forcible metamorphosis into an identity similar to the oppressors' one, but never the same. For Bhabha ". . . the colonial hybrid is the articulation of the ambivalent space where the rite of power is enacted on the site of desire, making its objects at once disciplinary and disseminatory; or in [the] mixed metaphor, a negative transparency" (1985:97). Like the mimetic colonial other, replicating the colonizer's sameness, even if it is always repetition with a difference, the hybrid subject remains invisible to the colonial eye (Bhabha 1984:125-133). Hybridity results from "the repetition of identity-effects" in the identity of the subjugated ones (Bhabha 1985:97), and this occurs in Nicolete's situation: she repeats Aucassin's Christianity and the amazing repetition of his ethnicity occurs in her body, fair-skinned and blond-haired, even if she remains a slave of oriental origin. Her Saracen corporeality becomes disciplined, but she simultaneously portrays the spreading of mutation rather than being the same as her masters. According to the text's ideology the mutation she represents ought to be spread and other Saracens should follow Nicolete's conversion and Europeanization, transforming themselves into hybrids as well. The girl's slave status transforms her into a subject of both disavowal and desire. The mutation consists here in the double status of Nicolete as a Christian, able to convince pagans to follow in her footsteps, and a subject of the imperial power of any slave master. In the conversation with David Townsend, Uppinder Mehan noted the duplicity of Bhabha's idea of hybridity in another context, Bede's *Historia ecclesiastica gentis Anglorum*, from which the author emerged as "a sharer of the metropolitan's power and the object of that power" (Mehan – Townsend 2001:8). Hybrids thus have to situate themselves simultaneously inside and outside the system which generates their mutant identity, with their self continually shifting between the colonizer-like identity, never fully available to them, and the identity of the other, necessary for the system of domination to be perpetuated. Hybridity, however, not only signals mutated identity, but implies subversion, whose strategies "turn the gaze of the discriminated back upon the eye of power" (Bhabha 1985:97). The slave of Saracen origin is not only subjected to scrutiny by the slave masters, but also performs ocular inspection herself, reversing the oppressing gaze and turning it into a look which could possibly demonstrate dissent.

As for physicality, Nicolete looks Europeanized, but her actual self proves to be more complex in the end. There exists within her a potential for rebellion and for disagreement with the situation in which she had been placed as a child. Her hybridity should function as a disquieting presence for the non-Saracens who surround her. What remains dormant within her identity is authority, which materializes in the scene in which she unexpectedly reminisces of her distant past. The memories of her true origin return to her once she finds herself aboard a ship of the king of Carthage:

> Il nagierent tant qu'il ariverent desox le cité de Cartage. Et quant Nicolete vit les murs del castel et le païs ele se reconut, qu'ele i avoit esté norie et pree petis enfes ; mais ele ne fu mie si petis enfes que ne seust bien qu'ele avoit esté fille au roi de Cartage et qu'ele avoit esté norie en le cité (*AN* 163).
>
> [They sailed on until they arrived beneath the city of Carthage. And when Nicolette saw the walls of the castle and the surrounding area, she realized who she was and that she had been raised there and taken away as a small child; but she had not been too young to be well aware that she was the daughter of the King of Carthage and that she had been raised in the city] (*AN* 164).

Her otherness turns out to be a source of her power: here also political, as the previous "deformation and displacement" (Bhabha 1985:97) of a Saracen slave metamorphoses into the authority of a princess of Carthage (possibly Phoenician if we consider the origin of the city as a settlement of the ethnic group). Obviously, Nicolete's hybridity is only signaled by her new religion and physicality, but her actual ethnicity testifies to the complexity of identity. Nevertheless, her mutated self becomes transparent only when she discovers another part of the old identity, her memories, while aboard the ship. Carthage turns out to be Nicolete's home, even though the image of Phoenicians as merchants also trading in people disconcertingly mingles with her predicament as a slave herself. Fortunately, despite the frequency of such situations in past ages, but also in the modern world, as the king's daughter Nicolete had not been sold into slavery by her father.

Earlier, when Nicolete is still a slave, her misfortune increases through her secret imprisonment by Count de Biaucaire. He separates her from Aucassin, who intends to marry her. Nicolete metamorphoses into a prisoner, heightening the misery she has already been subjected to. The disappearance of a slave might not be a matter of high importance; here, however, it is, but the rumours reported in the narrative testify to the frequency of such situations and the fate that often befell slaves then:

> Nicolete fu en prison, si que vous avés oï et entendu, en le canbre. Li cris et la noise ala par tote le terre et par tot le païs que Nicolete estoit perdue. Li auquant dient qu'ele est fuie fors de la terre, et li auquant dient que li quens Garins de Biaucaire l'a faite mordrir (*AN* 123).
>
> [Nicolette was, as you have heard, imprisoned in the chamber. The cry and the rumour spread throughout the country and over the entire region that she was lost. Some said she had fled the country, others that Count Garin of Beaucaire had murdered her.] (*AN* 124)

Leading the life of a fugitive or being murdered appear to be two types of predicament frequently experienced by slaves who disappeared. Many people fret about Nicolete's lot in all likelihood only because she is the beloved of the count's son and this romance renders her story more interesting to the count's subjects. Very probably an ordinary slave would not attract so much attention. Nevertheless, when confronted by Aucassin, her godfather the viscount criticizes the youth's amorous intentions by stating that his marriage to Nicolete, a slave, would have been impossible even if she had not disappeared, and making her his mistress would have been sinful. As Menocal notes, according to the poem's ideology slavery, in contrast to adultery, is not morally wrong. The *chantefable* demonstrates double standards: the sacrament remains out of reach of slaves, but their bodies may be freely used by their Christian masters, also sexually, which is supposedly not sinful (Menocal 1989:501).

Equally twisted is the issue of ethnicity and gender. As for Nicolete's undoubted physical femininity, it contrasts with Aucassin's equivocal psychic masculinity. While riding in search of his beloved, he presents a stalwart military attitude only to give a different impression as he loses control over the situation when dreaming about his beloved:

Aucassins fu armés sor son ceval, si con vos avés oï et entandu. Dix, con li sist li escus au col et li hiaumes u cief et li renge de s'espee sor le senestre hance! Et li vallés fu grans et fors et biax et gens et biens fornis, et li cevaus sor quoi il sist rades et corans, et li vallés l'ot bien adrecié par mi la porte.

Or ne quidiés vous qu'il pensast n'a bués n'a vaces n'a civres prendre, ne qu'il ferist cevalier ne autres lui. Nenil nient! onques ne l'en sovint; ains pensa tant a Nicolete sa douce amie qu'il oublia ses resnes et quanques il dut faire. Et li cevax qui ot senti les esperons l'en porta par mi le presse, se se lance tres entre mi ses anemis; et il getent les mains de toutes pars, si le prendent, se le dessaisisent de l'escu et de la lance, si l'en mannent tot estrousement pris; et aloient ja porparlant de quel mort il feroient morir. (*AN* 129)

[Aucassin sat upon his horse fully armed, as you have heard. God, how his shield around his neck suited him and the helmet on his head and his sword belt on his left hip! He was a tall, strong youth, handsome, noble and well-built, and the horse on which he sat was swift and fleet and the young man rode it straight through the gate.

Now do not think that he was intent on catching oxen, cows, goats, or on striking knights or being struck by them. Not a bit of it. Such a thing never occurred to him; for his mind was so firmly fixed on Nicolette, his sweet friend, that he neglected his reins and everything he was supposed to be doing. And the horse, feeling the spurs, carried him right to the throng and launched itself into the midst of his enemies; and they flung out their eyes on all sides and seized him, dispossessed him of his shield and lance and carried him off as a captive; and, as they departed, they were already discussing the means by which he would be put to death.] (*AN* 130)

His amorous longing leads to the change in his status, which becomes similar to that of Nicolete, who remains permanently enslaved and temporarily imprisoned. It is this languor, portrayed as unmanly and depriving him of the qualities needed for a warrior, that causes his capture. It appears that a man, if he intends to stay free, cannot abandon a masculine competitive attitude to life and devote all his thoughts exclusively to romance. There exist limits to the desire to be reunited with one's lady and if a man does not heed those limitations, his liberty will be imperiled along with his relationship. A slippage of gender categories is observable in this scene, because too much interest in love renders the youth not masculine enough for the chivalric world he lives in. Aucassin's confrontation with his father does not help much in the family conflict and the youth ends up in prison, sharing the plight of Nicolete:

Aucasins fu mis en prison, si com vos avés oï et entendu, et Nicolete fu d'autre part en le canbre. Ce fu el tans d'esté, el mois de mai, que li jor sont caut, lonc et cler, et les nuis coies et series.

Nicolete jut une nuit en son lit, si vit la lune luire cler par une fenestre ; et si oï le lorseilnol center en garding, se li sovint d'Aucassin sen ami qu'ele tant amoit. Ele se començca a porpenser del conte Garin de Biaucaire que de mort le haoit, si se pensa qu'ele ne remanroit plus ilec, que s'ele estoit acusee et li quens Garins le savoit, il le feroit de male mort morir. Ele senti que li vielle dormoit qui aveuc li estoit. Ele se leva, si vesti un bliaut de drap de soie que ele avoit mout bon, si prist dras de lit et touailes, si noua l'un a l'autre, si fist une corde si longe conme ele pot, si le noua au piler de le fenestre, si s'avala contreval le gardin; et prist se vesture a l'une main devant et a l'autre deriere, si s'escorça por le rousee qu'ele vit grande sor l'erbe, si s'en ala aval le gardin. (*AN* 135)

[Aucassin had been put in prison, as you have heard, and Nicolette was still in her chamber. It was summer in the month of May, with warm days, long and fair, and nights which were tranquil and serene. Nicolette lay in bed one night and saw the moon shining clearly through a window and heard the song of the nightingale in the garden, and she thought of Aucassin, her friend whom she loved so much. Her mind turned to Count Garin who had a mortal hatred for her, and she decided she would remain there no longer, because, if she were accused and Count Garin found out, he would subject her to a painful death. She realized that the old woman who lived with her fell asleep. So she rose, put on a very fine tunic she possessed, took sheets and towels, knotted them together to make as long a rope as possible, and tied it to a pillar near the window. She climbed down into the garden, held her dress at the front with one hand and at the back with the other, and pulled up the hem because she saw how heavy was the dew which lay on the grass, and she made her way down the garden] (*AN* 136).

If love was capable of turning a valiant knight into a powerless dreamer, the will to live transforms Nicolete into a fugitive, equally aware of the two options gossiped about on her disappearance, her escape or being murdered by her lover's father. The fugitive's ways also demonstrate a gender role reversal, since she skillfully devises her means of escape and carries out her plan with agility, leaving her previously passive and docile, stereotypically "feminine", comportment behind her. A slave's body is capable of more than a free person's, even in the sense of transcending gender boundaries, whenever necessary. Nicolete's escape marks yet another physical displacement in this narrative about the burdensome nature of captivity, while the shifts in the characters' behaviour demonstrate a symbolic displacement in the gender roles culturally assigned to them.

The *chantefable* revolves around the characters changing their place; not only does it demonstrate that displacement is inseparable from thralldom and domination by other people, but it also makes this displacement central to the adventures of the two lovers. The geographical landscape changes in the narrative, passing from Biaucaire, through the forests and seas, to Torelore and Carthage. The emotional landscape of the characters' minds changes as well. Having escaped, Nicolete hears a demonstration of her imprisoned lover's sorrow:

Li tors estoit faelle de lius en lius, et ele se quatist delés l'un des pilers, si s'estraint en son mantel, si mist sen cief par mi une creveure de la tor, qui vielle estoit et anciienne, si oï Aucassin qui la dedens pluroit et faisoit mot grant dol et regretoit se douce amie que tant amoit (*AN* 135).

[The tower was cracked in several places: and she pressed herself up close to one of the pillars, wrapped herself in her coat and put her head through a crack in the tower, which was old and ancient, and within she could hear Aucassin weeping and bewailing his fate and mourning his sweet friend whom he loved so much.] (*AN* 136)

The dejection, however, is provoked by the separation from Nicolete rather than by his captivity. He appears unmoved by his own imprisonment, which proves to be transitory and does not affect his status within the social hierarchy. But even when liberated by the Count, he grieves over his lost love:

Quoi que li feste estoit estoit plus plaine, et Aucassins fu apoiiés a une puie, tos dolant et tos souples: qui que demenast joie, Aucassins n'en ot talent, qu'il n'i venoit rien de çou qu'il amoit (*AN* 145).

[Whilst the celebration was at its height, Aucassin was leaning against a balustrade, plunged into grief and sadness: others may have been rejoicing, but Aucassin had no desire to do so, as he saw no sign of the one he loved.] (*AN* 146)

Humans metamorphose not only through the experience of slavery and incarceration, but also as a result of the symbolic captivity of love. Slavery emerges from the narrative as an experience constituting an important part of Nicolete's life and a short span in the life of Aucassin, which paradoxically brings them closer to each other.

Still, the idealized vision of slavery as an experience spiritually uniting these lovers considerably differs from the realistic account of medieval serfdom introduced into the plot while Aucassin's searching for Nicolete in the forest. The churl that Aucassin encounters even physically differs from beautiful aristocrats and their beloved ones:

Grans estoit et mervellex et lais et hidex. Il avoit une grande hure plus noire q'une carbouclee, et avoit une grande hure plus noire qu'une carbouclee, et avoit plus de planne paume entre .ii. ex, et avoit unes grandes joes et un grandisme nes plat et unes grans narines lees et unes grosses levres plus rouges d'une carbounee et uns grans dens gaunes et lais; et estoit cauçié d'uns housiax et d'uns sollers de buef fretés de tille dusque deseure le genol, et estoit afulés d'une cape a .ii. envers, si estoit apoiiés sor une grande maçue (*AN* 151).

[He was tall and strange, ugly and hideous; he had a large head, blacker than a piece of coal, and there was more than a palm's breadth between his two eyes, and he had large cheeks and a huge flat nose and thick lips, redder than grilled meat, and huge, ugly, yellow teeth; he was dressed in leggings and shoes made of ox-hide held up, above the knee, with lime-bark, and he was muffled up in a cape with two wrong sides, and leaning on a huge club.] (*AN* 152)

Beauty cannot characterize serfs, whose position is much lower than that of Nicolete; after all, she is the type of a slave about whose plight people care and who has been chosen by the count's son. Even the serfs' physicality does not allow them to aspire to anything but what they are subjected to: penury, toil, and ultimately death. Love and sorrow over its loss are a secondary issue in a world where people lack food despite their drudgery, the serf claims as he tells the story of his life in poverty and the lost ox:

> J'estoie luiés a un rice villain, si caçoie se carue, .iiii. bués i avoit. Or a .iii. jors qu'il m'avint une grande malaventure, que je perdi le mellor de me bués, Roger, le mellor de me carue, si le vois querant. Si ne mengai ne ne buc .iii. jors a passé, si n'os aler a le vile, c'on me metroit en prison, que je ne l'ai de quoi saure ; de tot l'avoir du monde n'ai je plus vaillant que vos veés sor le cors de mi. (*AN* 151)
>
> [I was hired out to a rich peasant and was driving his team with four oxen. Now three days ago a great disaster overtook me, for I lost the best of my oxen, Roget, the finest of the team; I am looking for him. I have not eaten or drunk for three days now and dare not go into town, as I should be put in prison, for I have no money to pay for it. All I have in the world is what you see on me.] (*AN* 152)

Nonetheless, living the life of a serf does not denote ultimate misery, because a serf, occupying the position similar to that of a slave in the feudal system, may also be imprisoned, which worsens his bondage. The realism of the account ends, however, with the romance-like outcome of the encounter, when Aucassin proves to be courteous and generous to the serf by giving him money to pay for the lost ox.

Predictably, if we consider the medieval prohibition against marrying a slave, Nicolete's status metamorphoses from that of a commodity-like slave to that of a monarch. The girl regains her status as the rightful heiress of Carthage through the sudden hindsight she experiences aboard the ship of the king who is her lost father, as has been noted earlier. Once she has regained her long-lost position, she is free to return to Aucassin. Implying her actual ethnic identity, she smears her face brown in the forest and returns to her lover unrecognized, revealing to him the nature of the metamorphosis from a slave to a royal she has gone through. In the manner that medieval audiences loved, as Bynum maintains, the *unitas* of Nicolete's identity remains unchanged, but the elements of the *structure*, ethnicity (not Saracen, but Phoenician), social status, and wealth, metamorphose into those that are as socially acceptable as possible under the circumstances (2001:28). Significantly, not only does Nicolete regain her freedom, but she also enjoys the unrestrained liberty of a monarch's daughter, free to marry whomever she chooses. The narrative resists the notion that one may marry a slave, transforming the girl into a free person instead of questioning any rules observed in the society in which the text is set. Nicolete's possible rebellion against the system of control and subjection is cancelled, displaying her willingness to be incorporated into Christian society by marrying Aucassin, who is now a count.

In the introduction to a collection of articles devoted to the inner limits of the body and those limits designated for it by society, Jeffrey Jerome Cohen and Gail Weiss emphasize what they call "porousness" between bodies and world; this is the body's ability to integrate itself with the surrounding world (2009:8). Nicolete's hybrid identity does not allow her body to be porous enough and to fully unite with the Western world. Only once the status of a slave is abandoned can the body entirely become a part of the surrounding reality by being reintegrated with the society. The lovers are reunited and wedded in church, and the burdensome parts of the *structure*, Nicolete's originally Saracen identity and her position of a slave, are ultimately annulled. Slavery does not leave any mark on her identity, it seems, with the text idealistically claiming the possibility of complete transformation with no aftereffects resulting from the previous position. A slave's body is capable of much, but the body of the princess of Carthage knows no limitations; finally she can enjoy her liberty as the wife of a count. Diverse parts of *structure* appear to be shifting for the happy ending to become possible.

Identity shifts and hybridity are also a large part of the world represented in Middle English romance *Floris and Blancheflour*, even though one could not detect effeminacy in Floris or any masculinization in Blancheflour's comportment. Blurring of gender can only be noted if one considers how youthful both of them are, because the gender boundaries are less visible in a young boy and a girl than in a man and a woman. Nevertheless, shifting gender roles such as occurred in *Aucassin et Nicolete* do not occur in *Floris and Blancheflour*. Conversely, according to N.H.G.E. Veldhoen, Floris represents the ideal of vigorous masculinity in spite of his Saracen origin, which according to orientalist stereotypes could make him more effeminate (1988:59). In contrast to the somewhat pensive and distraught Aucassin, Floris attempts to actively end Blancheflour's captivity and prevent the situation in which as a slave she could change hands in the manner which would indicate her status as an object. In comparison with *Aucassin et Nicolete*, the combination of gender and cultural identity is reversed, because here Floris is a free Spanish Saracen and Blancheflour an enslaved Christian, but the pattern of the lady held captive remains unchanged, testifying to a fairly permanent status of women within the institution of slavery. They are made doubly captive: through their ethnicity and through their gender, rendering their enslavement more "natural" and the liberation through marriage with a free man more frequent than it would have been in the case of men permanently held captive.[69]

---

69 What comes to one's mind is Gayle Rubin's famous *Traffic in women*, dealing with the continuing position of women as tokens in the patriarchal world of exchange (1998), which supported the argument in Kelly's study on *Floris et Blancheflour* (1994:104).

Yet again, as in *Richard le Coer de Lyon*, the historiographic context of the plot, here that of the relatively less painful slavery, demonstrates that real life differed from the fantasies recorded in oriental romances. Crusading reality led not only to Christian victories, as happened at the beginning, but also defeated and enslaved by Muslims. John V. Tolan starts his discussion of the Saracen imaginary in medieval Europe with a quotation from Riccoldo da Montecroce's *Epistolae V de perditione Acconis*, published in 1291:

> And so it came to pass that I was in Baghdad, "among the captives by the river of Chebar" [Ezek. 1:1], the Tigris. This garden of delights in which I found myself enthralled me, for it was like a paradise in its abundance of trees, its fertility, its many fruits. This garden was watered by the rivers of Paradise, and the inhabitants built gilt houses all around it. Yet I was saddened by the massacre and capture of the Christian people. I wept over the loss of Acre, seeing the Saracens joyous and prospering, the Christians squalid and consternated: little children, young girls, old people, whimpering, threatened to be led as captives and slaves into the remotest countries of the East, among barbarous nations (Tolan 2002:xiii).

As with the actual starvation crusaders suffered, here the historian records the dire experiences of Christians becoming prisoners of war of the Saracens, who often enslaved Franks and sold the captives further. This is not what Blancheflour suffers in the romance under consideration, but the historical context of Arabs building wealth and political power on the institution of slavery remains important.[70] "The rise of Islam was made possible by slavery," writes Orlando Patterson, "for without it the early Arab elites simply would not have been able to exploit the skilled and unskilled manpower that was essential for their survival and expansion. Even more than the Western states, the Islamic world depended on slaves for the performance of critical administrative, military, and cultural roles" (1982:viii). This must be the reality that the text alludes to.

Despite their ethnic and gender difference, Floris and Blancheflour are introduced in the romance as children similar to each other through their birth and nurture, inviting some critics to consider it as yet another text about incest.[71] The part of the plot missing from the Middle English version has Blancheflour as the daughter of a Christian lady of aristocratic origin who was captured by Saracens and gave birth to the girl while in captivity. Included in the Saracen queen's retinue, she befriended her and they subsequently gave birth to children

---

70 The etymology of the word "slave", *sklabos*, shows that the first slaves brought into al-Andalus by Jews and Muslims were Slavs; it was discontinued after Slavic peoples were Christianized.

71 Carol F. Heffernan argues that rape was a frequent type of violence to which female slaves were subjected; hypothetically, Blancheflour could have been the extramarital child of Floris's father, which would make her union with him incestuous (2003:83-107).

on the same day, which was the festival of flowers. This coincidence resulted in the floral names of the children, Blanchefleur and Floris, making them even more related to each other through the compatibility of that primary identification (Sands 1986:280). Karl P. Wentersdorf, however, identifies the festival of flowers in the French original as a Christian holiday, pointing to *Le jour de la Pasque florie* or Palm Sunday as the actual day of the children's birth (1981:76). Not only is the similarity of the two signaled by their names, but also by their appearance, which the French *version aristocratique*, Middle English translation, and Boccaccio's *Il Filocolo*, emphasizes (Grieve 1997:65). In the Middle English romance the anonymous author dwells on the similarity most likely in order to confirm the care that the children received:

> Ne thurst men never in londe
> After fairer children fonde.
> The Christen woman fedde hem tho;
> Full well she loved hem both two.
> So longe she fedde hem in fere
> That they were of elde of seven yere.
>   (*FB* 1-6)[72]

The fairness of the two does not necessarily signify merely their beauty, but may also be ethnic and, ultimately, cultural; gender seems to be a question of minor importance in the case of such a similarity. The medieval conviction of the nurturing woman's influence on the baby whom she breastfed may have contributed to this image of Floris and Blancheflour being very much like each other, regardless of their respective genders and ethnic origins. Christian mothers were careful about the choice of the nurse who was believed to transfer some of her qualities onto the nursed child, while the Saracen mother in the romance appears to be unaware of the possible influence. Clarissa W. Atkinson cites Bernardino of Siena, who claims that "the child acquires certain of the customs of the one who suckles him. If the one who cares for him has evil customs or is of base condition, he will receive the impress of those customs because of having suckled her polluted blood" (1991:60). The ancient and medieval theory of lactation physiology, claiming that blood metamorphosed into maternal milk during breastfeeding, strongly connected nature with nurture because the milk was expected to transfer the wet nurse's character onto the baby. In *De proprietatibus rerum* Bartholomew Anglicus even propounded the idea that the mother was the woman who put forth her breast, which encouraged him to state that: "The nurse is instead of the mother . . . glad if the child is glad

---

[72] All the quotations from *Floris and Blancheflour* come from Sands' edition (1986) and the number of the lines refer to it as well; they are preceded by the abbreviation *FB*.

and sorry if the child is sorry, and takes him up if he falls, and gives him suck if he cries, and kisses him if he is quiet" (Atkinson 1991:61). Nurturing, according to Bartholomew, forms a permanent relationship between the wet nurse and the baby, somehow obscuring the link between the baby and the actual mother. Perhaps then Blancheflour's mother as the wet nurse of the two children equally distributed her civilized quality, European mores, and even her ethnicity between the two of them. This would make Floris's conversion to Christianity, otherwise not mentioned, but evident at the end of the narrative, a natural consequence of being nurtured by a Christian.[73] European identity could exercise a strong influence on heathen children, producing the effect of Floris's invisible hybridity, since due to his nursing he metamorphoses into a Christian in the disguise of a Muslim prince. The psychological similarity between the boy and the girl, very likely resulting from the nurture they received, becomes transparent even in school education they share: "To scole they were put;/ Both they were good of witte" (*FB* 25-26). The French *version aristocratique* indicates the reading they were doing together at the moment when they fell in love with each other, emphasizing the triumph of nurture over nature in their relationship (Krueger 1983:67). Then their mutual love grows, annulling the boundaries between their backgrounds and producing the effect of Cohen and Weiss's porousness, but this time not with the surrounding world, but between the two of them, due to the lack of distinct boundaries separating them.

Nonetheless, like Nicolete, Blancheflour cannot integrate herself with the surrounding reality or another person fully, as she is not only formally a captive, but also becomes a commodity that can be sold to another slaveholder. In contrast to the *version aristocratique*, where the role of nature and nurture are elaborated on, the Middle English version emphasizes the fact that Blancheflour is marketable very strongly. Kelly even claims that the girl's status of a slave is "essential to the poem" (1994:102). When she is given a name similar to that of Floris, the act stresses her humanity. Then she is sold to merchants trading in slaves, which must alter our perspective on her humanity in the society in which she was born. She acquires the in-between status of neither a free human being, because she represents a specific pecuniary value once she has been sold for the first time, nor an object. Patterson highlights the fact that a slave "had no socially recognized existence outside of his master", which amounted to his

---

[73] Grieve insists that in most versions Floris actually converts to Christianity before marriage (1997:2), while Pearsall notes that "scholars draw the identification of Floris as heathen and Blancheflour as Christian from the French tradition; there is no explicit identification as such in the Middle English manuscripts" (2011:77); it cannot be presumed from the Middle English text that Floris is Christian (Pearsall 2011:77).

status of "a social nonperson" (1982:5). Slavery entailed the status of "a socially dead person" and someone "secularly excommunicated," as Patterson insists (1982:5). As a result, slaves became "a subcategory of human proprietary objects" (Patterson 1982:21), "neither dead nor alive" (Patterson 1982:48), as they were entities situated neither inside the society nor outside it. They formed the category of an internal alien, foreign to the rest of the society, but excluding their masters from the relationship of alienation.

As chattel, Blancheflour can be replaced with a specific monetary equivalent already in the first scene in which she is traded:

> Well sone that maide was his betaught
> And to the haven she was brought.
> Ther have they for that maide yolde
> Twenty mark of reed golde,
> And a coupe good and riche;
> In all the world was non it liche.
> (*FB* 159-164)

The description of the cup, featuring Paris's abduction of Helen "the Queene" (*FB* 168), humanizes the object, creating the illusory impression of it also having, like Blancheflour, a physicality and distinct history, since it "was stoole fro King Cesar" (*FB* 181). On the other hand, Kelly stresses the idea that all three of them, Helen, Blancheflour, and the cup, become merely articles of trade as a consequence of the enumeration (1994:106). Subjected to further trading, the Christian girl's value increases as if she were a commodity, because the Emir "gafe for hur, as she stood upright,/ Sevin sithes of golde her wight" (*FB* 195-196). The price paid for her and her future role of the Emir's mistress seal her social death. Blancheflour's double status as neither a human nor an object, so characteristic of later slavery in the Western world, produces the effect of ambiguity. The shifting identity based on the dialectic of neither-nor does not result in the grotesqueness of body that Leonard Cassuto observed in representations of slavery in American culture (1997:xv). Still, like African slaves in American culture, she cannot be fully objectified, either. The obstacle to objectification is both her humanity and Floris's affection, which drives him to try to purchase her back. Blancheflour, like Native Americans and African Americans in the texts Cassuto analyzes, returns to the full human identity in the end (1997:xvii). Nevertheless, for the girl it is the actual liberation that is the humanizing experience, while in American culture based on slave systems the return to humanity remained mainly symbolic, since no liberation happened (Cassuto 1997:xv).

Yet Blancheflour's yoke is not the only one in the romance. The text nuances diverse forms of bondage and comments on the modes in which they may limit a human body. The question of slavery forcefully materializes here, as bondage impinges on Blancheflour's life, and simultaneously remains a highly metaphorical situation. In *Aucassin et Nicolete* the theme of symbolic thralldom was signaled by the subplot of Aucassin's father as someone enslaved by his old body and ultimately dying, which allowed for the reunion of the lovers to occur (Shahar 1994:166). The dialectics of slavery and liberation thus combine in the *chantefable*, and the motive of parental death liberating lovers who have been separated by slavery is repeated in *Floris and Blancheflour*:

>Was it nought longe after than
>That to Floris tiding cam
>That the King his fader was deed.
>The baronage gaf him reed
>That he shuld wende hoom
>And fonge his faire kingdoom.
>   (*FB* 1074-1079)

In these two narratives the soul remains metaphorically enslaved by an old or possibly diseased body, while both of the fathers emerge from the texts as brutal persecutors bent on torturing their sons' beloveds. After all, Blancheflour's status as a commodity sold dearly and then as an object which changes hands to generate further profit for her owners results from Floris's father's intention, firstly, to murder her, and then, once he has been dissuaded by the mother, to keep her out of Floris's sight. The father's callousness perhaps springs from his decrepitude, which compels him to make those subject to him enslaved (this time literarily) and miserable like himself. With its inevitable aging and the mental condition resulting from it, the human body appears in the narratives in question as continuously metamorphosing and changing its shape and qualities. The old body both is captured within its own limits and imposes limitations on those who surround it. Despite its decrepitude, the father's diseased body can still inflict much harm. The slave's body, whose capabilities and instruments remain limited, functions as a foil to this metaphorical enslavement of senility.

Not only does old age generate enslavement; love metaphorically binds a lover as well, pleasant as the experience may be. The seven-year-old Floris, already infatuated with Blancheflour, reacts vehemently to the very thought of attending school without his love: "Floris answerd with weeping,/ As he stood bifore the King" (*FB* 15-16). Furthermore, he is not governed by the positive aspects of love only. His parents keep dominating him, leading to his immense sorrow over the supposed death of Blancheflour and to a heart-rending scene at her grave. The darker side of love is, after all, the possibility of a lover committing suicide due to the demise of his beloved. Only later do Floris's parents allow him to learn the truth and search for the girl. He tries to buy information about her from merchants and others. The sale of Blancheflour leads to the metamorphosis of her identity, since her earlier enslavement at the Spanish court was formal, while the actual status of a commodity she acquires even leads to a linguistic change whenever she is discussed. When searching for her, Floris talks to a burgess, who believes the youth to be a slaveholder considering a purchase of more property:

> "Ow, child, me thinketh welle
> That muche thou thinkest on my catelle."
> "Nay, sir, on catel thenke I nought"
> (On Blancheflour was all his thought),
> "But I thinke on all wise
> For to finde my merchaundise;
> And yit it is the most wo,
> When I it find, I shall it forgo."
> (*FB* 459-466)

Confessing love for a slave is unacceptable, so even Floris employs trade vocabulary when he refers to Blancheflour. This represents an example of the "cunning and ingenuity" traceable in the text that Geraldine Barnes finds (1984:10-25), but also displays the mercantile reality of the poem. Floris searches for Blancheflour with a cup of gold which was the pecuniary equivalent of Blancheflour's value, somehow adapting to the harsh reality of the world in which he lives. The cup was given to him by his father, who had become more despondent than tyrannical when his son intended to take his life in grief for the allegedly dead girl. During his quest Floris continues trading in Blancheflour, since he intends to exchange the cup of gold for her. Cups are a frequent currency in the lands to which he travels, as he exchanges "a coupe of silver clere,/ A mantil of scarlet with menieure" (*FB* 475-476) for the information about the girl that the burgess possesses. In order to gain or regain a slave, other possessions are necessary. The slave's own capabilities and instruments, a subject of Deleuze's divagations on the human body (1990:217-234), do not matter at this point, because an enslaved body functions here as an immovable object that requires the deployment of other instruments (here pecuniary) so that it can change hands. In *chansons de geste* women also tend to acquire the status of objects to be owned, traded, and exchanged (Kay 1995:38). This indicates a more general pattern in the treatment of women as commodities.

Simultaneously, other obstacles are introduced into the narrative as though to prove that instruments in the form of valuable objects may not suffice to regain a lost commodity, even if this commodity is human. Floris must show himself to possess complex capabilities if he wants to win Blancheflour back, as in the episode of the Emir's porter, "cruel and feloun" (*FB* 658), who is obsessed with chess playing, a game which symbolized the threat of mortality.[74] Advice about the Emir's porter is given to Floris by Daris, a bridge porter or toll keeper, who tells him the following about the Emir's servant:

> Well sone he will com thee nere
> And will bid thee play the chekere.
> When thou art at cheker brought,
> Without selver be thou nought;
> Thou shalt have redy with thee
> Twenty marke beside thy knee.
> Yif thou winne ought of his,
> Thou tell therof litel pris;
> And if he winne ought of thin,
> Loke thou leve it with him.
> So thou shalt, all with ginne,
> The porters love forsoth winne
> That he thee help on this day.
> (*FB* 669-681)

A human body can do much to release another, enslaved, body, from the burdensome position of a traded object. Here the slave is portrayed as a person with a body marked with social disability, which does not follow from impairment but is the result of a convention dividing people into free men and slaves. The social disability does not allow people to decide for themselves, but enforces on their bodies the status of chattel. Actual thralldom denotes not just frequent change of physical place and geographic displacement, but also a displacement of will, since all volition is granted to the slaveholder. Blancheflour, educated like Floris, cannot undertake any decisions about herself. The necessary instruments for such responsibility are theoretically at her disposal, as she is not lacking in intellect, but in practice her social position constrains her. According to the ideology of the romance, the incongruity of this situation is stressed for European readers on the level of *structure*, because the girl is both Christian and civilized.

Slavery is portrayed here also as displacement from one's ethnic group and culture. After all, Blancheflour first undergoes objectification by Saracens, who will sell her to anyone willing to pay enough. The system forces her to obey any future owner, which she indeed conforms to in the Emir's harem, where becoming the master's choice is all subject to chance. A culture which allows a man to choose his wife at random, depending on whose head the flower falls

---

74 Apart from being popular chivalric pastime in the Middle Ages, chess allegorized human life with the possibility of the devil playing chess for the human's soul (Reiss 1971:347); chess could betoken sin and damnation (Wentersdorf 1981:83).

upon from the "Tree of Love" (*FB* 631), appears unpleasant, but it indicates the fairy-tale quality of the setting: "And which so falleth the floure/ Shall be queene with muche honour" (*FB* 635-636). Paradoxically, flowers which once brought Blancheflour a name and a peaceful childhood equal to Floris's now may bring about her disgrace and sexual thralldom. The romance harshly criticizes the slave system of the Saracen world, demonstrating the corrupted rules and values observed within it. To cite Winks, "Slavery [is] . . . an indication of the cultural values upon which a dominant people bases its attitude towards those subservient to its culture" (1972:xii). Muslim slavery is grounded in the exploitation of women. Oriental excess demonstrates itself in the promiscuity of the Emir, intent on collecting beautiful women and apparently disinterested in their humanity. Human life, especially of a beautiful woman, has a pecuniary value and serves merely sexual purposes. Slavery exhibits instrumental treatment of any human body, especially a female one, because it affects even its sexuality. In this context white-skinned and Christian Blancheflour adopts the identity of the other, whose body becomes a property one can dispose of freely if one has the status of being its owner. Slavery denotes a displacement not only from one's own culture but also, more radically, from one's own body, especially if one is female.

The portrayal of the Saracen slave trade as a ruthless mechanism, however, may be exaggerated. Pierre Dockès writes that Arabs enslaved only those who did not agree to convert to Islam (1982:238); by contrast, the usual route of enslavement and conversion in medieval Christian culture consisted in enslaving enemies and forcibly converting them only afterwards. Furthermore, baptism did not necessarily entail true conversion, as for instance the missionaries dispatched to Tartary knew too well (Ryan 1997:162). The Middle English author of the romance emphasizes the fact that "merchaundes of Babyloin [were] full riche" (*FB* 147), obscuring all the wealth that was generated by the European slave traders who based their fortunes on human misery and social, and sometimes also physical, death. Still, he portrays the oriental merchants as "kindly, perceptive, and helpful," as Kelly notes (1994:107). Perhaps the writer transfers the relatively high social position of all merchants in English society onto the slave merchants portrayed in *Floris and Blancheflour*, regardless of their origin. Christian conquerors of heathen lands were very much interested in generating revenue, but also in converting pagans. Forcible conversion to Christianity oftentimes preceded the death of infidels at the hands of the converting Europeans, which can be seen in the dreadful reality of raids on Prussia and Lithuania, vaguely suggested in the portrayal of the Knight in the *General Prologue* to *The Canterbury Tales*, who:

Ful ofte tyme he hadde the bord bigonne
Aboven alle nacions in Pruce;
In Lettow hadde he reysen and in Ruce,
No Cristen man so ofte of his degree.
In Gernade at the seege eek hadde he be
Of Algezir, and riden in Belmarye.
(I:52-57)

Chaucer presents this character as a paragon of virtue, but our modern perspective has to be different. Nevertheless, this is not the reality that the author of *Floris and Blancheflour* recreates, because he resorts to the propagandized division of Western slavery as a necessity and Arab slavery as dehumanizing, uncivilized, and even lethal for the slaves.

As for the hybridity of a slave, in *Floris and Blancheflour* slavery does not produce the effect of double identity; Blancheflour is, after all, European and Christian, which does not force her to adopt any other identity but her primary one. According to the logic of the Middle English oriental romance, there is no need for change. Hybridity operates merely when one represents a culture different from Western. Everything becomes subservient to the drive to spread Christianity. According to medieval writers, religion permanently marks the self, not receding before other cultural influences. Blancheflour takes up the missionary, i.e. culturally colonizing, agenda from within the Saracen society in which she had been placed as a child. It is Floris, a free man, who abandons his primary self and subjects himself to metamorphosis; as a result, considerations of hybridity arise when the reader turns his or her gaze onto him. What happens to Floris is a displacement from his original culture; yet the change from Islam to Christianity appears here to be fortuitous, since it stimulates a closer relationship with Christian Blancheflour. Significantly, Floris's previous religious identification leaves no residue on his identity. Once "converted" to Christianity through the nurture of the girl's Christian mother, he does not illustrate colonial hybridity with all its complications: he cannot be characterized as somebody situated between two religions and cultures, whose identity constantly mediates between them with no permanent position possible.[75] His situation is that of a hybrid only in the sense of his having kept his social and political position in the Saracen world; still, it does not generate any hybridity of the self. The change of his identification arguably consisted in his gradual metamorphosis, with the transformation from a Muslim into a Christian proceeding in stages while he was an infant. In what Patricia E. Grieve

---

75 The ramifications of colonial hybridity could be, according to Bhabha, the problematization of the colonizer's identity and the "tongue-tied" quality of his discourse towards the colonized ones (1985:97-98).

actually dubbed "a tale of conversion" (1997:87), Floris's conversion conforms to the pattern of evolution frequent in medieval texts rather than to the more unusual abrupt transformation. Gradual change was perhaps more natural and conducive to permanent metamorphosis than were sudden transmogrifications of monsters and other supernatural creatures. Oddly enough, in the romance conversion there is neither what James Muldoon termed an "emotionally intense search for God" nor "the corporate or communal acceptance of a new God" (1997:vii). It consists in the gradual transformation from one set of religious beliefs to another, which is beneficial in the end as it leads to a happy love with a Christian. The lack of conformation to the norms and definition, however, may be explained by the simplified rationale of popular narratives, which tended to avoid psychological complications in the description of the characters' motivations. Floris's conversion could thus be read as one of its many non-standard varieties, which medieval intellectuals discussing the subject hesitated to term "conversion" (1997b:3).

Christianity reveals its highly contagious nature in the *denouement* of the romance. The Emir catches the lovers in bed and sentences them to death. As he tells the story of his property, usurped by Floris, to his barons:

> ... "Lordinges, with much honour,
> Ye herde speke of Blancheflour –
> That I bought hur dere aplight
> For seven sithes of gold hur wight.
> For I wende, without wene,
> That faire maide to have had to quene.
> Among my maidons in my toure
> I hur dide, with muche honoure;
> Bifore her bedde my self I coom;
> I fonde therin a naked man.
> (*FB* 924-933)

The Emir's legalistic attitude, however, impels him to seek advice among members of his court rather than avenge himself at once on the two lovers: on Blancheflour, who dared to dispose of her own body as if she had ceased to be her master's property, and on Floris for using this "object" without its master's permission. Death appears inevitable but Floris says he intends to protect Blancheflour against punishment with a magic ring "that his moder him gaf at her parting" (*FB* 967), while the girl refuses, choosing to protect her lover rather than herself. The romance logic of conversion to Christianity makes the Emir vulnerable to such heart-rending scenes and he apparently decides to change his religion in a moment, because for him the lovers' selflessness must stem from their religion. It looks as if he converted to Christianity in this moment, as the lovers are immediately taken to a church by the Emir and wedded there:

> The Amiral gaf him his leman;
> All that there were thankid him thanne.
> To a chirche he let them bring
> And dede let wed hem with a ring.
> (*FB* 1062-1065)

The Emir is instantly transformed into a Christian clergyman who legally weds them, abandoning his previous religion and culture; Islam as his primary religion becomes erased from his identity. Under the influence of the selfless young love he had witnessed, he metamorphoses into a Western ruler, quite unexpectedly convinced of the rightfulness of the Christian way of life with its sacraments. His attitude to Blancheflour transforms itself from the materialistic idea that a slave is a material property to the sympathetic treatment of her as a person who must be liberated. The uneasy forcing of the girl into the category of an object terminates with her regaining the status of a person. Even the Emir cannot deny that she is fully human through her culture and behaviour which probably stemmed from the Christian ideal of self-sacrifice. Floris, earlier freed of sorrow once he had found Blancheflour and had declared "Of all my care I am unbounde" (*FB* 832), even though she was then a concubine of the Emir, now acquires the status of an entirely free man, as he has been released from prison and allowed to marry his love. As a matter of fact, his twofold identity contradicts the theory of colonial hybridity in that it gradually leads to full immersion in the other culture. According to Bhabha, "hybridity . . . is not a third term that resolves the tension between two cultures" (1985:98), since the tension continues, pulling the one subjected to it in these two directions. *Floris and Blancheflour* as a popular romance does not include many psychological intricacies; as an ideologically laden text, it prefers to present Floris as someone entirely converted to Christian religion (and culture). Her one-time status as a slave does not leave a trace on the psyche of Blancheflour, while Floris, previously bound by his old culture, gains liberty as the husband of his beloved. Social death almost caused the physical death of the lovers, but instead they are granted freedom and the kingdom of Floris's father, as if to reward them for their Christianity.

Slavery appears to be a force that disciplines all desire and restrains it until the fortuitous moment of liberation. It legally entails social death, but also brings about the production of a new body: tamed, orderly, and treated instrumentally. Yet the ultimate discipline of the body results from Christianity, which shapes all sexual desire and makes it a subject of the sacrament of marriage. Characteristically, also the Emir subjects himself to the requirements of Christians; he disciplines his lust and undergoes instantaneous transformation into a priest able to wed Floris and Blancheflour in church. In this sense the dialectics of diverse dimensions of slavery go further in this romance than in *Aucassin et Nicolete*, which is by contrast more realistic in the treatment of the actual medieval bondage, if not in that of the status of human bodies that were enslaved.

Chapter Four
Black giantesses as communal flesh in the *Firumbras* romances

"Black skin splits under the racist gaze, displaced into signs of bestiality, genitalia, grotesquerie, which reveal the phobic myth of the undifferentiated white body"
(Homi K. Bhabha Of mimicry and man: the ambivalence of colonial discourse) (1984:218)

In a collection of essays devoted to the idea of corporeality, William A. Cohen writes that it is skin which remains the most liminal part of the human body, because it both separates it from the outside world, constituting a border which cannot be crossed by others, and integrates that body with what is outside (2009:63). Unfortunately, this sounds false in the case of black skin, which also protects the body against what remains outside, but makes the body more vulnerable due to the colouring which is still, even in our age, ideologically laden and possibly a marker of difference. In white racist environments, it is presumed that black skin does not integrate the one who is endowed with it with the white-dominated world at all, not to mention the "phobia" that Bhabha alludes to in the epigraph above, which is the panic fear of otherness still for some embodied in a black person. In the colonial discourse blackness has denoted bestiality and grotesquerie, a phenomenon known all too well from representations of racial others in the times of black slavery. Cassuto calls the phenomenon the "tension of the grotesque, the anomalous treatment of cultural anxiety . . . born of the violation of basic categories" (1997:6). According to Cassuto the grotesque "occurs when an image cannot be easily classified even on the most fundamental level: when it is both one thing and another, and thus neither one" (1997:6). The most thought-provoking example functioning as a point of departure in Cassuto's text is the lynched body of an African American, neither a human nor an object, but a presence positioned at the cross-section of the two (Cassuto 1997:6). Our example of racial grotesquerie will be different: it is going to be provided by black giantesses from oriental romances who are neither beasts nor humans. We will explore here the complex relationship between the giantesses' blackness, grotesquerie, and their communal life, both of their own race and that of Franks.

The crucial thing is to note is that medieval culture appears to be rife with racialism or rather racialisms, which are sets of beliefs that Appiah discusses in the context of Victorian culture, but he does not deny their existence in previous epochs. According to these beliefs people are divided into groups and share qualities that are not only biological, but also moral and intellectual (Appiah 1995:276). In contrast to racism, racialism does not entail negative judgments passed on groups characterized by difference markers, but, nevertheless, it essentializes ethnic difference (Frederickson 2002:153). It must be distinguished from racism, which in its developed form is "a combination of group hatred and an extreme mechanism justifying such hatred as rational and based on an objective reality" (Isaac – Ziegler – Eliav-Feldon 2009:1). Appiah does not condemn racialism as a morally wrong attitude (1990:5); Frederickson, however, stresses the inadequacy of this "romantic racialism", but the lack of adversarial contact makes such racialism tolerable also for him (2002:153). Frederickson detaches racialism from the historically later racism,[76] because he emphasizes the idea that ethnocultural differences have to be "regarded as innate, indelible, and unchangeable" for racism to be spotted (2002:5). The foregoing allows us to believe that medieval racism perhaps did not exist before the fifteenth century. For any racism or racialism, in his discussion of the two Appiah questions the validity of racial discourse, giving the opinion that too many people do not fit any racial categories and that even if you assign someone to a specific race on the basis of certain criteria, it does not account for their other biological characteristics (1995:277). Frederickson suggests that modern concepts of racial types emerged at the end of the eighteenth century, but, again, he does not contravene the idea that the late Middle Ages already knew racialist attitudes. According to Frederickson the two main types of modern racism, what he terms "the color-coded racist supremacy" and "the essentialist version of antisemitism", appeared in the late medieval and early modern periods (2002:46), probably after *chansons de geste* and their Middle English versions, here represented by the *Firumbras*-group, had been created. Earlier Christianity safeguarded Western culture against racism by propagating the belief in humans being of "one blood" and all otherness disappearing upon baptism. Writes Frederickson:

> It is possible that relations among peoples before the late Middle Ages were sometimes characterized by the kind of hostility and exclusiveness that betokens racism. But it was more common, if not universal, to assimilate strangers into the tribe or nation, if they were willing to be so incorporated (2002:46).

---

76 Frederickson reminds us that the term *racism* started to be used in reference to Nazi racial theories as late as the 1930s (2002:5).

In this discussion of black giantesses in Middle English oriental romances and their direct textual sources of origin, French *chansons de geste*, we should then consider whether externalizing those characters is a racialist gesture, which denotes here more than merely a xenophobic one. No doubt here racism does not express itself "in the practices, institutions, and structures that a sense of deep difference justifies or validates" (Frederickson 2002:5); it is racialism that metaphorically "blackens" the giantesses. Yet it is open to question whether the black giantesses confirm the validity of Bhabha's "phobic myth", or their difference should be seen as more a cultural one, which could be annulled through baptism. On the other hand, Frederickson's definition of racism (and perhaps also of racialism) encompasses both *difference* and *power*; if both of them can be found in the narratives about the black female giants, perhaps the notion seems applicable to our considerations (2002:9).

What might problematize the giantesses' existence in the *chansons de geste* and, consequently, in the oriental romances that are based on their plots, is the issue of community and those giants' role in it. Can they be interpreted as Esposito's *flesh*, an entity different from that of the social *body*? The functioning of the racialized flesh of giantesses in the community, or rather, to rephrase it, of giantesses as the racialized flesh of the community, is particularly pertinent to *chansons de geste*, which are ostensibly texts describing the masculine world of Western knights who continually confront religious and ethnic others. The almost exclusively masculine community of Franks emerges from these texts as a foil for the uncivilized groups of Saracens. By necessity, the Franks have to be idealized; consequently, the communal spirit flourishes among them. Their sense of togetherness is strengthened through what Esposito terms "a paradigm of immunization", where paradoxically the "pathogens" that are externalized from the community fortify it; without its others, a group would not experience such unity. The immunizing process appears to be another step in what in *Communitas* Esposito describes as exteriorization of others. The exteriorized others, he writes in *Immunitas*, simultaneously destroy community and strengthen it (2004:35). In another study, *Bios: biopolitics and philosophy*, Esposito develops the idea even further; he describes the community's others as pathogenic and simultaneously beneficial for the strength of the group. The mechanisms of immunization designate flesh as a symbolic category different from the more literal Saracen flesh in *Richard le Coer de Lyon*. Esposito names it flesh in order to distinguish it from the social body, which apparently interiorizes the others in order to make them the exteriorized flesh: "The violence of interiorization – the abrogation of the outside, of the negative – could be reversed into an absolute exteriorization, in a complete negativity" (2008:12).

Disturbingly, the externalized flesh of the community may also integrate itself and form groups. Still, it remains arguable whether those others may form communities analogous to the ones from which they have been ousted. After all, if the integrity of the communities accumulating those who are "the same" depends on the existence of the others, those others' presence on the margins of the community will be crucial. They will not be allowed to abandon what are the margins as opposed to "the core", since they guarantee the maintenance of this core. It is an open question whether the black giants and giantesses are allowed to form their own communities if they are compelled to inhabit the margins of the civilized world of Franks. The giants' difference is an extreme manifestation of otherness, in which the difference of all the Saracens becomes intensified, enhanced, and emphasized. Their case consequently deserves a thorough analysis, because it illustrates the handling of all ethnic others in oriental romance.

The corpus of texts for our discussion of black giantesses can be labeled as Middle English oriental romances due to their "oriental" setting, even though they derive from French *chansons de geste*. The French narratives may be divided into the Guillaume cycle, Roland and Otuel, and Fierabras (the two latter have been translated into Middle English as, respectively, *Roland and Vernagu, Otuel*), and *The romance of Duke Rowland and Sir Otuell of Spayne*, and the group of texts discussed earlier in this study as the *Firumbras*-group, *Firumbras, Sir Ferumbras*, and *The sowdone of Babylone* (Cowen 1996:149-168).[77] There also exist non-cyclical romances, *The sege of Melayne* and *The tail of Rauf Coilyear*, which develop the themes of *chansons de geste*.[78] The generic incompatibility between *chansons de geste* and romances may be initially noted, because the former derive from oral literature, represent folk historiography, and "lack fixity of form, unity of authorship, or narrative cohesion" (Kay 1995:10), whereas the latter were largely written texts and posess both a fixed form and cohesion. The impression, however, is contradicted by the authors of *Fierabras, Aiol*, and other *chansons de geste* themselves when they define the texts they discuss as both "chansons" and "romances" (Kay 1995:7). We can certainly interpret the two groups of narrative poems, *chansons de geste* and the Middle English oriental romances that are their translations, as strongly interconnected, so searching for giantesses in both of those textual corpuses appears justifiable. Our focus on women in those texts, and not just any women but a specific type,

---

77 See, for instance, the editions of the texts of *Roland and Vernagu* (Burnley – Wiggins 2003), *Otuel and Roland* (O'Sullivan 1935 [1987]), and *The romance of Duke Rowland and Sir Otuell of Spayne* (Herrtage 1880 [2008]).

78 See the editions of *The sege of Melayne* (Mills 1992) and *The tail of Rauf Coilyear* (Lupack 1990).

is justified by another remark made by Sarah Kay, namely that in traditional scholarship *chansons de geste* have been presented as a genre in which female characters were not portrayed "as an integral element in social relations, as gifts and givers of gifts" (1995:24). Predictably, the marginalization on the part of the critics followed from the marginalization of giants committed by the writers themselves. What is more, females from the monstrous race of giants were no doubt even more entirely omitted from critical interpretations. Perhaps this general critical tendency should be remedied, since the giantesses are also significant as they could metaphorically illustrate the community's externalized flesh and the role of this flesh in forming an alternative community; therefore, they should no longer be seen as marginal characters.

An obvious choice for how giants were portrayed in medieval culture is the widely popular *Mandeville's travels*. This masterpiece hoax provided its numerous readers with ready-made ideas about the Orient and its inhabitants and it exemplified what Ian Macleod Higgins called "worldmaking" (1997:vii).[79] The unknown compiler's discussion of giants begins with the enigmatic remark: "Ebron was wont to ben the princypall cytee of the Philistyenes And pere duelleden somtyme the Geauntz" (Seymour 1967:16-17) ["In Hebron was once the chief city of Philistines, and giants dwelled there"] (Moseley 1983:73). The text continues later with more proto-ethnographic observations. The discussion purports to be based on those found in the real ethnographic sources, but it does not go beyond repeating the stereotypes found in other sources. The chapter titled "Of the deueles hede in the Valeye Perilous, and of the customs of folk in dyuerse yles þat ben abouten in the lordshipe of prestre Iohn" features the following description of giants:

> After this beȝonde þat vale is a gret yle Where the folk ben grete GEAUNTES of .xxviij. fote longe or of .xxx. fote long. And þei han no clothinge but of skynnes of bestes þat þei hangen vpon hem And þei eten no breed, But all raw flesch & þei drynken mylk of bestes, for þei han plentee of all bestaylle; And þei haue none houses to lyen jnne. And þei eten more gladly mannes flesch þanne ony oþer flesch. In to þat yle dar noman gladly entren, And ȝif þei seen a schipp & men þerejnne, Anon þei entren in to the see for to take hem. And men seyden vs þat in an yle beȝonde þat weren GEANTES of grettere stature, summe of .xlv. fote or of .l. fote long. And as sommemen seyn summe of l cubytes among þo geauntes ben scheep als grete as oxen here & þei beren gret wolle & rough; Of þo scheep I haue seyn many tymes. And men han seen many tymes þo GEAUNTES taken men in the see out of hire schippes & broughte hem to londe .ij. in on hond &.ij. in anoþer, etynge hem goynge all raw & all quyk. (Hamelius 1919:189-190)

---

79 There existed as many as three hundred manuscripts of *Mandeville's travels*, including versions in Czech, Danish, Dutch, and Irish (Moseley 1983:10).

[Beyond that valley is a great isle where the folk are as big in stature as giants of twenty-eight or thirty feet tall. They have no clothes to wear except the skins of beasts, which they cover their bodies with. They eat no bread; but they eat raw flesh and drink milk, for there is an abundance of animals. They have no houses to live in, and they will more readily eat human flesh than any other. Thanks to them no pilgrim dare enter this isle; for if they see a ship in the sea with men aboard, they will wade into the sea to take the men. We were told that there is another isle beyond that where there are giants much bigger than these, for some are fifty or sixty feet tall. I had no desire to see them, for no man can go to that isle without being promptly strangled by those monsters. In these isles among these giants are sheep as big as oxen, but their wool is thick and coarse. I have seen those sheep; and some men have often seen those giants catch people in the sea and go back to the land with two in one hand and two in the other, eating their flesh raw] (Moseley 1983:174).

The giants of this account are portrayed as male savages, possibly cannibalistic if they relish raw meat. The final reference to eating, here the eating of travelers, confirms the impression the readers should have on first reading about their partiality for uncooked meat. The giants' physicality makes them brutal, dangerous, and uncontrollable in their reactions towards humans. Their size appears to be infectious, since their sheep grow excessively as though in order to match the size of their owners, which, however, means degeneration, because the wool is unfit for use. No females are mentioned among the apparently all-male giants, or perhaps even if there are females among them, they do not differ from males either in build or in behaviour. This testifies to the general hermaphrodite nature of all monsters, since they remain on the margins of the civilized world, both geographical and conceptual. Marginalization leads to lack of interest in their gender, hence the tendency to represent all of them as male. As for the question of giant communities, in *The travels* monsters appear generally incapable of cultivating any communal life. Humans are treated by them as merely another source of raw meat, which testifies to the giants' bestiality and their inability to transcend this quality by, for instance, forming communities similar to the human ones.

The tendency to discuss giants as male creatures entered modern scholarship with such critics as Cohen, for whom the giant represents masculinity which is conducive both to experiencing and provoking desire, not necessarily normative. The association with desire inspires Cohen to relate the giant to Lacanian psychoanalysis, because in the Middle Ages it "embodied a phenomenon that Lacanian psychoanalysis labels 'external intimacy' or 'intimate alterity'" (Cohen 1999:iv), a phenomenon occurring during the process of symbolization, problematizing the opposition between inside and outside when the real transforms itself into law and language (Cohen 1999:187). For Cohen the giant remains the source of enjoyment (as he translates *jouissance*), an abjected entity both desired and externalized due to the dread he evokes (1999:iv). Identification of giants with masculinity rather than femininity is made by literary texts themselves, since male giants predominate there: "The giant is a violently gendered body. While it is true that some medieval giants were female, especially in Norse tradition and in some crusader romances, where giants were then, as now *an exception*" (Cohen 1999:iv). For Cohen the giant's male body signifies "dangerous excesses of the flesh", excesses which are simultaneously forbidden and indulged in whenever possible (1999:v). The giantess's grotesque body is structured in opposition to the dominantly male body of a giant. If the giant's body characterizes itself by fragmentation, because it is never a totality, but always single parts that function as a synecdoche (Cohen 1999:11), the female body of a giantess is even more fragmented since the monstrosity of femininity is added to the deformity of the entire monstrous race she belongs to. Characteristically, not only races of monsters have to be looked on as metaphorically fragmented corporealities. Race as such, as one of the markers of social difference, entails fragmented selfhood. Ania Loomba highlights "very real difficulties involved in theorizing social difference – race, gender, class, caste, and other social differentials cannot be easily accommodated without seeking an endless fragmentation of subjectivity" (1994:18). The fragmentation of the self may be conducive to achieving the effect of the grotesque, in which the giantess's body is neither a uniform whole nor a group of separate body parts, but again is something liminal, situated between a clearly definable corporeality and bodily fragments without a common denominator. Racialization of giantesses and the portrayal of them as black should not be surprising, as it strengthens the effect of incomplete fragmentation, with the corporeal constituents still drawn to one another by some unfathomable principle which does not let them fall apart completely.

Nevertheless, even Cohen's male giants do not subject themselves to the mechanisms of desire easily. Their corporeality remains too exorbitant, placing them "outside the realm of the human, outside the possibility of desire" (1999:iii). Giants in romances are usually asexual and plots relating them to some sexual impulses rare, even though to Cohen the giants display the dangers of *jouissance*. One of the rare cases of sexual desire felt and possibly also inspired by a giant is the French *Prose Lancelot*, in which the giant Galehot pines for Lancelot's attention, but has to be rejected in order for the heteronormative relationship between Lancelot and Guenever to develop. In non-cyclic romance, the giant features as both a possible object of affection for ladies and an attractive companion for men. The effect of attraction is achieved through his physicality, described as:

Il fu de mout bele charneüre, ne bien blans ne bien bruns, mais entremeslez d'un et d'autre; si puet an apeler ceste sanblance clers brunez. Il ot lo viaire enluminé de nature[1] color vermoille, si par mesurez a raison que vilsement i avoit dex assise la compaignie de la blanchor et de la brunor et del vermoil. . . . Il ot la boiche petite par messure et bien seant, et les levres colorees et espessetes, et les danz petites et sarrees et blancheanz, et lo menton bien fait a une petite fossete (Mosès 1991:138).

[He had a beautiful complexion, neither completely white nor all dark, but consisting of those elements blended with each other: such colour of complexion may be called a lighter shade of dun. His face was lightened with natural blush, but moderately, so it seemed that God had achieved here an ideal combination of paleness, dun complexion, and blush . . . His mouth was rather small and prettily formed; his lips were red and a little plump; a beautifully carved slightly cleft chin.][80]

Galehot's affectionate attitude towards Lancelot strengthens the aura of attraction that surrounds any giant, despite his monstrous size and his belonging to a different kind of being than humans. The thirteenth-century *Prose Lancelot* features an untypical combination of monstrosity and comeliness, putting together what in other texts, such as *chansons de geste*, remains separate. In *chansons de geste* and their translations desire is expressed by a whitened ethnic other, the princess who pines for a Western knight, while a monster, typically a giant, represents the ultimate evil, even though he may be a relative of the enamoured princess. In some narratives the repulsive relative may be a black giantess, not a giant. In *Prose Lancelot* the giant is both white-skinned and alluring due to his physicality, as if those two different characters from the *chansons de geste* tradition were combined into one consistent figure. Furthermore, in *chansons de geste* any affection between the Franks and the giants is out of question, while here the giant remains a character potentially attractive to Westerners. Nevertheless, even in *Prose Lancelot* closer relationships between humans and giants remain impossible: Galehot dies of unreciprocated love for Lancelot, who obviously chooses Guenever.

The white enamoured princesses of oriental romances and their black counterparts, the giantesses, form a dyad testifying to a twofold image of a Saracen woman in these texts, as de Weever remarked (1997:55). The dichotomy of a whitened Saracen princess, in love, as has been said here earlier, with a Westerner, and her evil, monstrous kin appears in *Aliscans* from the *Guillaume cycle*, where the Saracen princess Orable is contrasted with her brothers Rainouart and Walegrape, and with her cousin Margot of Bocident, all of them threatening in their cultural otherness. Their blackness displays an obvious peril to the world of the Franks and to those who, like Orable, aspire to

---

80 The translation into English is mine.

identify with it. The aspirations are clearly signalled in, for instance, *Enfances Guillaume*, where Orable is portrayed as "la plu belle pucele" (1. 516) (Henry 1935:24), "dame Orable la cortoise et la gente" (1. 1232) (Henry 1935:54), "Orable . . . saige et cortoise et riche" (1. 1798) (Henry 1935:77). Not only is the peaceful, gentle Saracen princess contrasted with members of her own family, but also with the belligerent giantess Flohart:

> Ez vos Flohart corant de randonee;
> De sa bouche is une si grant fumee
> Trestote l'ost en fu empullentee.
>   (ll. 6730-6732) (Régner 1990, vol. II:247)
>
> [Behold Flohart, charging at a gallop;
> From her mouth comes a great cloud of smoke
> That pollutes the entire host.]
>   (de Weever 1998:223)

Breathing fire implies an association with dragons, which are monsters considerably different from giants. The giantess's body is polluting the world into which she was born, because she poisons the air, upsetting human health and attempting to destroy human bodies. Flohart escapes the category she has been assigned to and defies labeling; the question of non-specified categorization becomes particularly relevant when the issue of grotesquerie arises. If Orable, another enamoured Saracen princess, was elevated to such an extent that she was whitened and called "a dame", the giantess Flohart becomes degraded through not even belonging to the monstrous race she should be assigned to. Bakhtin's vision of popular culture, to which, after all, both *chansons de geste* and popular romances about the Orient belong to, involves the idea that degradation is the central idea of grotesquerie. "The essential principle of grotesque realism is degradation," he writes; "that is, the lowering of all that is high, spiritual, ideal, abstract; it is a transfer into the material level, to the sphere of soul and body in their indissoluble unity" (1984:19). Such degradation is the plight of the black giantesses.

The universal category of the grotesque approximates that of the feminine in Bakhtin's development of the idea:

> To degrade also means to concern oneself with the lower stratum of the body, the life of the belly and the reproductive organs; it therefore relates to the acts of defecation and copulation, conception, pregnancy, and birth. Degradation digs a bodily grave for a new birth; it has not only a destructive, negative aspect, but also a regenerating one (1984:21).

The implication that the female body subjects itself to the principle of the grotesque more readily than the male confirms that indeed femininity entails fragmentation as much as does a racially marked body. Bakhtin's enigmatic image of senile pregnant hags which is meant to represent grotesquerie only confirms this intuition, since the old women violate the principle linking a female body either with life, here birth, or with death, in that the figures symbolize both (1984:25). Those two aspects of their existence are clearly mismatched. The image of the hags may be read against the two cruxes of the grotesque, by Geoffrey Galt Harpham summarized as "negative powers" and "regenerative capacities" (1982:71). Nevertheless, as Ganim puts it, Bakhtin's idea of the grotesque as feminine was not a novelty, because it originated in Horace's *Ars poetica* (2005:19). The term itself was not employed there, but the principle worked in a similar manner:[81]

> Humano capiti cervicem pictor equinam
> iungere si velit, et varias inducere plumas
> undique collatis membris, ut turpiter atrum
> desinat in piscem mulier formosa superne,
> spectatum admissi risum teneatis, amici?
> credite, Pisones, isti tabulae fore librum
> persimilem, cuius, velut aegri somnia,vanae
> fingentur species, ut nec pes nec caput uni
> reddatur formae.

> [If a painter chose to join a human head to the neck of a horse, and to spread feathers of many a hue over limbs picked up now here now there, so that what at the top is a lovely woman ends below in a black and ugly fish, could you, my friend, if favored with a private view, refrain from laughing? Believe me, dear Pisos, quite like such pictures would be a book, whose idle fancies shall be shaped like a sick man's dreams, so that neither head nor foot can be assigned to a single shape] (Horace 1932:450-451, quoted in Ganim 2005:19)

Horace's grotesque is exemplified by a female body partly white and beautiful, partly black and fish-like. The body is a continuum, evolving from the aesthetically pleasurable to the repulsive in its bestiality. The division between that part which is acceptable and that which is detestable remains fluid, which enhances the effect of porousness that Cohen mentioned in his discussion of corporeal limits. Not only is the grotesque body ideally porous through the lack of clear distinctions between it and the surrounding world, but also because of beauty and turpitude as qualities which are attached to one and the same body. Bakhtin also postulated the grotesque body's porousness, but he restricted himself to arguing that grotesquerie is particularly conducive to melting itself

---

81 Harpham pinpoints the baroque as the epoch when the ambiguous term "grotesque" entered the lexicon instead of the *grottesche* of the Renaissance, which meant merely "beautiful" (1982:xviii).

with its surroundings: "The limits between the body and the world are erased, leading to the fusion of the one with the other and with surrounding objects" (1984:310). According to Aron Gurevich, this testifies to Bakhtin's fascination with the grotesque body as opposed to the unchangeable, statuesque "classical body" (1985:53) and to his affirmation of popular culture as the site of grotesquerie. Nevertheless, it cannot be ignored that his idea of the grotesque involved acts of lowering and degrading. The resulting image could be a combination of the affirmable and of what has been famously termed by Julia Kristeva as abject.

The amalgamation of the attractive and the loathsome in the grotesque body is even more obvious if we consider another of Bakhtin's theses, that "the grotesque body . . . is a body in the state of becoming. It is never finished, never completed; it is continually built, created, and builds and creates another body" (1984:317). The vision of the body as one subjected to the process of continual becoming entails another suggestion of the body's feminization. Such a body "builds and creates another body" by giving birth to a new life, rendering the grotesque corporeality even more "degenerate" through labour and through the female corporeality that is subsequently extended by that of the infant. A woman in whose body a foetus grows becomes even more grotesque for Bakhtin, while birth augurs the inevitability of death and the body which gives life demonstrates its own futility and the prospect of the inescapable decomposition of its parts. If the female body is, according to Aristotle, degenerate in itself, it is even more so through the act of procreation and its outcome, a new life. Again, the thesis that Bakhtin's grotesque body elevates and spiritualizes the material, which was proposed by Peter Stallybrass and Allon White, appears debatable (1986:23).

Stallybrass and White's influential *The politics and poetics of transgression* opens with an affirmation of the grotesque, since they emphasize the juxtaposition of the grotesque body and the "classical body" in Bakhtin. Not only do the critics stress the grotesque body's location within popular culture, but also its association with collectivity, because for them this body was "usually multiple, . . . teaming, always already part of a thing" (1986:21), an entity "never closed off from either its social or ecosystemic context" (1986:22), a site where "place, body, group identity and subjectivity interconnect" (1986:25). From this perspective the grotesque could be connected with community or communities rather than with an individual, like the "classical body" keeping everything that is not him- or herself at a distance (Stallybrass – White 1986:22). The ambiguity of grotesquerie dislocates all individuality, introducing it into the communal sphere, where peaceful individual contemplation gives way to what Stallybrass and White define as the "clamour" of collectivity and merry disorder experienced together (1986:23). The "classical body" of a knight on a quest from chivalric romances may be contrasted with the grotesque bodies of male and female monsters from popular romances, who are introduced into the plots as a collectivity; nevertheless, their functioning as a community remains ambiguous.

What problematizes the issue of communal functioning even further is the topic of noise and production thereof during hostilities. All military confrontations in these texts are accompanied by a background of noise that at all times matters; nevertheless, it is the Franks who shout in an organized manner, producing an aural backcloth which plays a specific role on the battlefield, as Cohen argues in reference to all Middle English Charlemagne romances and their French predecessors defined as *chansons de geste* (2004:4). The Frankish noise is orderly in that it performs the function of scaring off the enemy and sowing confusion in the minds of Saracens. The sounds produced by enraged heathens, among whom the giants figure prominently, remain an example of grotesque clamour that has to be judged negatively, despite Stallybrass and White's affirmative stance on it. The clamour here is neither the voice of humans nor that of beasts and it does not show the existence of any communal spirit which would encourage members of the community to organize themselves. The noise they produce disrupts the aural space that surrounds them. According to Gurevich, in the Middle Ages not only were relationships between people expected to be hierarchical, but space too was to be orderly and permanently arranged in a specific manner (1985:76). Sounds were also assigned a place of their own, whereas noise always implied aural matter which was out of place, to cite Cohen (2004:2). The disorder produced by unorganized sounds signaled the disorderly nature of the ones from whom the sounds issued. *The sowdone of Babylone* illustrates this well, as the Saracens prepare themselves for the military confrontations with Charlemagne by using clamorous instruments, such as the clarion that Lukafere blows in order to summon his military forces (*SB* 260) or the "hornes of bras" (*SB* 683) that are deployed for the same purpose.[82] The references to Saracen noise may be more indirect, as when they use military machines during the siege of Rome:

> To the toure a bastile stode,
> An engyne was i-throwe –
> That was to the cité ful goode –
> And brake down towres both hie and lowe.
> (*SB* 395-398)

---

82 The quotations from *The sowdone of Babylone* come from Lupack's edition (1990) and are marked by the abbreviation *SB* in brackets along with page numbers.

The execrable noise produced by the machinery which is employed to pull down towers can only be imagined, in contrast to the bestial noises of the Saracens slain during the battles. The giant Estragot "lai cryande at the grounde/ Like a develle of helle" (*SB* 435-436) and did not suffer silently like an exemplary Christian knight would, but exposed his base nature and uncultured quality. It appears from the text that an effect of grotesquerie is produced also by sounds issuing from ethnic others, not only by their physicality. The rare occurrences when Saracens shout in an organized manner, such as when "'Antrarian, antrarian,' thai lowde cryed/ That signyfied 'Joye generalle'" (*SB* 689-690), indicate the existence of a community, disorderly and noisy as it is, but cannot undermine the grotesque impression of their animal-like nature, in contrast to the Franks who cry in a comprehensible language.

To summarize the issue, confusion remains the principle that marks all Saracens from oriental romance, making any orderly communal life among them practically impossible. Within the world of *chansons de geste* and oriental romances the grotesque body stands for both a multitude, albeit disorganized, and for the confusion of the bodies, like those of the giants, that do not belong to any clearly designated categories and that contrast with the orderly and separate bodies of Franks, who are able to form model communities. The shouts of the Franks, such as the famous "Monjoi!", contrast with the bestial noises produced by the Saracens (Cohen 2004:3). The organized noise of Westerners on the battlefield contributes to the strengthening of their community, whereas the grotesque clamour of Saracens is neither productive nor elevating. Instead of elevating the base and the corporeal, the grotesque produces the effect of degradation and disintegration of any communal life. The mechanisms of the grotesque detectable in the *chansons de geste* and oriental romances are far more complex than it might be thought.

Nevertheless, the term "grotesque" invites complications rather than solving them. Even the etymology of the grotesque does not necessarily signal all the meanings which became attached to the term later. Wolfgang Kayser, a critic whose writing was influenced by Bakhtin's perspective, traces it to the technical term denoting a painted border and decorative detail fusing human and nonhuman elements, where symmetry is disregarded and size is distorted (1981:21). His definition derives from the concept found in Vitruvius, Horace's contemporary:

> On the stucco are monsters rather than definite representations taken from definite things. Instead of columns there rise up stalks; instead of gables, striped panels with curled leaves and volutes. Candelabra uphold pictured shrines and above the summits of these, clusters of thin stalks rise from their roots in tendrils with little

figures seated upon them at random. Again, slender stalks with heads of men and of animals attached to half the body (VII, 5) (Vitruvius 1985:106-109). What Vitruvius appears shocked by is the incongruity of a reed supporting a heavy architectural element such as a roof. What is missing for him from the grotesque is a balance and commensurability among various parts of a design. This combination of otherwise conflicting elements materialized the principle of the grotesque observable both in architecture, where it could firstly be found, and in other types of art. Undoubtedly, adopting the category of the grotesque, whose etymology dates to the sixteenth century, but whose real origin is traceable to an "ancient form of ornamental painting" (Kayser 1981:19), one risks being accused of ahistoricity. Nonetheless, medieval art was replete with representations similar to the early modern and even baroque grotesque (though the ornamental designs were not yet called *grottesca* or *grottesco* from *grotta*, a cave) (Kayser 1981:19); for Alessandra Zamperini, for instance, medieval monsters combined otherwise conflicting categories and reconciled the impossible (2008:91). The idea applied to black giantesses from oriental romance ought not to appear entirely anachronistic, even though complications associated with defining the grotesque remain. Over time the idea of the grotesque evolved, with more and more emphasis being laid on turpitude rather than on the amalgamation of the beautiful and the ugly. Frances S. Connelly summarizes the varieties of the grotesque as images that "combine unlike things in order to challenge established realities or construct new ones; those that deform or decompose things; and those that are metamorphic" (2003:2). The three categories then proceed from a continuum of conflicting categories placed together, through decomposition, to metamorphoses. Connelly also stresses turpitude when she defines grotesquerie as also describing "the aberration from ideal form or from accepted correction, creat[ing] the misshapen, ugly, exaggerated, or even formless" (2003:2). Black giantesses metaphorize the alleged nature of a different ethnicity through combining their potentially seductive ethnic otherness, implied by their frequent affinity with the princesses, with the revulsion of ugliness and death. In this sense they combine states of existence which are unlikely to appear together. Still, they also, according to Connelly's formulation, emblematize the degenerate, deformed body of a cultural other and are metamorphic through the metamorphosis their bodies are prone to and they are an ostensible aberration from the ideally perfect female body. They materialize the principle of the grotesque to the extreme, fulfilling all the requirements for this condition.

The dyad of a white enamoured priecess and her black counterpart is represented by two separate characters in the narratives in question. Nevertheless, if we see those two types of representations as one uniform commentary on the corporeality of a female other, that corporeality emerges from it as a continuum, ranging from a whiteness and hence acceptable entity to a black and repulsive one. It seems that only the combination of the two may form what we could call a truly grotesque body. There is a hint of the black giantess that is preserved in any portrait of a beautiful Eastern princess and there must be a suggestion of possible beauty and willingness to convert in any image of a black Saracen giantess, even if it is implied through negation, since the giantess will always refuse to be converted regardless of the price she will have to pay for it. After all, the giantess stands for everything the princess does not because the latter is the former's reverse image. The giantess' blackness symbolizes the unchangeable nature of her heathenness: she is repeatedly characterized as black and monstrous as she does not intend to become a Christian, that is, an acceptable member of the society. Her black skin plays the role of an indicator of the evil which lies dormant in her, preventing any possibility of good in her.

The evil that blackness not infrequently connoted derived from medieval theories that did not repeat ancient ideas of race, which juxtaposed the familiar and civilized with the barbarian. Antiquity did not recognize that skin colour was the basic marker of difference: ancient Romans believed that people's skin differed due to the varying position towards the sun, but ethnic difference was cultural rather than physiological. Africans were simply darker from overexposure, but they had to differ culturally in order to be recognized as others. In the classic *Before color prejudice*, Frank M. Snowden, Jr. even writes that blackness did not exist as any basis for individual distinction in ancient Greek or Roman cultures (1983:101-107). Dorothy Hoogland Verkerk repeats this thesis when she remarks that in the antiquity skin colour was not overemphasized (2001:59). In contrast, the Middle Ages must have emphasized colour difference, since numerous negative qualities were attributed to blackness. Unsurprisingly, positive characters were frequently described as white, like the Saracen princesses. Skin colour was stressed as a marker of negative difference inconsistently, because in art there also existed, as we have noted earlier, positive figures whose skin was black. Besides, medieval culturalism, i.e. the conviction that one's culture defined identity more importantly than one's ethnic origin, or racialism recognized a possibility of change from the negativity of heathenness symbolized by blackness to the positive image of a convert. Physical change could even befall a fortunate convert, as may be illustrated by the Sultan, whose skin acquired a patched quality as a result of baptism in *The king of Tars*. Still, medieval people were far from disregarding colour difference in the manner of people of antiquity.

Racialism became the reality of the epoch, affecting the characterization of ethnic others.

Black giantesses are not introduced into the plots of *chansons de geste* and Middle English oriental romances only as a foil for the beautiful princesses who were smitten with Frankish knights even before they see them for the first time. They exemplify physical and psychological potency despite the ends they meet in the narratives. The giantesses are grotesque, but grotesquerie is not a *sine qua non* for portraying powerful women who represent the cultural other for the West. The physical strength and belligerence of black giantesses may be undermined by the contradictions of the grotesque principle, but their initial authority is undisputed. As a result, making her grotesque is one of the ways of dealing with the authority represented by an ethnically different woman. The threatening effect produced by such a woman needs to be toned down, which either leads to making her grotesque or to questioning her gender. The latter strategy may be illustrated by the story of the Queen of Sheba, a character deriving from the biblical description of a diplomatic mission recorded by a chronicler (I Kings 10:1-13). She was variously described as both black- and white-skinned, but she always stood for power manifested by a female ruler in both Judaic and Muslim culture. With time the narrative about the Queen of Sheba and Solomon had to be reshaped in order to "accommodate contemporary values and newly defined concerns", as Jacob Lassner maintains (1993:1). Jewish and Muslim scholars gradually transformed the historical account about a clever and politically conscious monarch into a tale about a dangerous foe attempting to undermine all gender boundaries through her wiliness and rebelliousness (Lassner 1993:1). The story of Sheba dangerously approached the biblical narrative of Lilith, the first wife of Adam, who, according to the Judaic *Alphabet of Ben-Sira*,

> refused to recognize her husband's status and held out for sexual equality if not dominance. She insisted on reversing positions and mounting him. Being disrespectful to Adam was serious enough, but this haughty challenge did not satisfy her. Boldly pronouncing the ineffable name of God (Yahweh), she abandoned the earth and threatened to harm newborn infants. When confronted about this threat, which is seen as running counter to the instinct and purpose of women, she defiantly proclaimed her destiny: She will alter the basic design of the universe. It is no wonder that, even to this day, amulets are worn to keep her from harming childbearing women and infants in their cradles and cribs (Lassner 1993:21).

Female independence as achieved by Lilith seems to threaten to the divine plan for humanity. Women, called to giving life, may easily take it away from their offspring. Female authority denotes here freeing oneself from one's procreative duties and murdering those for whom one should care. The image of Lilith threatening to murder her newborn children may reverberate in the uncannily dangerous figures of black giantesses, who simultaneously stand for motherhood and for brute force and even political scheming, if they consciously participate in the hostilities between Charlemagne and Saracens on the side of the latter. Nevertheless, even if they abandon their offspring, they do not intend to expose them to imminent death, but rather fight with the futile hope of victory over the Franks.

In *Sir Ferumbras*, the giantess Amyote emerges as a character seemingly contrastable with the enamoured princess Floripas, only to develop later into a character whose plight is lamentable. Her husband Enfachoun appears horrible in his physically excessive body and violently brutal onslaughts on Franks. The violence and belligerence in battle escalates in the case of Amyote. The marginalization of Amyote manifests itself in the relatively ample scope which is devoted to her husband and the considerably little scope devoted to her. Yet before Enfachoun enters the stage in the romance, another monster, Agolafre, features prominently in order to exemplify the principle that giants breed easily so they have to be killed on the spot before they produce offspring. Agolafre's size and ugliness are exorbitant, but his physicality signals that the race of giants has to be eradicated because of their deformity:

> Agolafre, þe voule gome, Ful wel of-seȝ þus knyȝtes come,
>   Wyþ hure somers fayre.
> Out of þe tour þan cam he doun, And set hym on an heyȝ peroun
>   y-mad as a chayre.
> And Axe had he þan an-honde, A shrewedere wepene for-to fonde,
>   Was neuere non yfounde.
> Three fet of brede was þe blad, Of style y-tempred ful wel y-mad,
>   þe hylue wyþ yre y-bounde.
> þe Sarsyn was an hudous man, By-twene ys to browen was a span
>   largeliche of brede;
> Ys browes were boþe rowe and grete, & ys nose cammus, ys eȝene
> depe,   & glystyd as þe glede.
> Suþþe þe werlde furst by-gan, Nas neuer ȝut so lodly man,
>   y-mad of flehs & felle.
> Was he noȝt a godes helf þe deuel he semede al hym-self,
>   y come þo riȝt of helle.
>   (*SF* 4427-4442)[83]

Agolafre's physicality is crude, a depiction meant to ridicule what could otherwise be seen as fearsome. His degeneracy is emphasized by his demonic behaviour. Bent on tracing the enemies of Saracens, he interrogates Richard

---

83 All the quotations from *Sir Ferumbras* come from Herrtage (1879 [1966]); the numbers of the lines come from that edition and are preceded by the abbreviation *SF*.

about his identity and receives a false answer: "we buþ Merchaund;/ Of drapreye we ledeþ gret fuysoun" (*SF* 4456-4457). Then he insightfully comments on the treacherousness of Christians, which foreshadows his future plight: "Ac her passede wyþ-inne a wyle, Crystene men þat dude me gyle,/ þat come fram Char[lis] kyng" (*SF* 4475-4476). The giant is treated here with a touch of sympathy, because his characterization approaches that of a human, either gullible enough to be cheated or not having enough guile to avoid being outsmarted by clever Westerners. The stratagem is, however, discovered by the Emir to whom the way was guarded by Agolafre. Richard and his men attempt to flee, but they are waylaid by the loathsome giant, who beckons them: "Aȝeld ȝow anon to me" (*SF* 4518). Either they will surrender to the giant or he will attack them. Agolafre, however, demonstrates his unexpected clumsiness when his axe misses the Franks and falls on "a stilp of oke,/ þat bar vp ther a chayne" [one of the chains of the bridge] (*SF* 4553-4554) instead. Charlemagne's knights take control of the situation, but the giant manages to slay numerous Franks when he recovers after the initial blow dealt to him. The enormous destruction he wreaks equals his excessive size and monstrous comportment: he "had wyþ ys axe a-slawe An hep of freschemen þat leye arawe,/ Afforn hym on þe gronde"(*SF* 4605-4606). The heaps of dead Frenchmen well illustrate the giant's power, but they remain anonymous, while Agolafre is confronted by Charlemagne himself, a figure who could not be anonymous to the medieval audiences in any sense and a ruler who manages to attack the giant successfully. The Franks who confront giants need to be victorious according to the poem's ideology, especially when they are legendary rulers:

> With þat Char[lis] to hym wond, And gurd him a strok wyþ brond,   & on þe heued him sette.
> Ac for þat strok had he no dere, For no strok myȝt hym percy þere,
>   þat sory skyn dude him lette:
> And þan was Char[lis] wonder grym, And aȝeyn hym renneþ, & stokeþ hym   By-twene ys browes rowe:
> þan ran þat swerd in-to ys brayn, And whan he haueþ him so a-slayn
>   to þe ryuer was he þrowe.
> (*SF* 4611-4618)

Evil must be destroyed and only a cunning stab between the eyes is able to defeat the giant, whose body becomes merely refuse that has to be discarded into the river. Still, according to the rationale of oriental romance, if you manage to slay one giant, another one will come. Enfachoun "a mayl of Ire he bar an honde" [took into his hand an Irish mallet] (*SF* 4653). Gigantic size and monstrous cruelty become racial, if we consider the Irish origin of the instrument that the giant wields. The giant is portrayed here as someone using a foreign weapon, connoting barbarity and crudeness unknown to the civilized Franks. His mallet renders him partly savage, partly other in the ethnic sense, and it has to be remembered that the Welsh, Scots, and the Irish were those ethnic others who remained geographically the closest and tangibly real to the English author of this version of the narrative. The image of the fearsome monster is softened by the reference to his two twin sons, who are not even four months old but already seven feet three inches high. Again, however, the infants' size makes them less than human. Enfachoun is slain by the Frankish ruler himself: Charlemagne cleaves his head with a sword, ridding the world of the vicious monster.

The economy of those oriental romances requires that the monstrous foes be annihilated so that the Franks should come to dominate both physically and psychologically. A black giantess, Enfachoun's wife, is introduced into the plot only to be slain in an exemplary manner. This fragment is missing from the Ashmole manuscript (Bodeleian Ms. Ashmole 33), so the passage from the earlier French version has been incorporated by the editors:

> Quant Amiete oï le cri et la merlée,
> Ki gist de .ii. enfants sous une cheminée,
> (Ce est une gaiande plus noire que pevrée ;
> Grant ot la fourcéure, et la guele avoit lée,
> Et si avoit de haut une lance levée,
> Les ex avoit plus rouges que n'est flambe alumée ;
> Moult est de tout en tout laide et deffigurée).
> De ses enfants se crient, dout ele est effraée ;
> Se gesine avoit faite, nouvele ert relevée.
> (*SF* 4807-4815)

Amyote features as a caring mother, exemplarily tending to her infants even when she feels confused, frightened, and at a loss. The grotesquerie dormant in her portrayal looms large, however, in the very same scene, since when she hears about her husband's death, she abandons her children, whom she has quite recently brought to life, in order to grasp "sa crigne" [her scythe] (*SF* 4821) and at once seeks to avenge Enfachoun's death. She metamorphoses into a female warrior who wreaks havoc and destruction among the Franks and the latter like Charlemagne before them could probably refer to her as "une diable plus noire que pevrée" [a she-devil blacker than pepper] (*SF* 4826). Consequently, the giantess has to die a death similar to that of Agolafre. Charlemagne

> Entre les .ii sourcis a feru la dervée,
> Que parmi la cervele en est la fleke entrée.
> La gaiande versa, la fleke est tronchonnée ;
> Par la guele geta marvelleuse fumée.
> (*SF* 4832-4835)

When the brain has gushed out from the giantess's head, smoke miraculously transpires from her mouth. Nevertheless, this is smoke similar to a dragon's rather than any sign that the monster had a soul which fled from the body upon death. A grotesque effect is created by the direct juxtaposition of tender maternity with unscrupulous revenge taken on the Franks. Those two ingredients of this character strike one with their mutual incompatibility. Nevertheless, a more sympathetic perspective could entail treating the ruthless attack on Charlemagne's knights as a bid to protect one's offspring from a similar fate. The situation would have been tragic if not for its grotesquerie. The giantess's body is not only metaphorically, but literally fragmented here, materializing the corporeal fragmentation of the grotesque.

In the end, the twins are saved by the Franks, who yet prefer to convert them rather than murder them in the manner in which they slew their parents. This exemplifies the relativity of medieval racialism since, in contrast to the later set of beliefs known as racism, what we could term racialist attitudes could easily be accomodated by inclusion of others in the community of Christians. Not surprisingly then the two gigantic twins are baptized. ". . . Roland þanne he het þat on,/ þat other Olyuere" (*SF* 4865-4866), in order to emphasize the fact that they, as it were, were usurped by Franks, body and soul. All other communities are closed to the two infants and the Franks are the sole community which actively incorporates them. This questions the possibility of demarcating among the giants any collectivity which could be called an actual community. Once the parents have been slain, the care of the children is not transferred to anyone but the Franks. Enfachoun and Amyote's sons are firstly physically separated from their parents slain one after another by Charlemagne and then psychologically and symbolically detached from their roots and named after the very invaders who deprived them of their parents. Their ethnoracial difference is obliterated through baptism, symbolically transforming them into equal members of the Christian community.

Amyote's body needs to be interpreted as not only very probably black-skinned, but also hybridic, since she neither displays a fully human version of maternity (her corporeality and those of her children are too exorbitant for that) nor demonstrates a complete monstrosity, as the humane, maternal element of her nature prevents such identification. Bynum's idea of hybridity as "the joining of two incompatibles" matches the half-maternal half-monstrous characterization of the giantesses well (2001:17). Yet she pinpoints the question of hybridity as a "non-change", because something is only added to another thing and the consequent combination perdures (2001:17). What remains to be considered is the order of metamorphoses: is maternity an element added to the giantesses' monstrosity, or is the monstrosity a quality leading to the metamorphosis of otherwise benign gigantic mothers? It appears that the former is the case, so the status of the mother is easily dropped by them when they are invited to display their monstrous strength and supernatural belligerence.

It is arguable whether their grotesqueness is a subject of the carnivalesque principle, since carnival entails ridiculing the privileged rather than the marginalized. Carnivalization affects her only if we assume that she remains, after all, a powerful female affecting the lives of Frankish knights, rather than a monster inhabiting the margins of texts and a creature sentenced to annihilation in the world of expanding Western Christianity. The giantess's sexuality is indicated only by her maternity, but her femininity is subsequently supressed once she chooses to fight in the name of Islam rather than stay with her own children. Her figure exemplifies the phenomenon of liminality also in the sense of her being simultaneously powerful and powerless, an object of fear and a creature doomed to failure in a world where the Franks have to be victorious in their pursuits. Another issue entailed by the question of liminality consists in what Cohen defined as a giant's hybridity, comprehended by him as the figure placed "neither outside the society nor inside it" (1999:viii). This hybridity is neither a corporeal nor a psychological one, but social identification with the margins rather than the centre. The giantess differs from her male counterpart in numerous respects, because she is portrayed as simultaneously maternal and belligerent, physically and psychologically powerful and yet vulnerable when she has to abandon her infants. Her functioning in the society must also be different from that of the male giant. Due to her femininity she stands outside the society and even on the margins of any collectivity of her monstrous race, since she single-handedly takes care of her offspring. Nor does she dwell inside the society of humans, whatever her attempts to integrate her with that society could be. Her status within an imagined community of giants is also fragile, as there is no one who takes responsibility for her orphaned offspring; they may consequently be claimed by Christians and incorporated into that collectivity. Her status as a figure neither intrinsic to the collectivity of giants nor entirely external to it confirms her grotesque status. In Harpham's view, the grotesque, after all, continually falls between categories (1982:3), including, as here, the communal inside and its outside.

The question of acceptance and exteriorization becomes particularly focal to the discussion of the carnavalization of black giantesses. The carnivalesque affects the threateningly powerful, not merely in the conventional understanding of exercising authority, because medieval women seldom had political power, but such women as a "loathly lady" who could imperil the social order, which also aimed at controlling the lives of women. Conventionally, carnivalization would denote externalization of people potentially dangerous to that social order. Nonetheless, the idea of carnival entailed including representations of those threatening others, such as an old hag, into the festivities and thus making the figures part of the mainstream culture, but in accordance with the rules established by the majority so they did not violate it permanently. Within the carnival order of things a potentially powerful old woman, who for Bakhtin would be the essence of the grotesque, especially if she was simultaneously pregnant, is subdued, tamed, and made insignificant in the paradoxical gesture of presenting her to the public and in people celebrating around the puppet symbolizing her. The giantess's liminality is also of carnivalesque nature: she may be depicted as an angel of death wreaking destruction among Franks, but her femininity and her singleness among the Western knights make her an exteriorized other. Paradoxically, the carnival is believed to reverse the social order, at least for the limited time of the year, displacing the existing rulers and replacing them with otherwise marginalized members of the society. On closer inspection of, for instance, the fabliau as a certainly carnivalesque genre, we see that it operates in such a manner that women are customarily ridiculed in that world turned upside-down, since, like the old hag of the festivities, virtuous women, and not merely the unfaithful ones, are mocked in the end.[84] As Jean Emelina claims, according to carnivalesque principles, the world turned upside down (*le monde renversé*) has to be followed by the world rearranged (*le monde redressé*) (1994:62). To some extent Amyote, a mother of children and a wife, was virtuous in that she exemplarily tended to her children. She is subsequently made grotesque and possibly exposed to laughter as she has no chances to win in the struggle against the Franks. She pays the highest price for her monstrosity, since she needs to be slain for the world to be rearranged after the temporary triumph of the carnivalesque order, within which a female monster posed a threat to Franks.

The grotesque identity and carnivalesque character of a black giantess is made explicit also in *Firumbras*, where there is a passage devoted to a giantess, here the wife of Fycon. It is preceded by Fycon's confrontation with Charlemagne, ending in an expected manner:

> hys wyf lay in Chyldbed by-syde in a kaue,
> of too knaue children, – that sorowe most they haue!
> four fet of brede in the brest, y-tolde,
> And of to fethem hey, [hey] were a monthe olde, –
> ffycoun with beryl, – that sorowe mote hem betyde!
> And he ȝede to the gate and opened it wyde,
> And by-gan to crye in a sory part:

---

84 On the carnivalesque nature of the *fabliau* see, for instance, Benson (1987:8)

"where artou, charlys, thou sory fabelart?
wenestou so ly3thly oure relykes to wynne?
I schal do the to wete, ere thou come here-Inne!"
whenne charlys that herde, he kast vp hys scheld,
hys noble swerd, trenchaunt, in hys hond he helde.
he let it fle to fycon in that ylke stounde,
And clef hys heued in-to the teth, þat he felle to grounde.
(*F* 1324-1337)[85]

Intriguingly, the giant is decapitated, slightly confusing the design set out by Bakhtin, who associated the grotesque with triumph of the lower bodily parts. On the other hand, the grotesque body's orifices and protuberances made it prone to death by violence to which they are continually exposed: the severing of some of those protruding parts or the breaking of the continuity of flesh through the orifice. The head, the site of reason in humans, may be, after all, only a protruding part of flesh in a giant, who is perhaps unable to think rationally at all. Furthermore, if we accept that the head could be the site of the soul, the monstrous giants do not necessarily possess souls due to their devilish nature. Or perhaps all of the giants' body parts feature as loathsome and debased, in contrast to the Bakhtinian division into the "high" head and the "low" regions, the belly and genitalia. Maybe their amorphous bodies should not be clearly defined in accordance with the dialectic of the high/low.

Violence, frequent in those descriptions, provokes further violence, with the giantess Amyet humanized even further as her feelings of sorrow and grief are related: "sory sche was and nothing blythe" (*F* 1350). On the other hand, violence in itself includes a transgressive potential and the giantess's monstrous femininity only enhances the initial effect of transgression: violence, after all, offends against the social order and, since it is directed against bodies, it afflicts the human body in its "classical", orderly form. The tender human-like mother metamorphoses into a devilish beast, displaying the non-normative nature of her body and her grotesquerie. The aggressive nature of her husband was, as it were, transmitted to her after his death, forming a combination of masculinity and femininity within one and the same corporeality. A scene of challenging the foe analogous to the previous one confirms such an interpretation:

whenne amyet þat herde, þere sche lay in here bedde,
That here lord, fycoun, was brou3t to dethe,
Sory sche was and nothyng blythe.
Dwelled sche no lenger, but went forth swythe,
And as a deuyl of helle to þe gate sche 3ede,

---

85 The quotations from *Firumbras* come from O'Sullivan's edition (1935 [1987]) and are followed by the abbreviation *F* and page numbers in brackets.

That was of yren wrou3t with ful gret gynne,
The barrys endentyd with stel with-oute and with-Inne.
Sche brayed vp a vyket and hente vp a tre
"who ys now so hardy for to come to me?"
Was þere none dou3ty in þat ylke stounde,
And sche hym rau3te, þat he ne scholde go to the grounde.
(F 1348-1359)

Another name by which she could be called here is the mythological Fury, because she prefers to abandon her infants and to assault the Franks rather than attempt to save what has been left from the slaughter so far, herself and her offspring, perhaps due to the unrealistic judgment of the situation which makes her delude herself that she can be victorious. Amyete, a character whose grotesquerie is more complex than that of Fycon, is slain in a manner similar to that by which her husband is killed: "Charlys hent an arblast, and a quarrel he let flen,/ And in-to here heued, it wente thoru3 þe brayn" (F 1364-1365). The grotesque body of a giantess cannot be subjected to any permanent affirmation. Carnivalization denotes here a temporary triumph, which needs to be superseded by the fall of those who could represent a threat to the social order. Femininity, materialized in the ability to produce new life, enhances the giantesses' authority, which is so dangerous that it has to be eliminated along with the one who represented it. Those who are situated at the top of power structures within the texts need to reinstitute their authority and eliminate all the possible dangers to it, here materialized in a monster, who is not just gigantic, but female and racialized.

The racialization of the giantesses possibly ensues from the impossibility of their acculturation. As for medieval "racism", Frederickson compares it with culturalism, postulating that whenever culture has not been essentialized and fixed, it is possible to not resort to racism and to endow ethnic others with a possibility of assimilation into the majority (2002:7). In the world of *chansons de geste* and analogous oriental romances, culture has not fossilized, allowing the others to convert if they are willing to or cannot object to it, like the giants' offspring. Racialization operates only when on the ethnic others are not willing to become the subject of a cultural shift and to convert to Christianity. Black skin seems here a relative category, marking Saracens only if they do not change their cultural identification upon contact with the Franks. It appears then that medieval culture, especially popular culture, used to be more hybridic than early modern culture in that baptism allowed ethnic others to be fully incorporated into the society. Culture was still not an essentialized, but rather a more open and inclusive phenomenon. The thesis about the openness of popular culture finds support in what Bakhtin seemingly did not consider, namely upper class acceptance of "low" cultural phenomena before the sixteenth century, when a marked shift occurred. Berrong maintains that the diversification of culture into popular, exclusively a lower class phenomenon, and higher, more elitist, culture is observable in Rabelais' *Pantagruel* when compared to his earlier, more open *Gargantua*. The mistake of Bakhtin seems to have been his assumption that popular culture has perennially been the domain of the lower classes, while the power establishment did not stoop to participation in it, as Berrong argues it did (1986:13). Even though popular culture was distinct from the official culture, it did not bar access to itself for the upper classes; on the contrary, it welcomed all types of participants and different social classes willingly subscribed to it. Furthermore, Berrong argues that even the image of official culture recorded by Bakhtin is false: the example given by Berrong is the presence of excrement, so emphasized by Bakhtin as a part of popular culture, also in official culture (1986:24). Medieval culture, particularly the popular kind, did not close its doors to members of higher social strata, even though they simultaneously had access to the "official" culture, and popular culture was something they enjoyed.

Racialization appeared to be a quality of popular culture which could easily be annulled, since culturalism proved to be stronger than racialism in, for example, conversion narratives. There exist, however, also texts in which the effect produced by racialized giants and giantesses is strenthened through their association with animals. Estragot/Astragot of Ethiopia is not merely black but also beast-like in a different version of French *Fierabras*, *The sowdone of Babylone*. His "bores hede" (*SB* 347), black and dun, enhances the effect of ethnic otherness. The description of animal-like physicality foreshadows bestial reactions and brutality during military confrontations with Westerners:

> And Estragot with him he mette
> With bores hede, blake and donne.
> For as a bore an hede hadde
> And a grete mace stronge as stele.
> He smore Savaryz as he were madde,
> That dede to grounde he felle.
> This Astragot of Ethiop,
> He was a kinge of grete strength;
> Ther was none suche in Europe
> So stronge and so longe in length.
> (*SB* 346-355)

Estragot's closeness to the beast's physicality may be classified as grotesque, because the combination of the human and the bestial signals the monster's liminality, which produces the effect of an identity unfathomable in its unpredictability. Humans cannot even guess what to expect from a creature so dissimilar from them and yet so deceptively resembling the human form. The Middle English writer comments on the giant with the words" "I trowe he were a develes sone,/ Of Belsabubbis lyne" (*SB* 356-357). The anonymous author introduces the element of devilish characterization, developing the trope of animal nature through a subtle association with anthropophagy, as when the giant becomes "tho the grete gloton Estagote" (*SB* 427). Gluttony denotes here his insatiable appetite for human blood and flesh that he may any time extract from the Frankish bodies. Such grotesque characterization enhances the effect of uncivilized blackness described in our previous sources.

The trope of bestiality of not only giants, but also the Saracens, is stressed in the narrative as it continues with the memorable feast organized for the Sultan Laban, the Lord of Spain, where "serpents in oyle were fryed/ To serve the Sowdon with-alle" (*SB* 687-688). The Saracens resemble wild beasts here, so the threat they pose to the Franks, who are to be slain as hogs, sounds very real. The standard slur, "dogs", appears not in the context of heathen dogs, as elsewhere, but in reference to the Westerners. Laban prays to Mars, promising him

> ... myrre, aloes and frankensense,
> Uppon condicion that thou me graunte
> The victorye of Crystyn dogges,
> And that I may some hem adaunte
> And sle hem down as hogges.
> (*SB* 954-958)

The linguistic situation is reversed, as Saracens are shown using the very same wording in reference to their enemies as Christians, who often used the canine metaphors in speaking of Muslims, Jews, and even members of the Orthodox Church. The Sultan sees his foes through the lens of his own, incomplete and thus grotesque, bestial nature, hence the phrase he uses. The grotesquerie of the Saracens is exacerbated once they are forced to drink animal blood, as if in order to boost their wildness and fierceness in battle:

> All these people was gadred to Agremore,
> Thre hundred thousand of Sarsyns felle,
> Some bloo, some yolowe, some blake as More,
> Some horible and stronge as devel of helle.
> He made hem drinke wilde beestes bloode,
> Of tigre, antilope, and of camalyon,
> As is her use to egre her mode,
> When thai in were to battayle goon.
> (*SB* 1003-1010)

Human and animal blood mix within their entrails, forming a flesh that can be accommodated neither among humans nor in the animal world. Their corporeality becomes consequently polymorphous and no fixed meaning can be attached to it. The meaning which is missing indicates that their bodies are truly grotesque: Kayser argues that the crucial difference between the tragic and the grotesque lies in the fact that the former denotes something, while the latter intentionally lacks any meaning (1981:186). The liminal and grotesque giants, to whose bodies no sense may be attached, symbolize the entire Saracen world. Yet their "community" does not figure as a compound entity, but remains represented by single individuals, who are eliminated one by one by the valorous Franks. Giants consistently play the role of attackers, as Alagolofur, both black and bestial, slays the Franks:

> This geaunte had a body longe
> And hede like an libarde.
> Therto he was devely stronge;
> His skynne was blake and harde.
> Of Ethiope he was bore,
> Of the kinde of Ascopartes.
> He had tuskes like a bore,
> And hede like a liberde.
> (*SB* 2191-2198)

Again, racialization does not appear here as significant as the idea of beastly character and the comportment which ensues from it. Still, regardless of the source of the impression of grotesquerie produced by the giant, he features the idea of liminal corporeality. As for the concept of community, despite the symbolic association of the grotesque body with it, in the end Franks are portrayed as united in their communal military engagement, whereas the giants appear in it individually. For the Frankish all-male community to triumph, the giants have to fight against Franks separately even if, theoretically, a grotesque body should be a communal one. After all, as in the citation above, even though Alagolofur is of Ascoparts' kind, he does not belong to any uniform group. In the end, "the geaunte faught with hem alone,/ He was so harde and stronge" (*SB* 2917-2918), but the multitude of Franks customarily combated him. The giant as externalized flesh is doomed to failure; furthermore, even the family milieu in which the giantesses are situated, which suggests some communal relationships among the giants, does not override the impression of victory as something impossible in their lonely fight against Christians. Barrok, Astragot's wife, proves to be even fiercer than him, but her separateness makes her an easy target:

> Than came forth Dam Barrok the bolde
> With a sithe large and kene
> And mewe adown as thikke as shepe in folde
> That came byforne hir bydene.
> This Barrok was a geaunesse,
> And wife she was to Astragote.
> She did the Cristen grete distresse;
> She felled downe alle that she smote.
> There durst no man hire sithe abyde;
> She grenned like a develle of helle.
> King Charles with a quarel that tide
> Smote hir, that she lowde gan yelle,
> Over the frounte throughoute the brayn.
> That cursede fende fille down dede.
> Many a man hade she there slayn.
> Might she never aftyr ete more brede!
> (*SB* 2939-2954)

Also here the giantess exceeds her husband in monstrosity. The last line in the citation above signals the source of this enhanced dreadfulness: a giantess may breed, bringing even more monsters to life, which will compound her monstrosity even further. Barrok has already procreated, having offspring who will be equally fearsome in the future. Nevertheless, again the grotesquerie of the children is overcome by baptizing them; they will no longer combine the human and the bestial, but become full-blown Christians, with no trace of their previous heathenness preserved:

> Richarde, Duke of Normandy,
> Founde two children of sefen monthes oolde,
> Fourtene fote longe were thay;
> Thay were Barrakes sonnes so boolde;
> Bygote thay were of Astragot.
> Grete joye the Kinge of hem hade.
> Hethen thay were both, wele I wote;
> Therfore hem to be cristenede he bade.
> He called that one of hem Roulande,
> And that other he cleped Olyvere
> For thai shalle be myghty men of honde.
> To kepen hem he was fulle chere.
> (*SB* 3019-3030)

Their souls are symbolically healed, even though their bodies suffer, here from famine, since "thay myght not leve; her dam was dede" (*SB* 3031). The hunger ensues from their inability to eat adult food ("Thai wolde neyther ete butter nere brede") (*SB* 3033), which implies that they are still not unlike human infants, who cannot survive without a mother or a wet nurse. Despite Charlemagne's good intentions, they die, since "Here dammes mylke they lakked there;/ Thay deyden for defaute of here dam" (*SB* 3035-3036). Nevertheless, the goal of acculturation is achieved and their death does not provoke any anxiety, because they die as Christians.

In *Categories of medieval culture* Gurevich portrays the division into the microcosm and macrocosm as central to medieval culture, but not imposing itself on it thoroughly due to the relative fluidity of borders between the self and world in that period. He maintains that particularly a grotesque body exemplified that indeterminate nature of identity: the grotesque illustrated "the levelling of all barriers between the body and the world, the fluidity of transition between them" (1985:54). He attributes the development of the grotesque body to popular literature and culture, but it needs to be highlighted that "popular" was not reserved for the lowborn in the epoch. Elitist tendencies in culture could only be observed in the Renaissance, when it occurred that access to popular culture with all its representations of the grotesque became barred to the aristocracy, as they started to think that it was beneath them to enjoy the arts where the principles of carnival were the rule, not an exception. In the Middle Ages there still existed a more positive perspective on the racialized grotesque bodies of giants and giantesses: they could illustrate the fluidity of the relationship between the self and the surrounding world despite the negative aspects of their textual existence. The negativity, however, was the quality that marked those representations through the racialization of their bodies, their marginalization indispensable for the construction of what Esposito defined as the *immunitas* which contributes to the maintenance of the community, and the violence the giantesses had to succumb to. The giants, and even more the giantesses, are a negative presence in the world of the *chansons de geste* and their Middle English versions known as romance. Acculturation of ethnic others still remained possible in this textual world, even though it was inextricably related to the abandonment of one's original culture, so it never became the plight of the black giantesses, but rather that of their children.

Chapter Five
Genealogy and desire in *King Horn*

> Desire involves political, religious, aesthetic, and economic objects, as well as sexual ones.
> (David Aers and Annabel Wharton Preface to *Desire, its subjects, objects, and historians*, Special Issue of *JMEMS*) (1997:1)

The classification of *King Horn* in the category of popular romance poses a number of problems. An entire critical debate has taken place around the issue of the text being either an unsophisticated "minstrel's song", as W.H. Schofield argued (1903, quoted in French 1940:1), or a representative of what Walter H. French called "a poem of the court", situated in a courtly setting except for the moments of travelling from one place to another (1940:7).[86] French claims that the poem is "accomplished on the technical side" (1940:2), so it cannot be defined as a low genre. Furthermore, its diverse meanings appear fairly sophisticated in contrast to the language, which is early Middle English still linguistically close to Old English. Another version of the romance, *Horn Childe and Maiden Rimnild*, derives from the Anglo-Norman *Romance of Horn* more directly, which means that it does not include such elements important for us as Saracens as the invaders (Mills 1988:44). Nevertheless, these two texts, regardless of the fact whether they are popular or courtly, do not deal with the question of the body of the other as desirable, as something good to eat, or something that can be enslaved or made grotesque, as was argued in preceding chapters in our study of the corporeality of the other. *King Horn* and *Horn Childe* provide their audiences with yet another perspective on the corporeality of the other: in the narratives the exotic invaders carry out an overturning of the categories of the same and the other, making Horn's corporeality temporarily one which signals alterity. Horn as the central character of the plot is turned into the ethnic and cultural other in his own land, which is followed by making him the subject of diverse characters' desire. His own desire remains rather a desire for God and for death, as Clare A. Lees argued in reference to other texts, those still representing Anglo-Saxon culture (2007:22). The Real looms large in the

---

86 Also Mehl refers to "the courtly atmosphere" of *King Horn* (1968:34).

text as a category more important for Horn than any erotic desire could ever be. After all, in Lacanian psychoanalysis the *objet petit a* is only "a residue, a remnant, a leftover of every signifying operation" (Žižek 2008b:204) after the occurrence of symbolization, while the entire chivalric culture is grounded in an amalgam of military and religious symbols that constitute an ethos central to European medieval culture, which in psychoanalytic terms could be termed the Real.

King Horn, the earliest extant English romance (Sands 1986:15), involves a number of prototypical elements within its dense plot including numerous turns of fortune for the eponymous hero.[87] Horn's parents, king Murry and queen Godhild, are a couple that symbolize traditional kingship and archetypal parenthood. Their bodies are not stamped with any markers of difference and they continue to be exemplary rulers; consequently, their son will turn out to be equally exemplary in his future adventures. The identity of Horn's father as ideal knight and king will exert a strong impact on Horn; in Lacanian terms, he will identify himself with that Ego Ideal, which, according to Žižek, may be summarized as "I want to become such a knight as my father" (1992:120). The narrative proves to be a story of Horn's maturation, which denotes his progress from the status of a child and merely a youthful heir to the throne to the position of a knight, a king and thus a symbolic father to his community, and possibly a father to his own children in the future.[88] The anonymous author of the romance is engrossed in exploring the issue of desire as central to human lives, even if its fulfilment remains illusory. Ostensibly maturation makes the materialization of desire easier, but the intangibility of any desire is illustrated by the events developing within the romance's plot. The moment when desire becomes reality appears remote and the fulfillment of all that one wants is continually deferred, sometimes even endlessly. Once the object of desire is approached, the fantasy of fulfilment as possible is projected onto another object. This is complicated by the disruption of kingship and fatherhood resulting from violence inflicted due to cultural and ethnic differences.[89] When the father has been slain by the community's adversaries, the son has to subject himself to regulations of the symbolic order at the expense of remaining within the realm of the imaginary. Horn loses his childhood, subjecting himself to the requirements of the Name-

---

87 Pearsall classifies it as the earliest extant Middle English romance along with *Floris and Blancheflour* (1988:11); he calls *Horn* a "lyric romance" (1988:24), "the first narrative outgrowth from song or lay" (1988:25).
88 Brewer remarks that the narrative shows the development of such qualities as charity, maturity, and integrity in the title character (1988:9).
89 Elizabeth Fowler treats divestment and investment of the king as topics focal to *King Horn* (2000:106).

of-the-Father, the law, and he even attempts to approach the Real, unattainable as it always is, through his comportment of a righteous Christian knight.

The familial happiness of Horn's parents endowed with an heir to the throne proves to be transitory; those characterized as "the same" in the poem's dialectics of the same and the other are attacked by cultural and ethnic others, "Sarazins" (*KH* 42) invading Sudenne aboard "shipes fiftene" (*KH* 41).[90] The identity of those called Saracens by the poet remains obscure, particularly if we focus on the non-determinate reference to a "payn" [pagan] (*KH* 45), who threatens king Murry:

"Thy lond fold we shulle slon
And alle that Christ luveth upon
And thee selve right anon.
..."
   (*KH* 47-50)

The threat materializes all too easily, as the king and his companions who observe the invasion are slain by the enemies: "So fele mighten ythe/ Bringe hem three to dithe" (*KH* 61-62). With the land invaded and Christian churches ravaged, Sudenne becomes imprinted with marks of Muslim culture and politically dominated by the strangers, who imprison Horn along with "his feren of the londe" [his comrades of the land] (*KH* 86) with the intention to slay him because he is the rightful heir to the throne.

Even when Horn's father has been slain, the narrative keeps supplying its readers with other kings and fathers, because there are a lot of them in the romance so that they could form relationships with the title character. Apart from his own father Murry, Horn is confronted with Aylmar, the king of Westernesse and Rymenhild's father, and the king of Ireland, the father of Reynild. The many fathers enhance the effect of simultaneous kingship and fatherhood which is an idea focal to the narrative. Fatherhood is limited in the text to a phantasmatic category, since the relationship between a father and a son remains permanently incomplete. Even when the impediments between Horn and his substitute fathers, Aylmar and the king of Ireland, are overcome, there always appear other obstacles that make the relationship impossible. As for the literal paternity, Horn is orphaned prematurely, before any development of a more fully-developed bond between him and his father can be possible. Fathers often die without their children being able even to bid them farewell, as the romance author claims, and there are also impediments to symbolic paternity. The incompleteness of all types of fatherhood makes us perennial children to some extent, as we never separate

---

90   All the quotations from *King Horn* come from Sands' edition (1986) and will be followed by the abbreviation *KH* along with page numbers.

ourselves from our fathers entirely. The idea materializes in the Horn romances, where, regardless of the changing geographical location, there is always a king who plays the role of a father to him.

The significance of paternal genealogies becomes even more emphasized in *Horn Childe and Maiden Rimnild*, a romance deriving from the Anglo-Norman *Romance of Horn* (Mills 1988:44); in the former text more scope is devoted to Horn's father, here named Hatheolf. The royal genealogy of Horn is described, probably in order to stress the importance of his lineage for his subsequent motivations. As for Hatheolf,

> He no hadde no childre, as ȝe may here,
> Bot a sone þat was him dere;
> When þat he was born,
> þe king was glad & of gode chere,
> He sent after frendes fer & nere
> & bad men calle him Horn.
> (*HCMR* 13-18)[91]

The history of the king's struggle to maintain sovereignty is portrayed in detail. The invasion by the Danes had to be withstood, as they "Out of Danmark com an here/ Opon Inglond forto were,/ Wiþ stout ost & vnride" (*HCMR* 49-51). There was a consequent need for him to reorganize the kingdom and, in the end, to combat the Vikings from Ireland that were invading the land. As a result, "King Haþeolf slouȝ wiþ his hond,/ þat was comen out of Yrlond,/ Tvo kinges þat tide" (*HCMR* 190-192). He was vanquished by the Viking king Malkan, who "smot King Haþeolf to þe hert" (*HCMR* 224). The reign of Horn's father terminates with the seizing of his lands by the Earl of Northumberland, against whom king Houlac protects Horn, as he gives the child refuge in his land, situated in England as well. Once Horn has been orphaned by the father, his thoughts will continually revolve around gaining knighthood and regaining his lost position. It will be central to what his heart desires, making all other desire secondary, including even that for Houlac's daughter Rimnild, though their love is exemplary like that of "Tristrem or Ysoud" (*HCMR* 311), as the author makes clear; after all, the text stands alongside the anonymous *Sir Tristrem* in the Auchinleck manuscript.

Horn appears to be a character haunted, like his literary great descendent Hamlet, by the premature death of his father. Revenge becomes all-important for Horn and in *Horn Childe and Maiden Rimnild* this revenge materializes in his slaying of king Malkan towards the end of the story. As Horn confesses to Rimnild:

---

91 The quotations from *Horn Childe and Maiden Rimnild* come from Mills' edition (1988) and the numbers of the lines, preceded by the abbreviation *HCMR*, are taken from it.

> "King Malkan was mi faders ban,
> & now for soþe Ich haue him slan,
> þe soþe forto sain.
> Mi fader swerd Y wan today,
> Y kepe it while Y liue may,
> þe name in Blauain."
> (*HCMR* 799-804)

This is really the end of the plot, while the reunion with Rimnild had not sufficed to end it, which shows the marginality of the desire Horn feels for her in comparison with the task of avenging his father. Another dimension of revenge occurs in *King Horn*, where Horn very early manages to exterminate Saracens, when "The Sarazins he smatte/ That his blod hatte" (*KH* 611-612). After all, as Reiss comments, his actions cannot be reduced to acts of personal revenge: his ambition is "to defeat the enemies of God" (1986:115). The meaningful gesture of presenting "the maisteres heved" (*KH* 625), the cut-off head of the Muslim leader, to the king of Westernesse cannot be interpreted in any other way but as the fulfilment of a scheme of revenge:

> "King," he sede, "well thu sitte
> And alle thine knightes mitte!
> Today, after my dubbing,
> So I rod on my pleing
> I fond o shup rowe
> Mid watere al biflowe
> All with Sarazines kin
> And none londisse men
> Today for to pine
> Thee and alle thine.
> Hi gonne me assaille.
> My swerd me nolde faille:
> I smot hem alle to grunde
> Other yaf hem dithes wunde.
> That heved I thee bringe
> Of the maister-kinge.
> Nu is thy wile y-yolde,
> King, that thu me knighty woldest."
> (*KH* 631-648)

Successful attacks on Saracens aboard ships are more significant to him than other issues. Not only is knighthood indispensable for the improvement of his social status, but also for fulfilling the plan of taking revenge on his late father's enemies. In a manner analogous to *Richard le Coer de Lyon*, the head as the cultural other's most symbolic bodily part illustrates full victory on the part of Horn and becomes a metaphor for the relationship between all Westerners and the Orientals they encounter. The latter have no chance to survive the military confrontations since any successes of theirs will be turned into defeat and gruesome slaughter and annihilation of their Saracen bodies. Their violence will be met with even more violence, because this is what Christians actually desire more than any other things, as the Horn romances make clear. Domination of Westerners over Muslims is inevitable according to the ideology of the romance. Importantly, the Saracens of *King Horn* are not individualized, as Sebastian I. Sobecki noted (2008:101). As a result, they feature in the text as a "one-dimensional portrait" (Sobecki 2008:101) of cultural enemies who need to be wiped from the face of the earth.

As for Horn as a son, *Horn Childe* as a different version of the Horn narrative accentuates the other dimension of fatherhood that is merely suggested in *King Horn*. Paternity connotes not only closeness with one's children and protection of them, but also aggression which remains dormant in the relations with one's dependants. Houlac, otherwise protecting Horn against Malkan, his arch-enemy, openly uses violence towards his daughter Rimnild once he discovers her relationship with Horn, since:

> He bete hir so þat sche gan blede;
> þe maidens fleiȝe oway for drede,
> þai durst help hir nouȝt.
> (*HCMR* 499-501)

He also threatens Horn with a sword as the boy is the other culprit, because Houlac "seyd Horn schuld be slan" (*HCMR* 506). Apart from being sheltered from the hostile outside world by one's father, one also appears to be exposed to the same father's punishing hand if one's actions do not agree with the moral code imposed by the father. The Name-of-the-Father, in earlier versions of Lacanian psychoanalysis known as the paternal function, the function of the symbolic father, and the paternal metaphor, has to be comprehended here as the law that one becomes subjected to, regulates one's life, but also threatens one with possible punishment that will be meted out in case of transgression of that code. The aggression dormant in the maiden's father is also visible in *King Horn*, where he only chastizes his daughter without resorting to brute force:

> "Awey ut," he sede, "fule theof,
> Ne wurstu me nevremore leof!
> Wend ut of my bure
> With muchel messaventure.
> Well sone, bute thu flitte,
> With swerde ich thee anhitte.
> Wend ut of my londe
> Other thu shalt have shonde!"
> (*KH* 711-718)

Expulsion from the land of the symbolic father, however, is punishment severe enough for Horn, so he is deeply agitated by it. The symbolic order to which he had to subject himself knows no exemptions, so he metaphorically loses another father to whom he was probably attached. He will have to adopt the status of the other again, this time in Ireland, to which he must migrate. Nonetheless, Horn acknowledges his indebtedness to Houlac when he victoriously returns to his land and announces to him: "þou feddest me & forsterd to man" (*HCMR* 1102). It seems that, according to the ideology of this romance, the father remains the material and spiritual nourisher whom one may be deeply indebted to, despite the violence that may be occasionally directed by him against the offspring.

In *King Horn* the title character flees aboard a ship to Westernesse and then embarks for Ireland, which makes him change the status of himself and his companions like Constance in Chaucer's *Man of Law's tale*. Borders on land are easier to cross and appear more artificial, but crossing the sea emblematizes a real physical transfer from one country to another, with the status of voyagers changing once they alight on the new strip of land.[92] Such is the situation of Horn and other refugees from Sudenne once they leave the ship they sailed in and arrive in Westernesse. Their status changes into that of ethnic others, who are merely guests in the new land.[93] The status of others is not new to them, since the transfer of political power in Sudenne has already made them others to the Saracens, who adopted the privileged position of the same in the newly conquered land. The question arises whether the Saracens invading Horn's land appeared there as his others, or perhaps they illustrate how easily the same becomes the other owing to vicissitudes of fortune; then the invaders could be interpreted as Horn's doubles, because they also change their status, here from otherness to sameness. "The payns come to londe/ And neme hit in here honde" (*KH* 63-64), so the relationship between sameness and otherness is reversed.

The possibility of Saracens materializing otherness in the text and making Horn very close to themselves through othering him is perhaps so disquieting that the author keeps undermining this interpretation, emphasizing the boy's fairness and then describing him as the one who in his adulthood begins to fight against Saracens as his cultural others. Even the Saracen Emir notices the

---

[92] The topic of sea exile in the *Horn* romances and other Middle English and French texts has been analyzed by Sobecki (2008:100-113).

[93] Horn's status as someone who prefers exile rather than integration with the cultural others is clearly the exact opposite of what happens to Bevis of Hampton, who "uncomfortably deep[ly]" assimilates with the Saracens who abducted him (Calkin 2004:135-158).

difference between his own people and Horn that the boy's fairness makes, since the ruler argues:

> "Horn, thou art well kene
> And that is well y-sene.
> Thu art gret and strong,
> Fair and evene long.
> Thou shalt waxe more
> By fulle seve yere.
> ..."
>   (*KH* 95-101)

The king of Westernesse also predicts the fame of Horn, a future ruler "fair and strong", which becomes a formula for Horn in the romance, which like all popular romances very much depends on formulaic structures:[94]

> "... So shall thy name springe
> Fram kinge to kinge
> And thy fairnesse
> Abute Westernesse,
> The strengthe of thine honde
> Into evrech londe.
> ..."
>   (*KH* 215-221)

The adventures are subsequently summarized by the narrator as those of "Horn/ That fair was and noght unhorn" (*KH* 1537-1538). However, it requires scrutiny whether Horn's fairness is exclusively aesthetic here, that is implying beauty, or if it is also an ethnic and cultural characteristic distinguishing him from the non-fair, that is, possibly dark-skinned, Saracens. On the one hand, fairness may be a part of the characterization, which derives from the Neo-Platonic vision of beauty as a quality consistently accompanied by goodness. Neo-Platonic concepts pervaded medieval European culture and introduced into it the idea that beauty is inseparable from the good. As Plotinus argued in *Ennead* I, vi, passage two, unity is the primary virtue of the universe and Beauty resides in it, because "... on what has thus been compacted to unity, Beauty enthrones itself, giving itself to parts and to the one" and constituting oneness with good (Plotinus 1917-1930, quoted in: Winsatt – Brooks 1957:114). The unity, however, pertains to the relationship between the two in the world of ideas rather than the material world. In *Ennead* I (vi, 9) Plotinus, like Plato, observes that real beauty is that of the actions of humans, not of people's physicality or

---

94 For a discussion of formulaic diction in Middle English romances see Błaszkiewicz (2009).

the physicality of the world surrounding them: "Therefore the soul must be trained – to the habit of remarking, first, all noble pursuits, then the works of beauty produced not by the labour of the arts but by the virtue of men known for their goodness," as he comments on the distinction between two types of beauty (Plotinus 1917-1930, quoted in: Winsatt – Brooks 1957:116). Winsatt and Brooks summarize the point by arguing that he is "strongly inclined . . . to depreciate physical beauty, or at best to value it as an approach to the real beauty of Intelligence in the Yonder" (Winsatt – Brooks 1957:116). In the light of Neo-Platonic ideas Horn could be characterized as fair due to the continuity which might exist between beauty and kindness. His fairness may be internal, so his physicality merely demonstrates his inner virtue. Conversely, the physical beauty he is born with is a good point of departure for fashioning virtue in himself. In the end external beauty signals internal perfection that he has built within his own psyche. The final remark about Horn's physicality, "That fair was and noght unhorn" (*KH* 1538), may go deeper, since it does not merely have to be a reference to his beauty; it very probably summarizes Horn's moral attitude.

Nevertheless, fairness does not denote exclusively beauty in medieval culture. The emphasis laid on the adjective "fair" may be ethnically oriented here in the same sense as Chaucer's Constance was consistently characterized as pale-skinned, which was broached here in Chapter One. As was implied earlier here, Constance's pallor could be interpreted on several levels, ranging from the skin colour that implies beauty in medieval cultures, through the hue signaling strong affect provoked by the misfortunes afflicting her, to the indication of ethnic difference visible the most upon contact with others, Saracens and Northumbrians. Akbari investigated the ethnic difference of Constance's others, claiming that the North was almost as exotic a geographical and cultural location as the East according to Chaucer's vision in *The Man of Law's tale* (2000:19-34). The pale-skinned Constance constantly revealed her identity as a Westerner, in contrast to those who hosted her in, respectively, Syria and Northumbria, and who were expected to be darker-skinned like Saracens, barbarically swarthy, or excessively white-skinned like people inhabiting the areas close to the Ultima Thule. Consequently, Horn's fairness may also be ethnic if he receives the label of the other from those who differ from him both culturally and physically. *Horn Childe and Maiden Rimnild* also includes references to Horn's physicality, here described as more openly ethnic than in *King Horn*. "As white as milke he was naked" (*HCMR* 296), runs the explicit passage, which ostensibly implies the idea of standard ethnicity in the world of this romance rather than merely beauty and perfection. Rimnild is one who is "a feir may & a schene" (*HCMR* 305), as there probably arises no need for stressing her ethnicity. Even though no Saracens appear in *Horn Childe*, the title character's whiteness distinguishes him from the Vikings who have ruined his one-time peace and perhaps serves the function of reestablishing him within the category of sameness despite the change of geographic location and that makes him a cultural other. His cultured quality cannot be undermined as he is not merely "fair", but "white", which may suggest a specific racialism in this very early romance.

As for the division into "Sarazines" and Christians, the former category needs more investigation in *King Horn*, as has been said above. In *English medieval romance* Barron hypothesizes about the Saracens of *King Horn* as "late substitutes for Vikings originals", the pirates (1987:65), which follows the line of thinking in Daniel's *Heroes and Saracens* (1984). Speed summarizes that line of argument with the one found in Metlitzki's *Matter of Araby in medieval England*, where she indicated that occurrences of Spanish Saracens' travels to the British Isles were noted (1977:120). She makes us believe that the Saracens of *King Horn* could equally mean "pagans", "Muslims", and "Danes" due to the word's etymology, which derived from Latin in the form *Saracene* and from French in the *Sarazin*, appearing in the romance in question (1990:566-567). Still, Speed insists that the anonymous author of *King Horn* must have been aware of the functioning of Saracens in the *chanson de geste* tradition and may have accessed it through the Anglo-Norman *Horn Childe* and possibly through some French sources (1990:567). She even hypothesizes about a common ancestor of both the Anglo-Norman and Middle English romance (1990:567). Her line of argument identifying the "Sarazines" of *King Horn* as Muslims may be summarized in the list of elements which are indicative of that identification rather than any other. Speed lists the occurrence of the slur "heathen hounds" referring to the enemies, the leadership function performed by the emir, the occurrence of a giant familiar from the *chansons de geste* tradition, their blackness and religion, and, finally, the tradition of sea voyages undertaken by the historical Saracens (1990:573-591). Kathy Cawsey argues that some of these elements may not be exclusively indicative of the Saracen identity of the invaders of Sudenne: she shows that giants did not have to derive from the *chansons de geste* tradition, because they could also be included in the Arthurian romance, as for instance the case of *Sir Gawain and the Green Knight* reveals, while the ships called galleys were not sailed only by Saracens (2009:385). Still, the best of the argument remains with Speed, who identified the invaders as a specific ethnic group in *King Horn*, even though she did not address their different identification in other versions of the romance.

In *Horn Childe and Maiden Rimnild* the invaders are Danish and exoticism cannot be their chief quality. It appears, however, that the evolution that the narrative underwent in order to include some "Saracens" enriched its texture and allowed for a fuller development of the topic of otherness in the plot of *King Horn*. The process of making Saracens out of the invaders in the Horn-romances could be diagnosed as what Bartlett terms "Saracenization" when he studies visual representations of ethnic others in medieval manuscript illuminations (2009:132-156). What Bartlett detects is the strategy of portraying Asians, such as Mongols, but also Jews in a manner reminiscent of Muslims of the Mediterranean. The rationale behind it would be the physical closeness of the Muslims and relative familiarity of Europeans with their material culture (Bartlett 2009:146). These two factors made illustrators portray diverse ethnic others in those illuminations wearing "oriental" garb and headgear. In *King Horn* we probably witness the textual version of such Saracenization, making the invaders more "exotic" than Vikings, who permanently settled Anglo-Saxon England and whose settlements over time became an inseparable element of the landscape of the North, not to mention the Danish identity of such kings of England as Canute.

What could impress the readers of this romance is the shift in the identification of Saracens as outsiders who usurp power in Sudenne to the rulers who make Horn the other. Not only does he cross the physical borders between countries that he travels to, but he also transgresses the metaphorical border between the same and the other. Intriguingly, there exists a relationship between sameness or otherness and desire as either communal or individual ideas. Once Horn's social status is drastically lowered and he becomes the other in Westernesse, his desire becomes merely personal. Had he become king immediately after his father's untimely death, his desires would have been focal to the entire community. Temporarily deprived of leadership, he conceals his erotic desire, focusing on the question of survival, improvement of his legal status in the society he enters, that of Westernesse, and combating his enemies. In *King Horn* what Horn desires appears partly unfathomable, since, despite his partiality for the king's daughter Rymenhild, he refuses to express the sentiment openly, at first due to the intricacies of his status, very likely both social and ethnic, and then due to his position as king. His desire appears suppressed for some time, while such characters as Rymenhild openly voice their devotion for Horn and they desire what he represents both individually and socially. Then he continues to focus himself on his sovereignty.

The text simultaneously stresses his status of the other and questions his cultural difference. An adequate example of the strategy of undermining otherness is supplied by Horn's encounter with a giant, who visits the king of Ireland at Christmas:

> Hit was at Christesmasse,
> Neither more ne lasse;
> There cam in at none
> A geaunt swithe sone
> Y-armed fram paynime
> And seide thes rime
> . . .
>
> (*KH* 805-811)

Despite being a cultural and ethnic other in Ireland, Horn cannot be characterized by the same degree of otherness as the giant, armed like pagans and speaking to the king in an enigmatic manner about a threat posed to the kingdom.[95] There are diverse degrees of alterity, it appears, and the body of the other always reflects the position he or she has on this continuum of otherness. The giant's body is too exorbitant for him to be comparable to the other newcomer to the court, Horn, who has renamed himself as "Cutberd". Paradoxically, the arrival of the giant restores Horn to the category of sameness once and for all, despite the cultural isolation he may still be feeling in the strange land. The new name "Cutberd" becomes the name which implies affinity with the Christian culture probably observable in the realm of the Irish king, in contrast to the name "Horn", which is historically that of the Danish leader who arrived in Ireland in the year 851 (Mills 1988:58). The strong contrast created between the giant and Horn, who calls himself Cutberd here, enhances the impression that the latter controls all desire effectively, while the monster stands for unbridled desire and even primeval lust. In other romances, such as *Tristan*, such characterization of giants is put to the fore, as they are, to cite Sylvia Huot, "antithetical to civilization, both in their unspeakable viciousness and in their insatiable desire" (2007:381). The heir to the throne of Sudenne emblematizes everything that the giant cannot be: he practices the self-restraint of a good Christian and you can assume that he will always act justly instead of performing acts out of spite. Accordingly, he undertakes the challenge issued by the newcomer and victoriously ends the confrontation:

> "King," he sede, "cum to felde
> For to bihelde
> Hu we fighte shulle
> And togare go wulle."
> Right at prime tide
> Hi gudden ut ride

---

95 Metlitzki sees the same identity of a representative of the monstrous race in this giant and in the previously discussed here black-skinned giants from the romances whose plots were initiated by *chansons de geste* (1977:126).

And funden on a grene
A geaunt swithe kene,
His feren him biside
Hore deth to abide.
(*KH* 851-860)

Horn finally reaffirms his status of the same in announcing his chivalric readiness to defend Ireland against its others. He risks his life and may miss the fulfilment of his attachment to Rymenhild if he is slain by the giant.

The issue of identity, suggested particularly strongly by the self-renaming of Horn, becomes more complex even before the last self-exile of that character. Speaking the language of Lacanian psychoanalysis, in order to mature the subject needs to continually displace itself, which relates not only to the ideas of the maternal and the paternal, but also to the sphere of religion. Writes Fradenburg: "The subject is formed through its divine displacement from the material and partial place of the mother's body, through its positioning in that lack from which God will and may be petitioned" (1998:43). By abandoning the imaginary of the mother and entering the symbolic of the father, the character enters the sphere of continuing lack and proceeds from fantasizing about kingship, fatherhood, and political power to materializing those fantasies. He is transferred from what Fradenburg terms "the unbarred 'O'", "a fantasy of sovereign knowledge, jouissance, riches" into the "barred 'O'", "Ō", "multiple and open systems that structure subjectivity" (1998:267-268). The multiple and open systems in *King Horn* may be Christianity as opposed to Islam, knighthood as opposed to the status of a slave, whom Horn pretends to be in order to see Rymenhild, and political power as contrasted with subjection and deprivation of rightful sovereignty. The systems include the signifiers that subsequently define Horn's identity and, what is significant for us here, also determine his corporeality. His body, according to Lacanian theory designed by diverse signifiers (Fradenburg 1998:267), metamorphoses from the childlike corporeality of the young heir to the throne, through the potentially abused bodily frame of a refugee, that of a stranger to Westernesse, a knight, and ultimately to the twofold body of the king of Sudenne, who will be endowed both with his own physical body of a living king and the body politic. As for paternity, himself prematurely left fatherless, he will serve both as a father to his people and to his future offspring, substituting for his own lack of the father a developed version of his own paternity. These two, body and identity, mutually influence each other and the type of impact depends on the signifier determining them at a given stage of Horn's life.

Nonetheless, regardless of the character's progress from the imaginary to the symbolic, the Real continues to affect his actions. Fradenburg straightforwardly claims that in the Middle Ages God was the Real (1998:257), an intuition she shares with Žižek, who claims that the Real is "the brute, pre-symbolic reality which always returns to its place"; God must belong to that sphere from the perspective of psychoanalysis (2008b:182). The reality entails the symbolic existence of the Real, whose role in the symbolic remains paradoxical. To cite Žižek's *Sublime object of ideology*, "The paradox of the Lacanian Real, then, is that it is an entity which, although it does not exist (in the sense of 'really existing', taking place in reality), has a series of properties – it exercises a certain structural carnality, it can produce a series of effects in the symbolic reality of subjects" (2008b:183). Horn's identity as a Christian influences his body, which appears to be more immune to carnal temptations and more resistant to the negative effects of physical and cultural displacement and exile. When he arrives in Westernesse with his companions, he immediately introduces himself to king Almayr as a Christian:

"We beoth of Suddenne,
Y-come of gode kenne,
Of Christene blode
And kinges swithe gode.
Payns ther gunne arive
And duden hem of live.
..."
(*KH* 179-185)

He thus affirms his status as one whose religious and cultural "sameness" remains unquestionable despite his being ethnically different from the people of Westernesse. The Christians of Sudenne are even more integrated with their religion through the misfortune of the pagan invasion which has befallen them. Horn's Christian identity needs to be later reaffirmed in Ireland, where he even changes his name in order to reinforce this chivalric self. The trick of Horn renaming himself works, as Berild, one of the king's men, exclaims: "Ne saw I nevre my live/ So fair knight arive!" (*KH* 783-784). The name adds authenticity to Horn's aristocratic appearance and enhances his "fairness", here again a word with many denotations, as we already noted. Christianity, outer and inner beauty, and upper-class origin appear to be related attributes in the world of the *Horn* romances.

Once Westernesse is invaded, the characters start to emphasize their Christianity, as when Godhild, Horn's mother, secludes herself in order to practise Christian ritual despite the prohibition against it that is imposed by the Muslims: "Ther heo servede Gode/ Agenes the paynes forbode" (*KH* 79-80). Horn is consequently surrounded by the care exercised directly by Jesus Christ due to his mother's prayers: "Evre heo bad for Horn child/ That Jesu Christ him beo mild" (*KH* 83-84). The invaders are consequently defined as the Christian God's adversaries, as when queen Godhild speaks to "the payne king,/ Jesu Cristes withering" (*KH* 151-152). Christianity in the romance is irrevocable once someone has been christened. It appears to mark bodies permanently, even if the marking is manifested in the clothes someone wears, which signal this religious identification, or in the paraphernalia, such as a weapon. Once Horn returns to Westernesse to win back Rymenhild, he encounters a knight sleeping under a shield, whom he awakens when he notices that "O the shelde wes y-drawe/ A crois of Jesu Christes lawe" (*KH* 1313-1314). The knight confesses that, indeed, he is drawn to Horn's "Drighte" [Lord] (*KH* 1322), because he used to be Christian before being forcibly converted to the "paganism" of Islam:

> He sede, "Ich serve agenes my wille
> Payns full ille.
> Ich was Christene a while;
> Tho y-come to this ile
> Sarazins blake
> That dude me forsake-
> On Christ ich wolde bileve.
> ..."
>   (*KH* 1327-1334)

He follows his story with the account of the slain "King Murry,/ Hornes fader, king hendy" (*KH* 1347-1348), which confirms the centrality of kingship and fatherhood to the plot. The reality of the narrative appears to be entangled in the issue of sovereignty and in religion as the principle that validates the legitimacy of a sovereign. Horn is able to enhance his political position due to the air of religious authority which had surrounded his late father and which now gives him the aura of a legitimate ruler, drawing the former Christian knights back to the rightful sovereigns of Sudenne. Quite tellingly, Christianity connotes enjoyment, since it signals the future victories of Horn and his company and the triumph of what the forcibly converted knight judges to be the religious truth. After all, in the Middle Ages the categories of sameness and otherness revolved around religious identification, so it is not surprising that religion is a concept that connotes *jouissance*. In the world of the romance sameness, that is, ultimately, Christianity, will always allow for enjoyment to appear. Otherness is also constructed by use of religious signifiers, which determine both the psyche and the corporeality of believers, but any enjoyment is denied to those who are non-Christians.

As was noted in Chapter One, entering the symbolic means that we are constantly going to be afflicted by a feeling of lack.[96] Consequently, the materialization of any desire will always be deferred, which is especially true of Horn, a righteous Christian ruler, realizing his desire for Rymenhild, the daughter of the king of Westernesse. If he is to aspire to the status of a good Christian knight, he must never reveal his more mundane interests, such as his carnal desire for Rymenhild. He silences his desire and prefers to sublimate it into the pursuit of knighthood and then into the intention to regain political power and avenge the premature death of his father. His desire is very likely projected onto the people around him, because he inspires almost uncontrollable desire in Rymenhild. When she meets him for the first time, she exclaims:

> By God that me makede,
> A swich fair ferade
> Ne sauw ich in none stunde
> By westene londe!
> (*KH* 169-172)

It has to be noted that this admiration is inspired by a thirteen-year-old boy, who evokes such strong emotions with his physicality. Later, misled into thinking that Athulf is Horn, she declares her devotion with the words "well longe/ Ich habbe thee luved stronge" (*KH* 307-308). A phrase that summarizes her attraction to Horn is: "Heo luvede so Horn child/ That negh heo gan wexe wild" (*KH* 255-256). Despite her status as a Christian virgin, Rymenhild does not withhold expressions of devotion and strong attraction, including also physical attraction to the main hero of the romance. Certain of her position, she asks Horn to declare the same sentiments to her and offers herself to him in marriage:

> "Horn," heo sede, "withute strif,
> Thou shalt have me to thy wif.
> Horn, have of me rewthe
> And plist me thy trewthe."
> (*KH* 411-414)

Her desire can be expressed freely, since her social and legal position in Westernesse remains unquestionable. Perhaps some of the desire that Horn would express under other circumstances is articulated by Rymenhild, making her the only one openly voicing what both of them want. Social limitations might introduce this lack of balance into the relationship in which only the woman speaks about what she aspires to. When Rymenhild rejects Athulf by saying that no one can be like Horn, because "Horn is fairer and riche,/ Fairer by

---

96 Lacan discusses the lack as fundamental for the relationship between the self and the other (1981).

one ribbe/ Thane eny man that libbe" (*KH* 318-320), this does not improve Horn's position as an exile in Westernesse. He clearly realizes the lowliness of his position when he declares: "Ich am y-bore too lowe/ Swich wimman to knowe" (*KH* 421-422). The idea that Horn might be a lowborn person, however, can also be seen as a disguise for his actual cultural otherness and an excuse used by him in order to postpone materialization of his desire for Rymenhild. The desire must be postponed until the moment when he regains the social status that is due to him. Even when knighted, he defers the fulfilment endlessly, to some extent allowing such people as Finkenhild to take over Rymenhild, even if they can never usurp the warm feelings she reserves for Horn.

Horn's desire for Rymenhild seems to be regulated by the Name-of-the-Father, since he openly acknowledges his status as a thrall in Westernesse. "Thanne is my thralhod/ Y-went into knighthod" (*KH* 443-444), as he speaks about the change in his status which will occur once he is knighted. The bridled desire of Horn binds Rymenhild's desire within the confines of restraint. In *Horn Childe and Maiden Rimnild* the girl intends to stay a virgin for seven years "for þe love" of Horn (*HCMR* 534) so as to give Horn a chance to alter his social status and return to her. This restraint may also be of religious nature, as waiting for Horn can be used in order to achieve spiritual perfection before she is reunited with him. The quasi-religious image of a virgin who sequesters herself away from the world in order to develop spiritually stands in stark contrast with the portrait of Rimnild as a seductress. The latter image is initially given to the audience, because Rimnild firstly presents herself as surrounded by opulence and splendor to Horn's companion Haþerof; she performs the spectacle in order to attract Horn's attention to her:

> þe miri maiden also sone
> As Haþerof into chaumber come
> Sche wend þat it wer Horn
> A riche cheier was vndon,
> þat se[u]en mi3t sit þeron,
> In swiche craft ycorn.
> A baudekin þeron was spred,
> þider þe maiden hadde hem led
> To siten hir biforn;
> Frout & spices sche hem bede,
> Wine to drink, wite & rede,
> Boþe of coppe & horn.
> (*HCMR* 325-336)

Even though she does not meet Horn here yet, she performs this self-fashioning so that he will find her desirable. This is not the only use of the phrase "miri maiden", since Rimnild was also called a "miri maiden" (*HCMR* 313) earlier, when she attempted to make another companion of Horn's, Arlond, to come to her room and bring Horn with him. Maldwyn Mills emphasizes that in other Auchinleck romances, *Amis and Amiloun* and *Sir Tristrem*, the phrase "miri maiden" is attached to sexually aggressive and deceitful heroines (1988:113). Rimnild, later presented as a peaceful would-be recluse awaiting Horn, here appears to be bent on ensnaring him as he is placed at the very centre of her attention.[97] The food that she has ready for him and his companions may signal the immediacy of her desire and the physical aspect of the attraction she feels. Here alimentation symbolizes her social position and the need to share this position with Horn if he agrees to succumb to her desire, but also implies lust that she may feel for Horn. Once their relationship begins, the boy may be metaphorically devoured by her in the way that food can be devoured and digested. Fortunately for the religious content of the romance, Rimnild adopts the identity of a recluse-like virgin awaiting Horn.

In *Horn Childe* the young lovers are separated by the ruse of Haþerof, who betrays them to Houlac when their love seems closer to consummation. In *King Horn* Fikenhild spies on Horn and Rymenhild so as to expose their passion to king Aylmar. Fikenhild, "the wurste moder child" [the most evil mother's child] (*KH* 652), is overcome by his obsession with Rymenhild to such a great extent that he pretends to care about her when he betrays the lovers' plans to the father:

> "Aylmar, ich thee warne
> Horn thee wule berne!
> Ich herde whar he sede,
> And his swerd forth leide,
> To bringe thee of live
> And take Rymenhild to wive.
> He lith in bure
> Under coverture
> By Rymenhild thy doghter-
> And so he doth well ofte.
> ..."
>
> (*KH* 693-703)

So as to enhance the negative impression that the unlawful relationship of Rymenild and Horn makes, Fikenhild presents the latter as the future slayer of the lawful sovereign and a usurper of his political power. The accusations

---

97 Mehl cites this aggressiveness of the lady as an example of the romance's "uncourtly characteristics" (1968:213); nevertheless, it is questionable whether the wooing of Gawain by Bertilak's Lady in *Sir Gawain and the Green Knight* is also uncourtly, and, if it agrees with the code of chivalric culture, perhaps this example of uncourtliness in *King Horn* is not the best one.

cannot be proved, but the idea that Horn not only desires the king's daughter, but has already gained her favours is bolstered by the scene when Aylmar "fond Horn in arme/ On Rymenhilde barme" (*KH* 709-710). Even though Horn's love for Rymenhild remains pure here, the idea is undermined by Fikenhild who, strongly attracted to the virgin himself, suggests that the lovers are connected by lust as something that every love supposedly entails. The introduction of Fikenhild into the plot as the evil companion of Horn produces an effect of duplicity, because Horn acts nobly any time when he is described by the narrator, while the worst can always be expected from Fikenhild. Even though Fikenhild appears early in the plot as the double of Athuld, Horn's best friend, and is portrayed as "the werste" (*KH* 30) of the two brothers, as a matter of fact he is the reverse image of Horn. They are doubles in that they complement each other, but also in portraying the two faces of erotic desire. In a fairly psychoanalytical manner the romance relegates the dark aspect of desire onto Fikenhild, leaving its more admirable aspects for Horn. Once Fikenhild is slain by Horn ("Fikenhildes crune/ Ther y-fulde adune" (*KH* 1499-1500)), the hero may fully express his desire in lawful marriage to Rymenhild. Writes Ramsey: "Horn's defeat of the villain represents the control of his own lusts" (1983:33). The hero's location within the realm of the symbolic, which is controllable and where all transgression needs to be punished, is finally reaffirmed. If Fikenhild is to some extent like Horn, he illustrates the aspect of desire which is false according to the romance's ideology, since it is tantamount to lust; as a result, the character of Fikenhild materializes the possible "darker" side of Horn's relationship with Rymenhild.

The unattainable nature of all desire is restated by Žižek, who in *The sublime object of ideology* discusses "the whole Lacanian problem of the reflexivity of desire: desire is always a desire of a desire . . . Which desire should I desire?" (2008b:196). The displacement of erotic desire in *King Horn* occurs while accompanied by two other types of desire, the desire for God and that for death. When desiring God one approaches the Real, unattainable as it is, while the desire for death materializes here in the desire for the death of one's enemies, which may also entail one's own death on the battlefield. Slaying Saracens as one matures does not suffice, because Fikenhild functions in the plot as another enemy of Horn. The villain appears to be obsessed with Rymenhild that he intends to rape her:

> Fikenhild was prut on herte
> And that him dude smerte.
> Yonge he yaf and elde
> Mid him for to helde.
> Ston he dude lede

> Ther he hopede spede.
> Strong castel he let sette,
> Mid see him biflette;
> Ther ne mighte lighte
> Bute fowel with flighte.
> Bute whanne the see withdrowe,
> Mighte come men y-nowe.
> Fikenhild gan wende
> Rymenhild to shende.
> To wowe he gan hure yerne;
> The King ne dorste him werne.
> Rymenhild was full of mode;
> Heo wep teres of blode.
> That night Horn gan swete
> And hevye for to mete
> Of Rymenhild, his make,
> Into shupe was y-take.
> The shup bigan to blenche;
> His lemman sholde adrenche.
> Rymenhild with hire honde
> Wolde up to londe;
> Fikenhild agen hire pelte
> With his swerdes hilte.
> (*KH* 1401-1428)

Fikenhild's wicked intentions towards Rymenhild are thwarted, so he finally decides "to weden hire by nighte" (*KH* 1442) instead of raping her, obviously provided that we read the "wedding" as a legal act and not as the beginning of a natural marriage. As a consequence, Horn takes revenge on Fikenhild not only for the early betrayal of Horn, but also for the later intention to possess Rymenhild.

The significance of Horn's double, the villain companion who betrays him, probably due to envy as he is not able to gain Horn's beloved himself, emerges also from the narrative of *Horn Childe*, where the cunning traitor who informs Houlak about Horn's liaison with Rimnild is named Wikard:

> Wikard bi þe king rade,
> Wikel þat lesing made:
> Horn gan þai wray
> & seyd, "Sir, Y seiȝe ȝisterday
> Hou Horn bi þi douhter lay:
> Traitours boþe be þai".
> (*HCMR* 487-492)

In *Horn Childe* the traitor, however, does not attempt to approach Rimnild once the seven-year-span of waiting for Horn has come to an end. She becomes the object of interest for "Moging þe king/ Wiþ Rimnild at spouseing,/ þe kinges douhter dere" (*HCMR* 871-873). Other figures within the plot then appear to treat erotic desire as an important part of their lives, in contrast to Horn, whose pursuits are temporarily of a different nature before he may finally return to Rimnild.

Lees argues that the two types of desire, religious and erotic, are not always contrasted in medieval culture, especially in the early Middle Ages from which she takes her textual examples, but desire for God and for a lady coexist side by side, one merging with the other in various combinations (2007:17-45). Lees states that Caroline Walker Bynum's *Holy feast and holy fast* (1987) draws a rigid boundary between religion and "the erotics of pleasure and/or pain" (Lees 2007:39-40), while the distinction is questioned as artificial by Biddick in *Genders, bodies, borders* (Biddick 1993:389-418, quoted in Lees 2007:40). In *King Horn* the narrative fluidly progresses from Horn's Christianity and his drive to avenge his father to his intention to eliminate Fikenhild and regain Rymenhild, the object of his erotic desire. The writer does not indicate any conflict between the two manners in which Horn identifies himself, the manner of a devout Christian and that of a lover willing to do anything to win the lady. Characteristically, the romance appears to follow the Anglo-Saxon perspective on eroticism and sexuality, which distinguished itself from the later visions of religiousness with the idea that pleasure should be neither overvalued nor ignored, as Lees writes (2007:19).

Desire, religious and erotic, is highly gendered in *King Horn*, since virtuous men such as Horn tend to be religiously and martially oriented first, but their self-restraint is not matched by a similar attitude in women, who are more readily associated with sexual desire rather than the ways in which, according to Freud, it could be sublimated and transformed into culture (Lees 2007:19). Yet again, as in the Anglo-Saxon period, eroticism connotes more than sexuality detached from spiritual issues (Lees 2007:21). Erotic love is not merely sexual, hence corporeal, but it also involves the lovers' souls, while true fulfilment may be found in the sacrament of marriage, so Christian desire needs to complement the carnal kind. Such is precisely the message of both *King Horn* and *Horn Childe and Maiden Rimnild*: even if all desire is unfulfillable, one may approach it by uniting oneself in marriage with one's beloved. Significantly, the culture of male restraint cannot be attributed to Christian influence only; martial culture equally imposed limitations on male desire, making combat against the enemy central and love for a lady marginal (Lees 2007:22).

Naturally, one cannot argue that all sexual desire is absent from the *Horn* narratives, but the Anglo-Saxon emphasis on the desire for God and death and the implication that erotic desire may be directed towards the main character, but he defers it, are traceable in those early romances. The portrayal of Rimnild in *Horn Childe* as a seductress who lures the object of her desire with a feast she has ready for him illustrates this, as she is the reverse image of Horn. Horn will never approach her attitude of explicitly erotic interest due to his identity as a Christian knight and owing to his masculinity. This may be another reason why his desire will remain unfulfilled to some extent: as a masculine figure in the world of this early romance he will always be engrossed in military confrontations, following the ethos of a *milites Christi*, of his knighthood, and ultimately of his kingship and the metaphorical body of his state, rather than focusing on his own sexualized body and the pursuit of erotic desire. In the dialectic of various types of desire, Rymenhild, who actively desires, appears to be another object which may be incorporated into what Horn gains and what he owns. The status of Horn's desiring her as marginal is confirmed at the end, as she is granted to Horn along with the social status that was due to him and the crown to which he aspired.

Nevertheless, in Lacanian psychoanalysis it is argued that desire and sacrifice are not necessarily opposed terms. Horn does not sacrifice his desire for the benefit of greater causes, military triumph and kingship, but transfers this desire into the domain of suffering. L.O. Aranye Fradenburg claims that "psychoanalysis distinctively insists that we are capable of *desiring* suffering, for ourselves, not just for our loved ones or our enemies, because a subject *tout court* is a function of desire" (2002:3), hence it is established through desiring. The volition of Horn may be directed towards himself, as he does not sacrifice himself for the cause of revenge or for his people, but appears to willingly subject himself to suffering. What Fradenburg terms "the 'opposition' of pleasure and duty [which] is rarely treated in moral philosophy" (2002:4) exposes its very subjective nature here. As a matter of fact, Horn seems to derive pleasure from the fulfilment of his duties, because the latter are more important than the immediate erotic pleasure that he could experience if he did not pursue knighthood and kingship instead. The reality of duties as entangled with pleasure and desire for suffering as a self-perpetuating phenomenon is illustrated by the continuity of what Horn aspires to. When he achieves one of his goals, he smoothly proceeds to realize another goal he has designated for himself.

What Lacan defined as "the gift of death" becomes all-important for Horn. Having lost his father, the country which had been his patrimony, and then his beloved in Westernesse (due to the wrath of her father), he deals with loss by resorting to melancholy, which paradoxically does not stand in opposition to his actively pursuit of his goals. Frandeburg writes, "the gift of death is a melancholic incorporation of loss and a bid for the surplus provided by the psychic exchanges enabled by extimacy" (2002:30). As we noted in the previous chapter in relation to giants, the Real transforms itself into law and language through the process combining the inside and the outside. Fradenburg writes about "the uncanny inside-outsideness of the signifiers" that structure consciousness but are absent from it (2002:20). Horn's experience of the Real makes him go beyond the limitations of his individuality and transform himself not only into a user of law and language, but also into their author as a king and maker of political discourse. In order to accomplish his sacrifice which combines with desire, he deploys the symbol identified by Fradenburg as the "premier signifier of sacrifice in the Middle Ages, and mediator of the interchange between the laicizing of sacrifice and the sacrilizing of lay culture", the cross (2002:32). This is another aspect in which the scene of meeting the knight forcibly converted to Islam but still carrying the symbol of the cross focalizes the concerns of the romance. The religious emblem stands for the "gift of death": the amalgam of sacrifice and pleasure that leads Horn with his companions to fulfilment of his goals. Reiss claimed that desire and chastity are the romance's "warp and woof" (1986:115). Nevertheless, the desire remains almost exclusively the desire for death, while its other types are marginalized by Horn himself. What Mehl specified as "the religious seriousness" of the romance may be psychoanalytically explained (1968:179).

Despite the apparent simplicity of the plot, *King Horn* provides the readers with copious commentary on the question of sameness and otherness and didactically instills in one a sense of the righteousness of Horn's attitude, whether contrasted with the Saracens who invade his land, the wicked Fikenhild, or even his beloved Rymenhild. But the Lacanian ideas of the barred and unbarred Other and of the desire for death may place the text in a different light, particularly if we focus on the issue of the body desiring individually and communally as an important concern of this romance. Fatherhood and maternity start the list of topics treated by the Middle English narrative and they also symbolically end it, since Horn becomes the father in a number of ways, symbolically continuing the tasks undertaken by his own father, whose spectre will probably never abandon him.

Chapter Six
Transformation and regeneration in *Kyng Alisaunder* and *The wars of Alexander*

> Many gode citees þere ben in þat contree & men han gret plentee & gret chep of all wynes & vitailles (*The travels of sir John Mandeville*) (Hamelius 1919:136)
> [There are many other cities in that land, and also great abundance of food.] (Moseley 1983:138)

What binds together the diverse oriental romances we have analyzed so far is the vein of fantasy that flows through practically all of them, starting from the imagined Tartary of Chaucer, through the uneasy parentage and eating of the other in *Richard le Coer de Lyon*, to the Emir's wedding of Floris and Blancheflour and, in *King Horn*, the invasion of Britain by the Saracens. The giants and giantesses in the romances which are versions of the French *chansons de geste* are even more obviously products of fantasies about the other, so an effect of grotesquerie is produced in them. The relationship between fantasy, the grotesque, and the Orient has been observed by Bakhtin, who traces the onset of the two former cultural phenomena in the Middle Ages to the so-called "Indian Wonders" cycle, better known as the Marvels of the East, to the Prester John legend, and to other "exotica", including the myth of Oriental abundance from the epigraph above (1984:344-347). Importantly, Bakhtin reminds his readers that the tradition was started, on the one hand, by the description of the marvellous included initially in Ctesias' work, written in Persia in the 5th century BC and now lost, but incorporated, among others, into Lucian's, Pliny's, Isidore of Seville's work, and on the other hand it was included in the romances about Alexander the Great (1984:344). The Alexander tradition was continued in the English Middle Ages, because such artistic romances as *Kyng Alisaunder* and *The wars of Alexander* were written then. To be fair, these two texts may be said to heal the rift between the mostly negative orientalism analyzed so far and the positivity dormant in at least some medieval representations of the Orient. After all, the Marvels of the East may have represented the essence of a more nuanced medieval orientalism on which Ganim commented (2005:13-14), so negativity did not have to be the principle determining the medieval image of the Orient. The tendencies in presenting the Orient that are latent in the

Alexander romances should therefore be carefully studied. After all, medieval orientalism comes in at least two varieties, if not more, and distinguishing only its negative and positive varieties still remains a simplification; but viewing negativity as the exclusive manner of describing the East is even more so. The Middle English Alexander romances focalize the issues discussed in the chapters above: the chief concern of the conqueror is fascination with bodies marked by alterity, while his desire modifies his perspective on the Orient into a view subtly hinting at what much later became Romantic infatuation with the Eastern world.

The Alexander romances, with the first text written by Pseudo-Callisthenes in the third century,[98] unquestionably mark the beginnings of the romance as a genre, as is noted Elizabeth Archibald (2004:11). John Finlayson also writes about those texts, ancient and medieval, as belonging to the category of the romance:

> ... the amount of fabulous material in the *Alexander* narratives has led critics to call them romances, based on the assumption that the marvellous or exotic is a necessary and therefore definitive feature of the *romance*. However, the fabulous material in these works is drawn largely from their sources, occasionally originated from Mandeville's *Travels*, which are not usually described as romances (1980:169).

Nevertheless, if we dwell on the extensive inclusion of the marvellous in *The travels* and consider the role of adventure in the text and the possible impact thereof on the medieval Alexander romances, it becomes evident that we may take the liberty of reading *The travels of sir John Mandeville* along with the two Middle English Alexander romances that will concern us here, since the two groups of texts, the numerous versions of *The travels* and the Alexander romances, are undoubtedly interrelated. After all, Bakhtin observed that the tradition of writing about the body made grotesque and stressing the role of extraordinary corporeality arose within the Wonders of the East cycle, which was continued by *The travels* in their various linguistic versions and manuscripts (1984:347). A crucial thing for us then is to read the Alexander romances and *The travels* together, regardless of their respective genre classification.

One element that the medieval Alexander romances and *The travels* share is the audience that they address. *Kyng Alisaunder* performs the meaningful gesture of indicating its audience in the most open way, but all of these texts

---

98 The version of the narrative by Callisthenes, a pupil of Aristotle, was not preserved; the so-called Pseudo-Callisthenes and its derivatives include the story of the magician Nectanabus, the last independent king of Egypt, who is driven from his throne by Persians and goes to Macedon in order to seduce Olympias with his magic tricks (Cary 1956:47).

indicate a similar readership. In the fourteenth-century romance both "lurid men" and "lewed" (*KA* 2) are invited to listen to the romance about Alexander, which implies that the needs of diverse people will be met by the text.[99] Both the learned and the unlearned, as the idiomatic phrase still employed in English conveys it, are going to be lectured on various differences that distinguish Europeans from peoples in the parts of the world that are remote. Furthermore, in modern audience the differences may give rise both to wonder and to reflection on what the same is and what the other is, and how the two may be interrelated. The discourse on this in these medieval texts will probably entail the premise that the title character of the Alexander romances belongs to the category of the same, as opposed to all that is exotic, bizarre, and potentially threatening, but also captivating in its otherness and potentially altering the same whenever the two meet.

As George Cary once argued, there existed diverse Alexanders in medieval literature, not European, because some of the sources came from the Arabic culture, even if they were, like the *Arabic Life of Alexander* (Gómez 1929) or the *Aljamiado Alexander* (Nykl 1929), i.e. the Rrek written in Aragonese Spanish using Arabic alphabet (Zuwiyya 2011:76), written in what is Western Europe nowadays.[100] The authors of *A companion to the Alexander romances in the Middle Ages* have recently confirmed the existence of a wealth of Alexander texts and the collection gives no priority to texts originating in European cultures over other cultures (Zuwiyya 2011). The scope for our analysis, however, will be restricted to two Middle English Alexander romances, and we shall exclude from our considerations what appears in the Old English *Epistola Alexandri ad Aristotelem* (from the 16th century onwards included in the so-called *Beowulf*-Manuscript along with the Old English *Wonders of the East*, *Beowulf*, and *The life of St Christopher*), and the Middle English poems *Alexander A* and *Alexander B*, the prosodic Thornton *Life of Alexander*, and *The dicts and sayings of the philosophers* (Ashurst 2011:256-257). The reason for

---

99 All the citations from *Kyng Alisaunder*, as well as the page numbers, come from Smithers' edition (1952a); the page numbers are preceded by the abbreviation *KA* and the manuscript version that is used here is Ms. Lincoln's Inn 150 (whereas the other manuscript version available in this edition is Ms. Laud Misc. 622).

100 Cary argues that "these two Spanish Arabic works were neither influenced by, nor had any influence on, Western textual tradition" (1956:61), but does not provide any evidence for the separate nature of these two traditions; on the contrary, in the light of what was said at the beginning of this study, we could argue that the relationship between the two Alexander traditions, Spanish Arabic and the one established in other European countries, could be fairly natural; Cary himself notes that the Arabic text must have given rise to one of the Hebrew translations of the *Historia de preliis* (1956:51).

our choice of texts is simple: this study practically limits itself to interpretations of what we might term oriental romances, and none of the above listed works could be classified as such. In contrast to *The travels*, they do not fulfill any of the criteria indispensable for a text to be categorized as a romance.

Kyng Alisaunder was written earlier than *The wars of Alexander*, namely around 1330, and must be treated as an adaptation of the Anglo-Norman *Roman de toute chevalerie*, attributed to Thomas of Kent and based on the *Res gesta Alexandri Magni* written by Julius Valerius in the fourth century (Cary 1956:37). G.V. Smithers argues, however, that even if the main source of the Middle English romance is followed quite closely in some passages, the anonymous author's "handling of it is in general highly independent", which produces an original artistic effect (1952b:15). Smithers as a matter of fact argues that *Kyng Alisaunder* has to be considered

> among the best of the Middle English metrical romances. The native vigour and liveliness which were within the range of the authors of *King Horn* and *Havelok* are here enriched by a sophistication of tone and of technique which were beyond them ... the world of courtly values and romantic love is here ... unobtrusively laid open in English poetry more than fifty years before the advent of Chaucer and the author of *Sir Gawain and the Green Knight* 1952b:40).

Cary voices similar praise for the text, writing that it is "no close translation but a skillful adaptation by a writer of originality and power, and the best of the English Alexander-books" (1956:37). This admiration for the anonymous author, to whom *Richard le Coer de Lyon* has also been attributed, may lead us to ask how intricate the vision of the Occident and the Orient is in this romance and, more importantly, whether the discourse on sameness and otherness and their role in the community formation and its maintenance could resemble that in *Richard*.[101] It would be interesting to see if the poet writes denigratingly about others, or, to be more specific, about their bodies, as it happens in *Richard*, or perhaps a degree of positivity may be spotted here. In the portrayal of Alexander as the same rather than the other the issue of bodies may be central, especially if the vision of the Marvels of the East in this text is considered.

The wars of Alexander was written later, in the early fifteenth century, but artistry as high as that of *Kyng Alisaunder* is absent from it, even if it is also a poem "of considerable merit" (Cary 1956:57). As Cary writes, it is a translation of one of the manuscripts of the *Historia de preliis* with the author's addition in the form of an introduction, an abridged version of the *Fuerre de Gadres*, and some connecting passages (1956:57). Nevertheless, despite the differences between the earlier and the later Middle English romance, similar ideas of

---

[101] Mehl attributes also *Arthour and Merlin* to the same anonymous author (1967:33).

otherness and sameness and an equal focus on corporeality are traceable in them, as both of the narratives derive from various versions of the life of Alexander, where these topics generally keep reappearing. The boundary between the European self and the non-European other is blurred to a great extent in both of these romances and may become a matter of considerable controversy in the course of interpretation. Nevertheless, this does not make these two Middle English Alexander romances special within the corpus of texts that includes the topic of the Marvels of the East. Linda Lomperis comments on *The travels of sir John Mandeville* in the context of the culturalist, or here even racialist, ideas of "us" and "them". She postulates that in criticism there should emerge

> ... [a] strong tendency to stop seeing "Mandeville" and the society that produced "him" as entities that are purely and simply "Christian", or purely and simply "male", and to undertake instead an investigation how the homogeneous category "purely and simply x" got produced in the first place (Lomperis 2001:163).

In the case of the text putatively written by the traveler "Mandeville", but in fact by an anonymous writer who created a hoax as a result of his extensive reading interests, there has been a tendency to describe it as a product of the Occident treating the Orient in a highly biased manner. Perhaps, however, the matter is not so simple, since *The travels* records amazement and fascination with what one may find in the East and does not have to be diagnosed as uniformly Western- and Christian-oriented. As Lomperis plausibly argues, the extensive travels of "Mandeville" place him outside the allegedly uniform Christian Europe, questioning the simplistic distinction into some imaginary "us" and 'them" (2001:151).

With the Alexander romances the temptation to categorize people into some "us" and "them" is not so great, either. It is impossible for us to determine how medieval audiences imagined Alexander: whether he was for them a barbarian or a civilized character. The latter image appears more likely, because he used to be counted as one of the Nine Worthies. Nevertheless, from our modern perspective his partly Illyrian origin[102] makes his uniformly Greek identity less pure.[103] In the antiquity, when the barbarians' ways were thought to be highly uncultured as a rule, Alexander's civilized status was not undermined (Tarn 1956:9). Ivan Hannaford emphasizes the idea that the ancient Greek categories

---

102 Illyria, which refers to the modern-day Balkans, later inspired the creation of another variety of orientalism, as Maria Todorova argues in *Imagining the Balkans* (1997).
103 Chism tentatively writes about Alexander's "proto-European" identity in *Wars of Alexander*, as opposed to that of his biological father, who has been "othered" in the narrative (2002:112).

of the civilized and the barbarian were not hereditary, but depended on someone being either an inhabitant of a city-state or of the countryside and on the political consequences thereof, since these two conditions guaranteed life in democracy or under despotism (1996:17-57). An association between Alexander and uncivilized Asia was drawn when he was alive, because he became Lord of Asia, the liongryphon of Persia, and king of some of his Asiatic territories as a consequence of his conquests (Tarn 1956:59), but the historiographic writing of his times did not even vaguely suggest that he was seen as the other. The close political link with Asia suggested by the titles above was nothing but a demonstration of his power as a conqueror. The medieval perspective could be different: he could be seen as both a pagan, hence someone not belonging entirely to the civilized world, and a figure that could be a model of chivalry despite his non-Christian beliefs.

In what follows we will not firstly focus on Alexander's conquests, but on his identity. In the ruler's lifetime a legend of his association with the supernatural was created. As W.W. Tarn writes, Callisthenes (or rather Pseudo-Callisthenes) came up with the idea of Alexander's divine descent (1956:77), which medieval romance writers developed to the full, creating a complex narrative of the ruler's supernatural origin. *The wars of Alexander* narrates this story in considerable detail, since its author delineates an oriental background for how Alexander was sired. The divine origin of the future ruler is signaled by the form of his biological father's physicality, which he, the Egyptian magician Anectanabus, adopts before secretly meeting Olympias (here given the name "Olympados") in her bedroom. His two horns imply an association with god Amon, whom he intends to impersonate:

> How he was merkid & made is mervaile to neuyn,
> With – tachid in his fortop – twa tufe hornes;
> A berd as a besom with thyn bred haris,
> A mouthe as a mastif hunde vnmetely to shaw.
> (*WA* 318-321)[104]

He sires Alexander disguised as a dragon which flies into the bedroom, very likely inspiring in Olympias the quasi-religious awe, less religious wonder, or perhaps even some erotic fascination. This is how women in the text of the romance react to extraordinary bodies, especially if those bodies are supposedly divine. Not surprisingly, Christine Chism remarked that the author "revels in mysterious eastern seductions" (2002:114):

---

104 All the citations from *The wars of Alexander* come from Skeat's edition (1936 [2002]) and the subsequent page numbers, preceded by the abbreviation *WA*, are taken from it.

> þer worthid he by his wiche-craft into a wild dragon,
> And to the ladi lere he lendid in haste,
> Fliʒand in his fethire-hames & ferly fast sletus,
> And in a braide, or he blan he þe bed entris.
> Quen he was laide be-lyfe his liknes he changis,
> Worthis agayn to a wee fra a worme turnys.
> (*WA* 378-383)

The corporeality that is alien is more likely to seduce a Western woman, as though this masculine body were also endowed with what was hypothesized to connote the Lacanian *objet petit a*. The body of Anactenabus is not only fantastic, but may also be an embodiment of the fantasy of a supernatural, deified lover. Žižek insists that fantasy is the primordial form of *narrative* (2008a:11) and the story of Alexander's begetting indeed becomes a narrative focalizing the psychoanalytical issues of attraction and repulsion towards, respectively, a husband and a lover, and the question of fatherhood and its repercussions. The biological father will determine Alexander's physicality, at least in his infant years, while the father who acknowledges him as a son, Philip of Macedon, is going to grant him a kingdom and political influence. The scene of the supernatural begetting illustrates the two parallel relationships of Olympias and the double fatherhood of Alexander, who will benefit from both of the connections that are made once he has been begotten. Importantly, perhaps, like Canace in Chaucer's *Squire's tale*, the Egyptian magician is made more attractive by his exotic background and supernatural tricks. What in the case of Canace was only an entity we called the "body marvellous", that is, her corporeality complemented by a supernatural object, is taken to the extreme here: Anactenabus's body becomes such a magic entity himself and his real identity is fully obscured by the form he adopts.

Anactenabus, the shapeshifter, achieves what he aspires to. The birth of his son is preceded by a series of some more supernatural occurrences, as if to confirm the marvellous dimension of Alexander's identity. The biological father returns to Olympias as a dragon, which Philip of Macedon witnesses, and a bird lays an egg in the king's lap:

> þis egg, or þe kyng wyst to þe erth fallis,
> Brak, & so it wele burde & brast all e-soundir;
> þan wendis þar-out a litill worm & wald it eft enter,
> And or scho hit in hire hede a hard deth suffris.
> (*WA* 509-512)

It is prophesied from this occurrence that Alexander will be a powerful conqueror, but death will prematurely end his career. The entire question of Alexander's half-supernatural origin through his father situates the narrative close to the controversial topic of the mother of Richard le Coer de Lyon. As has been argued here in the discussion of *Richard*, the Mélusine narrative entered the Middle English romance, but only partly, so as not to undermine the ruler's position within the category of natural rather than supernatural. A similar strategy is applied both in *The wars of Alexander*, where the topic of origin is developed in detail, and in *Kyng Alisaunder*, which like *Richard le Coer de Lyon* attempts to obscure the question of the unusual parentage of the central character. Nonetheless, in *Richard* the purpose of obscuring the question of the actual identity of the king's mother became more ideological, as we said earlier; Richard had to be classified as "the same" in order to confirm the validity of his combat against the cultural and ethnic others and his portrayal had to separate him from the category of Frenchness that his historical mother represented. Here a different solution to the problem of the natural or supernatural origin is applied: Philip acknowledges Alexander as his own son despite the child's actual roots, which the king may be at least dimly aware of. What is more, in the Middle English Alexander romances the issue of otherness is more tangled than in *Richard*, as they do not have *Richard*'s openly ideologically laden, proto-nationalistic, ring to them and no questioning of national or cultural origin is even vaguely alluded to.

In *Kyng Alisaunder* Neptanabus first charms the Greek queen Olympias with his herbs before he seduces her, which at least partly exculpates the woman, because she cannot fully control herself under the circumstances:

> His leue tok Neptanabus
> To his yn wel irrous
> Herbs he tok in an herber
> And stamped heom in amorter
> And wrong hit in abox
> After he tok virgyn wax
> And made apopet after þe quene
> His ars table he can vn wreone
> þe quen is name in þe wax he wrot
> Whil hit was sumdel hot
> Jn abed he hit dyȝt
> Al aboute wiþ candel lyȝt
> And spreynd þer on of þe herbus
> þus charmed Neptanabus
> (*KA* 327-340)

Only sophisticated magic tricks, it seems, could force the queen to obey the will of Nectanabus in disguise, so he imitates Amon, here the Roman god Jupiter Ammon (Smithers 1961a: xv).[105] All this happens so that the Egyptian could

---

105 Chism claims that it is rather the Macedonian sun-god Amon here (2002:138).

gain access to the queen's body. Importantly, Neptanabus drugs her and only later enchants himself in order to become a dragon ("Hire þouȝt adragon a doun lyȝt/To hire chaumbre he made his flyȝt") (*KA* 345-346) so that Olympias believed that she was visited by the deity.[106] The scene of the quasi-supernatural amorous encounter is graphic and suffused with eroticism:

> Mony siþes he hire kust
> And faste in his armes he hire þreost
> And went away so dragon wild
> And grete he laft hire wiþ child
> (*KA* 349-352)

Alexander's body will therefore be a hybrid between the Greek identity of his mother and the complicated identity of his biological father, combining in itself Egyptian blood and a curious mixture of the horned god Amon with a dragon, whose form the alleged god adopts.

The son of a quasi-god and the queen of Macedon is born with accompanying "lascis fra þe heuyn,/ thonere" (*WA* 553-554) and his physicality is accordingly supernatural:

> þe fax on his faire hede was ferly to schawe,
> Large lyons lockis þat lange ere & scharpe;
> With grete glesenand eȝen grymly he lokis,
> þat ware as blackenand briȝt as blesand sternes
> (*WA* 601-604)

His "wald-eȝed" (*WA* 608) face, that is, characterized by *heterophthalmia*, expresses otherness, even if the otherness is positive as it will manifest itself in great deeds and imperial victories (Gerritsen – Melle 1998:17). When Alexander grows up, "in anters of armes all men he passes" (*WA* 656). This could suggest the skills of a typical hero from the ancient Greek culture if it were not for the bizarre nature of his physicality that the the text impresses on the audience. Alexander is neither an entirely alien figure in the culture into which he is born nor an entirely familiar one, since the uncanny elements of his body imply that he cannot be just like any other son of a powerful ruler in the Greek world. In *Politics* Aristotle claimed that a Greek body was perfect, as it was unaffected by the extremities of the cold North or those of the sultry South. The bodies of barbarians, by contrast, were thought by him to be more "embodied, because the mark of deviation is imprinted upon flesh and soul", as Cohen summarizes the thesis (2006:32). As a result, the physicality of Alexander could indicate his

---

106 Smithers specifies the magician's corporeality as the lower bodily parts resembling those of a dragon and the upper ones adopting the likeness of a ram, clearly designating the deity as the first identification of whom Nectanabus enchants himself into (1961a:xv).

partly barbarian origin, if not for the fact that he was necessary as the heir to the throne of Macedon and his otherness could not be emphasized under the political circumstances.

As has been argued above, there are many medieval Alexanders and the Alexanders we possess are those of various faces. Z. David Zuwiyya insists that the Arabic texts about Alexander were numerous and they included the image of the ruler that originated on the one hand from a Persian legend and on the other hand from those written in al-Andalus; they were also mingled with elements from Pseudo-Callisthenes (2011:73). The Arabic authors customarily gave Alexander a lineage from Spain or North Africa and made him a Muslim hero (Zuwiyya 2011:74). The image of Alexander in those texts was entirely positive, in contrast to the ancient sources and their medieval descendants. The Stoic, i.e. Seneca's, and the Peripatetic, i.e. Ciceronian, criticism of Alexander entered the medieval European vision of the ruler, because medieval moralists relied heavily on those sources (Cary 1956:81).[107] In the ancient tradition Alexander was vicious due to the influence of Fortune, which was later difficult to reconcile with the medieval idea of Divine Providence (Cary 1956:81). In oriental texts Alexander accomplished miracles on behalf of God (Cary 1956:81), which could explain the rift that exists between that tradition and the medieval one. In the latter Alexander was usually portrayed as the epitome of pride (Cary 1956:141), a vice that had to be chastized, in contrast to humility and ascetism, attributed to Alexander's interlocutor Diogenes. As a result, some Christian elements could be found in Alexander's biography, even if those elements could not be attributed to the ruler himself (Cary 1956:83). Nevertheless, neither *Kyng Alisaunder* nor *The wars of Alexander* are works of Christian moralists. Instead, they offer a narrative of adventures that lead to political power in a world which is uniformly heathen. What remains highly debatable is the issue of Alexander's pagan or "proto-Christian" identity, which anachronistically appears in those medieval texts, despite his having lived before the advent of Christianity.

Alexander was usually given the type of identity which was convenient for the authors of a given text; for instance, as we have noted above, in Arabic texts he was a Muslim hero whose religious orthodoxy was taken for granted. It is intriguing how the Christian authors of *Kyng Alisaunder* and *The wars of Alexander* handled the historical fact that Alexander predated Christianity. The usual manner of coping with this problem was either to direct criticism against the ruler's pagan pride and arrogance (as the Church Fathers, Fulgentius and St. Jerome, did) (Cary 1956:141) or to acknowledge his virtues despite his heathen

---

107 Cary adds Valerius Maximus to the list of Alexander's critics, writing that the philosopher's attitude anthologized the Stoic and the Peripatetic approach (1956:82).

identification, which denoted a non-anachronistic perspective on those who lived before Jesus was born. After all, most writers admitted that Alexander must have been entirely pagan (Cary 1956:181). Cary writes about two groups of medieval religious authors, the moralists and the theologians, who were not entirely critical of Alexander, either: even though the moralists followed the Peripatetic approach, the theologians slightly softened the import of the Stoic disapproval of the ruler (1956:142). This meant that late medieval writers understood that Alexander had lived in times when Christianity was unknown. To be sure, some of them attempted to attach a Christian meaning to a narrative which was primarily pagan. David Ashurst comes up with a fine example of the Christian outlook inherent in the Old English *Letter of Alexander to Aristotle*, where the issue of power and mortality is touched upon; he writes that the *Letter* includes a Christian perspective when the king calmly meditates upon his imminent death and reminisces on his past glory (2011:262). "And to me the swift ending of my life was not so much pain as the fact that I had achieved less glory than I would have wished" (Orchard 1995:253) is a phrase that sounds both Stoical and spiritual in a more Christian manner. No one achieves everything they aspire to in life, but all people should look upon death with the same composure as Alexander, the medieval writer seems to be saying.

The issue of Alexander's heathenism appears to have been a part of a wider debate. When discussing oriental romances and whether they could be situated within the historical context of medieval Europe, a place pervaded by Arabic learning and literature, it is advisable to remember the image from Dante's *La divina commedia*, in which Avicenna and Averroes are also situated in the Inferno, like Mohammad and his son-in-law Ali, but the former can be found in its First Circle, where virtuous heathens reside, rather than in the regions where the disembowelment that happens to the Prophet is not uncommon.[108] The more lenient punishment that the Arabic philosophers receive has usually been interpreted as an illustration of the idea that even pagans deserve salvation if they have enriched the Christian European world of philosophy and proto-science, at the time understood as two co-existent undercurrents of learning. The Muslim thinkers had the right to be seen as less hostile to the Christian world than Mohammad and Ali, respectively a false prophet and the perpetrator of a schism within Islam itself, Shiites. According to most medieval Christians, the two sowed disorder and chaos and built a complex religious system that threatened medieval Europe politically, if not religiously. However, these stereotypes did not account for the influence of Arabic learning on Europe at the time. In the Inferno Avicenna and Averroes do not belong to the makers of

---

108 Interestingly, Saladin is also granted a place in this less atrocious circle of the Inferno.

discord, but to the poets, "the noble school of that lord of loftiest song that flies like an eagle above the rest" (Sinclair 1961:63)[109] and the philosophers, Socrates and Plato, "Democritus, who ascribes the world to chance, Diogenes, Anaxagoras, and Thales, Empedocles, Heraclitus, and Zeno . . . Orpheus, Cicero, Linus, and Seneca the moralist, Euclid the geometer, and Ptolemy, Hippocrates, Avicenna, Galen, and Averroes" (Sinclair 1961:65).[110] The lenient treatment of the "virtuous heathens" in *La divina commedia* must be Dante's commentary on a discussion which was conducted from the twelfth century onwards: the question was whether to "incorporate the pagan and Hebrew past into the Christian cultural framework", as Schildgen summarizes it (2001:14). The gist of the argument consists in the thesis that "moral Jews and pagans, who had lived before Christ, had equal access to salvation" (Schildgen 2001:14). In Dante no equal access to salvation is postulated, but the noble heathens are partly acquitted, since their learning constitutes one of the cornerstones of medieval culture. In the debate in question the group is extended to "those who . . . never encountered Christianity but were nonetheless just" (Schildgen 2001:15). Dante enlarges the group even further, to include those who had access to Christianity because they lived in the territory of Europe: they remained Muslim, but their learning was valuable for Christians.

To cope with the problem of Alexander's heathenism we should adopt a broader perspective. If the Arabic philosophers who transferred ancient learning to the Christian Middle Ages were viewed fairly liberally by Dante (and Menocal argues that the Arabic commentaries on Aristotle were more widely read than translations of Aristotle through the Arabic language) (Menocal 1987:10), the pagans who did not have access to Christianity since they lived before Christ's birth could receive even more indulgent treatment and be quite artificially incorporated into the Christian culture. To exemplify this with a well-known text, *The Physician's tale* offers a fairly tolerant perspective on the ordeal of the pagan character, Virginia, even if this tolerance amounts to comparing her to Christian figures.[111] In the tale a fair daughter of judge

---

109 ["... la bella scola/ di quel signor dell'altissimo canto/ che sovra li altri com'aquila vola" (IV:94-96)] (Sinclair 1961:62)
110 ["Democrito, che 'l mondo a caso pone,/ Dïogenès, Anassagora e Tale,/ Empedoclès, Eraclito e Zenone/ . . . Orfeo,/ Tullio e Lino e Seneca morale;/ Euclide geomètra e Tolomeo,/ Ipocràte, Avicenna e Galïeno,/ Averois" (VI:136-143)] (Sinclair 1961:64).
111 The topic of sympathy to pagans in *The legend of good women* appears more multi-faceted, since it could be shown that hagiography is only one of the numerous sources of inspiration and, apart from minor subjects such as the association between the Dreamer's daisy and St. Margaret (Delany 1994:67) or as suffering as an exculpating condition, the Christianizing of those tormented women by Chaucer cannot be proved.

Virginius did not allow judge Apius to possess her; in the manner of Christian female martyr saints she chose death rather than the ignominy and dishonour of becoming the mistress of a man who was obsessed with her. In accordance with Chaucer's politics of religious sameness and difference, Virginia was not inferior in her sacrifice to the Christian virgins who later experienced similar plights, even though she could not have access to the truth of the Christian God. Despite those chronological impediments to seeing her as a martyr for faith, Chaucer grants her a number of qualities which could easily pertain to female saints:

> As wel in goost as body chast was she,
> For which she floured in virginitee
> With alle humylitee and abstinence,
> With alle attemperaunce and pacience,
> With mesure eek of beryng and array.
>   (VI:43-47)

Furthermore, she is described as "so prudent and so bountevous" (VI:110) and, most importantly for the message of the tale, a " gemme of chastitee" (VI:223), because carnal purity appears to be more important than human life.[112] In contrast to the shameless, "lecherus", Apius (VI:266), she prefers to be slain by her own father rather than to submit to the judge's carnal desire. Apius argues that Virginius's daughter is in reality a slave that he stole from the judge; the dishonest lawyer passes a verdict requiring a remittal of Virginia to her alleged owner, namely himself. She anachronistically evokes the Christian God ("Blissed be God that I shal dye a mayde!") (VI:248), prior to being cold-bloodedly executed of her by her father. Subsequently, Apius is punished for his immorality. Chastity emerges from this tale as a quality that absolves Virginia from the sin of paganism. The pattern of a "consecrated virgin" narrative is artificially applied to the plot, making Virginia more than just a "righteous heathen", since she adopts the status as a proto-Christian martyr saint, in spite of the narrative having come from Titus Livius' Roman history. She is absolved of heathenism and the absolution probably stems from her sacrifice.

If one ruminates on how such a non-moralist writer as Chaucer imposed a Christian message on a pagan story, one finds it not surprising that religious writers seriously debated Alexander's heathenism. However, Cary controversially claims that secular writers composing texts about Alexander, such as the two authors of the romances we are considering here, hardly ever dwelt on the issue (156:181). Indeed, it needs to be admitted that instead of

---

112 Lomperis notes another contradiction, namely that the tale focuses on the attractiveness of Virginia's body only to condemn the carnal desire of Apius afterwards (1993:21).

some thorough consideration of the ruler's heathenism they presented a confusion of images referring to Alexander's religious beliefs. In *The wars of Alexander*, more obviously based on Pseudo-Callisthenes, or rather on the narrative's reworking in *Historia de preliis*, Alexander persists in his paganism as he prays to the Egyptian god Amon, around whom Anectanabus's trick revolved:

> Seches þar to a synagoge him-selfe & his princes,
> Amon þar awen god at þai honoure myȝt.
> And so to þe temple as he tiȝt with his tid Erles,
> þan metis him myddis þe way was meruale to sene,
> A hert with a huge hede þe hareest on erthe,
> Was to be-hald as a harrow for-helid ouer þe tyndis;
> . . .
>
> (*WA* 1058-1064)

Alexander shoots the hart with an arrow, symbolically breaking the association that exists between his own body and the world of beasts, in his life represented by the ram-headed body of god Amon, whom Anactenabus impersonated in order to sire the ruler.[113] Then the hound is "aires . . . on ser Alexander till Amon temple" (*WA* 1072) and subsequently a new relationship is formed between the ruler and Amon. Alexander no longer owes his existence to this god, since Olympias accepted Anectanabus in her bedroom only because he was disguised as Amon. Instead, the ruler voluntarily subjects himself to this deity, making his companions and all who belong to his people subservient to it. The natural relationship between the bestial body of Amon and Alexander's origin is broken and it gives way to a more political one. Alexander as a political leader will be helped by Amon, as it happens when he dreams about the god giving him useful advice:

> þe same niȝt in his slepe to him soda[n]ly a-perid
> Amon, his awen god in aung[e]ls wyse,
> In a mery mantill of mervailous hewis,
> Meuand as a Messedone in Marcure fourme;
> Said: "vn-to Susys my son na sandisman þou send,
> Bot fange my fyngour to þe fast & fand furth þi-selfe,
> Clethe þe with my conyschaunce & for na care drede,
> I hete þe haly my help na harme sall þou suffire."
>
> (*WA* 2862-2869)

Alexander cannot be Amon's son in any sense, even a symbolical one, any longer, but he remains under the god's protection as his acolyte. Praying to the

---

113 Amon could also be represented as bull-headed or symbolized by a goose.

god works wonders, because the dream visions that the Macedonian ruler experiences allow him to wage wars and administer his lands more efficiently. The non-Christian perspective on Alexander was undoubtedly realistic if we consider the historical ruler's intention to be deified himself, which for religious authors accentuated his central vice, pride (Cary 1956:110). He probably believed in the existence of a close connection between himself and gods that was confirmed by his victories, which were quick and ended in the death of his antagonists, Darius of Persia and Porus of India.

Nonetheless, even though *The wars of Alexander* were relatively free from openly Christian elements, it relies to some extent on *Fuerre de Gadres*, where the pagan (or, more probably, Muslim) ruler Balaam appeared. *The wars of Alexander* includes this episode as well, which makes it approach the medieval Christian ideology, since Alexander attacks Tyre and breaks through the wall of the city to kill his enemy:

> þe first modire son he mett oþire man outhire,
> Was Balaan þe bald berne as þe boke tellis,
> And him he settis on a saute & sloȝe him belyue,
> And werpid him out ouir þe wall in-to þe wild streme.
> (*WA* 1429-1432)

Jettisoning the enemy's body as if it were merely litter to be discarded is a scene repeating what befalls many other Saracen bodies in the romances that are Middle English renderings of the *chansons de geste*. In the *Firumbras*-group Floripas dumps the bodies of her enemies from the window: this is the fate that befalls her female servant Brytamon and the prison guard who bars her way to Charlemagne's knights. Not only does the name of the adversary imply a connection with the *Firumbras*-group; so does some conventional behaviour adopted towards him, which was probably intended to be humorous. The scene, however, subtly questions Alexander's paganism. The episode is not an example of one pagan ruler attacking another, but the case of a righteous monarch, who stands for "us", ravaging the forces of the ruler whose name sounds not only like Laban, the name of Jacob's uncle who was conventionally portrayed in oriental garb, but also like the name of one of the biblical devils, Balam.[114] Yet the difference between "us" and "them" does not run along the lines of religion here, but again uses the paradigm of the civilized and the barbarian deriving from the ancient Greek culture. This is what distinguishes this subplot from similar scenes recurrent in the Middle English versions of *chansons de geste*.

---

114 Rembrandt van Rijn's etching *Three oriental figures (Jacob and Laban)* (1641) pairs the biblical Laban with the figure of an Easterner with a headgear.

Kyng Alisaunder also includes a reference to the ruler known both from the *Firumbras*-group and *Fuerre de Gadres*, even though here, as in *The sowdone of Babylone*, Balaam becomes Laban. Alexander is not the one who confronts him in battle, but one of his men, Philotas, "mette Laban þe duyk/ And baþed his spere in his bouk" (*KA* 3234-3235). The separation into the civilized "us" and the pagan, demonic "them" is also preserved in this romance. Even though in *Kyng Alisaunder* the question of Alexander's paganism is not as clear as in *The wars of Alexander*, in a semi-moralistic manner the anonymous author refers to the legendary ruler's religion when he ends the romance with the phrase "Alisaunder me reowiþ þyn endyng/ þat þou nadest dyȝed in cristenyng" (*KA* 401-402, from the Auchinleck manuscript). Cary summarizes this important passage by stating that Alexander's death is lamented because he did not die a Christian (1956:239). The overall impression that is unexpectedly imposed on the romance's audience is that Alexander could hypothetically be like Christian heroes and that his paganism deprived him of an even more valuable life that he could have lived. At the end of the romance paganism is therefore presented as a minor condition which prevents one from developing one's virtues to the full. When the hero dies, it is as pity that his body has not been christened, as the sacrament keeps the soul from perishing after death.

The Christian perspective emerges in the very characteristic ending of *Kyng Alisaunder*, but, if we look into it more closely, it is also implied in other places in the plot. What distinguishes the ruler from other potent monarchs is his relative chastity which agrees with Christian ideals, especially if we analyze the episode with queen Candance, the archetype of an oriental seductress. She embodies the myth of Eastern lasciviousness which is, according to Said, present in orientalism as a manner of thinking about the Orient, as we have already seen. In the Middle Ages the myth of female seductiveness was repeated in what has been termed *la belle juive* or *die schöne Judin* type, a representation reminiscent of orientalist stereotyping, though it did not refer to others inhabiting remote regions of the world, but to Europe's familiar others, the Jews.[115] If Candance is presented as an oriental seductress, her portrayal does not radically depart from other women embodying otherness, namely Jewish women living in medieval Europe. Candance may be a development of the idea that medieval Christians had of Jewesses as women who lived near them, but belonged to a different culture. Apart from her highly attractive appearance, *la belle juive* was also expected to be treacherous and to change sides easily, like Floripas from the *Firumbras* romances. Her disloyalty towards her own people was excused by Christians, but

---

[115] This character type in later literature has been thoroughly discussed by Lampert (1998:254-270).

it never made the Jewess exactly the same as the Christian she became smitten with. Candance from the Alexander romances continues this type of representation: she combines seductiveness and treachery. However, unlike the beautiful Jewesses or the Floripas-type characters, she does not betray her own people, but tries to suborn Alexander to her own scheme of political domination.

Significantly, there exists no association between oriental women and the phenomenon of Courtly Love that Lacan probed with his theory in *The ethics of psychoanalysis* (1992:139-154), but the two types, the Lady and the seductress, undoubtedly must be situated on the two opposite ends of the continuum of female otherness. This is how Žižek comments on it: "the Lady in courtly love loses concrete features and is addressed as an abstract Ideal . . . However, this abstract character of the Lady has nothing to do with spiritual purification; it rather points toward the abstraction that pertains to a cold, distanced, inhuman partner – the Lady is by no means a warm, compassionate, understanding fellow-creature" (2005:89). An Eastern woman such as Candance also belongs to the world of the court, even if it is an oriental one, but she is no cold partner, but rather a self-conscious seductress. She does not employ what Lacan termed "the techniques of courtly love", that is, "techniques of holding back, of suspension, of *amor interruptus*" (1992:152). On the contrary, what may thwart the love between the European and the woman are only external circumstances, such as the arrival of a son who bears a serious grudge against the conqueror. The politics of difference shows a face unfamiliar to us so far in this study: Alexander is separated from the love-crazed Candance not because of her different religion or ethnicity, but because the circumstances are not propitious for their union. In this sense her character is not modeled on *la belle juive* or the figure of Floripas and her like, because they attempted to transcend the borders separating them from their loved ones by becoming like them (including the treachery that they committed because of the love).

Cary writes that ancient historians attacked real-life Alexander for his lechery, which was, after all, a type of behaviour tolerated in a powerful conqueror (1956:99). But both the anonymous authors of the Middle English romances abandon this tradition, presenting instead a relatively chaste Alexander juxtaposed with a lecherous woman. Cary describes the tradition that was conveyed in *Historia de preliis*:

> In the legend . . . , Candance is a queen who has a portrait painted of Alexander, and who, by a series of complicated events, manoeuvres him into an embarrassing position, and recognizes him by means of his portrait when recognition may mean death to him from her angry son Carator. No words of love pass between them; on the contrary, Alexander is furious with himself for having let a woman get the better of him (1956:219).

In *Kyng Alisaunder* Candance has the portrait of the ruler painted and then she meets Alexander in person. She wants to spend time with him, which makes her another seductress of the Middle English oriental romance, similar to Rimnild, the "miri maiden" from *Horn Childe*. Candance appears to be courteous, but her openness towards strangers reveals to the readers that she is interested in ensnaring them:

> He dude al þe ladyes wille
> Vundur couertoure ful stille
> Mony ny3t and mony day
> þus þey duden heore play
> Jn halle a day he sat hire by
> And any3t in bedde sikirly
> (*KA* 6441-6446)

The encounter must certainly end in love according to the romance author, which ultimately reveals the seductive nature of the Ethiopian queen. Alexander submits to her desire, but, very characteristically, is not active in relationships with her; nor does he cling to the relationship. The bliss of Candance ends when her son Candulek, married to the late king Porus's daughter, arrives in order to expose Alexander's real identity as a conqueror and usurper, so the ruler needs to leave. *The wars of Alexander* presents the episode of an interrupted love affair in more detail, since first Alexander exchanges letters with Candance, then adopts the identity of an "Antiochus" and visits her after she has adorned herself with a "Robe all of rede gold & þan a riche mantill,/ A croune & a corecheffe clustert with gemmes" (*WA* 5248-5249). After her initial diplomatic behaviour towards him, Alexander has to be slain and is led by Serapis into the wilderness, where the appearance of snakes and griffons thwarts the plans of Candance's men. The letters to Candance, the queen of Meroe (the present-day Ethiopia) (Stoneman 2011:5), undoubtedly imitate a similar episode, previous to it, when "to þe qwene of Amazoyne þan makes him þis pistill" (*WA* 3708). Alexander's chastity is clearly emphasized in all these passages, in contrast to the stereotypical oriental lechery. Eastern women either inhabit places where strange creatures, such as griffons, may be met, or they are monstrous themselves, like the Amazons.

The issue of Alexander's religion and potentially Christian virtues may be complicated, but what undoubtedly places him on the side of the same rather than the other, despite his confused background, is his conquests. The episode most readily associated with Alexander in various sources is the scene of the encounter with Gog and Magog and the handling of these two tribes. The Marvels of the East, another topic related to him, deserves separate attention. Gog and Magog were believed to be two uncivilized, hostile tribes after the biblical references to them in Ezekiel, xxxviii, 1-6, and in the Apocalypse, Revelations xx, 1-7. There the names meant all the kings and tribes that were hostile to Israel. The Christian perspective is puzzling, as it somehow puts the equal sign between the biblical people of Israel and the peoples governed by Alexander and imperiled by the savage tribes. An account of this part of the story can be found first in Josephus, where Sythians are separated with a wall by Alexander and where they are identified with Gog and Magog (Cary 1956:130), and the account from the Jewish tradition became popular in the Middle Ages due to the version in *Reuelationes*, ascribed falsely to Methodius, bishop of Patara (Cary 1956:18). The medieval legend coalesced in it with the concept from the Apocalypse, in which Gog and Magog were said to be separated from the civilized world by a wall that would be broken down by them upon the end of the world (Cary 1956:130). Testifying to the existence of medieval anti-Judaism, the myth of Gog and Magog was combined with the legend of the Jewish Ten Tribes confined beside the Caspian Sea, who besought Alexander to liberate them, but he refused as he was aware of God's anger towards them (Cary 1956:132). As Benjamin Braude writes, the legend of the Ten Tribes was based on "the prophecy that in the time of Antichrist the Ten Lost Tribes of Israel, after centuries of captivity in a land beyond Cathay, would finally emerge and aided by their co-religionists throughout the world wreak vengeance upon the Christians, treating them as they have been treated" (1996:140).

Kyng Alisaunder groups the legendary Gog and Magog with the "Getas", Turks, and other uncivilized tribes together, ommitting altogether the association between Gog and Magog and the Jewish Ten Tribes:

> He by sette þe see and þe lond
> Wiþ botemay and mace strong
> Taracoutes and Magogecas
> And afolk me clepiþ Vetas
> Al blak so cole brond
> And row3h as beore to þe hond
> Turk he by sette wiþ heom
> Grete werriours and dou3ty men
> (*KA* 4980-4987)

The tribes that need to be confined in the regions that Alexander reaches by the sea seem more specific than the mysterious "Gog and Magog" would have been if they had appeared there by themselves. The latter are made more historical by reference to Turks, who became central to Western thinking about the Orient in the Renaissance, when they started to pose a political threat to Europe. It should be recalled that the Turks replaced the less specific "Saracens" at the turn of the

Middle Ages and the Renaissance (Daniel 1984:8).[116] The security of Europe against those tribes that Alexander guaranteed confirms his status as a civilized ruler whose orderly reign is contrasted with the disorder and confusion among the barbarians whom he separates from the rest by building a wall. They are separated from those whom Alexander represents, restating the idea that the mixing of Western people with Eastern is really a sign of the Apocalypse approaching. Alexander's identity as a ruler whose ethnic background could situate him between savagery and civilized quality is finally linked with his cultured position in the world he inhabits. The dichotomy between the European ruler with his army and the exotic peoples whom he conquers is reaffirmed in the passages that follow: "Jn Egipte is folk of selcouþ kynde/ Jn oure boks as we fyndiþ" (*KA* 5028-5029), "Oure boke saiþ þat ilke men/ Buþ ycleped Garmacien" (*KA* 5033-5034), "Anoþer folk is by syde þis/ þat beon y cleped Cenophalis" (*KA* 5042-5043), "Anoþir folk þer is by syde/ Azachy men clepiþ heom wyde" (*KA* 5048-5049). The last group listed by the narrator, "Azachy", sustains itself with "olifans" (*KA* 5051), which makes it even more distant from the European habits and mores, as those people do not feed on "civilized" foodstuffs at all. The fact of one "monstrous race" feeding on another, this time consisting of animals, is significant. It is not enough that they represent a monstrous race themselves; they also have to enhance this effect by sustaining themselves with the flesh of other monsters. It needs to be restated that medieval Christian writers were obsessed with the eating habits of cultural others, as Beckett claims in her discussion of Old English literature. She exemplifies this point with descriptions of Muslims fasting (2003:1), but, as has been noted above, the interest did not refer exclusively to Saracen religious practices. It involved other cultural and religious groups, such as the Mongols of *The Squire's tale*, where the account of feasting includes theories put forward by missionaries to Tartary. After all, as has been argued in preceding sections of this study, your diet was deemed to shape who you were. The case of monstrous Indian races devouring one another is no exception to this assumption.

The author of *Kyng Alisaunder* grades otherness, adding to what has already been called a monstrous race of creatures walking on their hands:

Anoþir folk þer is stronge men and foule
þey buþ long and blak and lokiþ as an houle

---

[116] It does not mean that Turks were not identifiable as ethnic others in the Middle Ages, since, after all, it was the Seljuk Turks who ended the existence of Byzantium; the recipe for a Turk's head that McDonald quotes before proceeding to a discussion of *Richard le Coer de Lyon* as one of the "pulp fictions of medieval England" shows that Turks were thought to be as alien to European culture as other groups of Muslims (2004:130).

þey no haueþ camayle no olifaunt
No kow no hors auenaunt
On hold þey creopuþ at o word
(*KA* 5054-5058)

"Mauritymy" (*KA* 5065), who "ale þey beon Saracyns" (*KA* 5072), are portrayed as perhaps even stranger than the hand-walking people, since they pray to Bacchus and Apolyn, in an allusion to the myth of Muslim idolatry. The list is made complete with "Agriofagy" (KA 5081), "Archapites" (*KA* 5083), and *cenocephali*, whose "visege after hound y wis" (*KA* 5091) and who bark in order to communicate among themselves. The mores of those various "tribes", and others who are treated more descriptively, are discussed, but the overall aim of this introduction of the people inhabiting India is likely twofold: on the one hand such fictional reports are intended to provoke wonder in the audience, because they are distanced from the world described here, even if physically the "Saracen" world of al-Andalus was relatively near them at the time when *Kyng Alisaunder* was written. After all, as Cary insists, "the principle intention of all this [secular Alexander- A.C.] literature is to amuse" (1956:163). On the other, however, Danielle Buschinger noted that romances about Alexander the Great could have a political aim behind them (2011:301-306). The Wonders of the East stories, as much as generally all medieval Alexander romances, could also inspire some commentary on the audience's present or at least on some phenomena which did not have to be directly related to the topic of the Orient. The reference to "wild men of þe wast & women e-bland/ With sex handis" (*WA* 3910-3911) in *The wars of Alexander* may be therefore read as a statement about the normativity of the body of Alexander and those of his men, and about the consequent validity of his conquest. The political aim behind this presentation of the diverse "monstrous races" that Alexander encounters seems to be mostly to negate the otherness of the ruler that was first implied by the story of his supernatural begetting and on creating the impression that the world ruled by Alexander is really "ours". However, the act of westernizing Alexander is not artificial, but very likely offers us a different version of orientalism from that which was postulated by Said; negativity is not its dominating principle here, but negative references are marginal, especially if we compare them with the positivity embedded in the fascination with the marvellous.

The confrontation of Alexander with the Marvels of the East is precisely the point at which we must realize the inadequateness of what Said himself called the "reductive formulae" employed by the West towards the East. The standard gesture of degrading the Orient cannot be spotted here; instead, a fairly nuanced vision of all that is not Western Europe, whether we subsume it under the label "the Orient" or divide it, after Akbari, into Asia and Africa as contrasted with

Europe, or into the West, the East, and the North (2000:19-34), emerges from this confrontation. The West does not seem to be all that exists or everything valuable that exists. Instead, the self has to renegotiate its identity upon meeting with the other. This is precisely a type of thinking about the same and the other that originates from the same tradition as *The travels of sir John Mandeville*. Lampert-Weissig cites Benjamin Braude, who claimed that Said could not have written *Orientalism* had he read *The travels* (1996:135, quoted in Lampert-Weissig 2010:103), while she herself plausibly argues that *The travels* would have reshaped Said's theories into something more nuanced (2010:103). Again, Said's dichotomic thinking is questioned and the need for another take on orientalism, more focused on the specificity of the Middle Ages, postulated. The existence of the Marvels of the East tradition testifies to the heterogeneity of medieval texts treating of the Orient. Even as a textual construction, the Orient of medieval literature remains incomplete without a more positive perspective on the Marvels of the East and the pleasure that the Westerner takes in witnessing them and participating in this world. Even though the monstrous races are mostly misrepresentations rather than representations, since mimesis is not their goal, they inspire positive emotional reactions and portray the Orient as neither evil nor even slightly warped.

Still, even though it does not affect the Marvels of the East section, racialism is present in various other contexts in the two Middle English Alexander romances, because the issue of blackness reappears in them. Positivity and negativity about the East are consequently interspersed, since the Orient of the Alexander romances could not be fully detached from the more common representations of Eastern things as negative and even threatening. The racialism flows through the romances as a subtext, as in this passage from the Laud manuscript:

> þo com þere goande a men ferlich,
> Also blak as any pycch.
> Caluȝ was his heuede swerd
> And to his nauel henge his berd.
> He ne had noiþere nekk ne þrote-
> His heued was in his body yshote.
>   (*KA* 5938-5943)

The blackness of the adversary is complemented by an unusual beard and, which makes this character fairly monstrous, he has no neck. What Frederickson defined as medieval "Negrophilia" cannot be found here in any respect, and his skin colour makes this antagonist of Alexander monstrous and terrifying (2002:26). The first impression upon contact with the black man could be that of fear and uneasiness about the unknown that he represents. Perhaps blackness connotes ominous qualities as much as the black colour of the water in the lake does, from which "of þe water drynk ne taste" (*KA* 5061), as it is dangerous. The Muslim adversary is here a real person rather than a fantasy object. Even though the black Muslim is not a giant, as we could be led to believe if the text were one of the Middle English versions of the *chansons de geste*, his body is portrayed as repugnant rather than promising anything, as was the case with Canace in *The Squire's tale*. No ambiguity may be found in his characterization, even though ambivalence is traceable even in the presentations of the black giantesses from the *Firumbras* romances, because they are both monstrous and tender towards their offspring.

The conquest of India also includes episodes that recur in diverse other renderings of the Alexander narrative. The defective fragment of the M text includes a reference to "two quenes of Amazeyne/ Wiþ twenty þousand to hire banere/ Faire maydenes of whyte chere/ þat weore wyȝt in bataile/ And comly in bed saunfaile" (*KA* 4775-4779), but it is not preceded by any reference to the context in which Alexander meets the Amazons, since this is how the preserved M text starts.[117] The list of unusual women continues with women growing, like mandrakes, from the ground:

> Verrament þer he fond
> Wymmen growying out of þe ground
> Of somme þe hed pud owt
> Somme to þe breost wiþ owte dout
> And also somme to þe knowe
> And somme to nauel y growe
> And some weore y growe al out
> And ȝeode and romed al aboute
> Faire wymmen heo buþ of pris.
> (*KA* 5210-5218)

The difference possibly makes the women more attractive in the eyes of the Westerners visiting India. Even if they are compared to manticores, the Sphynx-like creatures from Persian legends, they are not manticores themselves, as the latter belong to a different group of marvels of India, "addren and monecores/... worm cales and manticores/ Broune lyouns" (*KA* 5815-5817). "Vnicornes" (*KA* 5819) are another species, enhancing the exotic quality of the place even further. Eastern women can be attractive even if, or perhaps precisely because, they grow like plants from the ground, as the text implies. Their bodies amaze the Westerners with their hybrid quality: they may be situated at an intersection

---

[117] The M version of the text are printed leaves in the British Museum, contained in the *Bagford Ballads*, vol. i, no. 27.

between humans and plants, which enhances their attractiveness, as they provoke wonder, which was considered highly desirable in medieval society.

To add another issue to this discussion of the function of the marvellous in Alexander romances, *The wars of Alexander* portrays *in extenso* the physicality of Porus, the king of India, who emerges from the text as a giant, that is, another representative of the monstrous races of India. The narrator attaches considerable importance to the question of physicality, which confirms the impression that Porus must be a giant or even a representative of the people who are quite monstrous, since "thre cubettis fra þe croune doun his cors had a lenghte" (*WA* 3987). Alexander is certainly more human than the king of India, which overcomes the previous, highly discomforting, first impression of his baby hair which resembled a lion's mane or that one of his eyes was different and had the qualities of the evil eye. "þe person of ser Porrus past him þat hiʒt twyse" (*WA* 3988), writes the author, excluding Porus from the category of fully human beings and admitting Alexander into it, even if this occurs somehow through the back door, because the Macedon ruler's humanity is not restated openly, in contrast to Porus's extra-human bodily size. Alexander is "litill & laghe" (*WA* 3985), which has a positive dimension, and these qualities by no means make him monstrous. Those whose bodies are marvellous may be admired and deemed attractive or feared, but they very often only establish Europeans within the category of the same more firmly, and the case of Alexander demonstrates this.

In *Kyng Alisaunder* Porus is slain by Alexander so that the Western hero could occupy the throne of India:

> Now is ded kyng Pors
> Alisaunder is kyng glorious
> He ʒeueþ londis he ʒeueþ rentis
> Stedis tresours warentmentis
> And makiþ iustice and constable
> And ouer al his lawe stable
> (*KA* 6160-6165)

Alexander cannot be seen as a stranger to the land any longer. He dominates it politically, taking over the treasure and, according to the proto-colonial discourse employed in this passage, giving the peoples of India justice and a stable law. He peoples the land (which should be identified with what is now Pakistan rather than with India itself) (Stoneman 2011:1) with his officials, introducing civilization to the place. The categories of the same and the other are blurred further, because the land is culturally conquered, but does this conquest make the monstrous races mentioned above less monstrous? Physical deformity is permanent, but what about the non-civilized nature of those peoples? And, returning to the issue of religion in the two Middle English romances, is Alexander's ultimate conquest of India a metaphor for the Christian expansion in heathen lands, so desirable for many religious and political leaders in the Middle Ages?

What also needs to be examined in a discussion of the same and the other in these romances is the functioning of various monsters in them, both in the short enumeration of monsters in the romances and in their long catalogue in *The travels of sir John Mandeville*. When broaching the monsters of *Kyng Alisaunder*, David Ashurst notes that "the long list of strange people may strike the modern reader as tedious"; the enumeration was cut shorter in the Lincoln's Inn Ms (Ashurst 2011:265). It is uncertain to what extent the catalogue of monsters in *The travels* could bore the text's audience and whether it could develop in them a positive image of the Orient. Various monstrous species appear both in *The travels* and in such romances as *The wars of Alexander*. In *The wars* there are women with "berdis to þe pappis" (*WA* 4117), who also appear in *The travels* as "women [who] shave their beards, and not men" (Moseley 1983:124). The phoenix, "the bird [who] comes and alights on the altar . . . and there he burns himself to ashes" (Moseley 1983:65), is granted more scope in *The wars*:

> þar bad a brid on a boghe a-bofe in þe topp,
> Was of a port of a paa with sike a proude crest,
> With bathe þe chekis & þe chauyls as a chekin brid,
> And all gilden was hire gorg with golden fethirs,
> All hire hames be-hind was hewid as a purpure.
> And all þe body & þe brest & on þe bely vndire
> Was finely florischt & faire with frekild pennys,
> Of gold graynes & of goules full of gray mascles.
> (*WA* 4982-4989)

Such sights make the king muse on the beauty of the Orient (since the king "wondire him thinke") (*WA* 4990) and they display the political and economic dimension of the conquest. Only such riches or the display thereof will make Alexander a truly powerful ruler in the eyes of the civilized world. Again, the question of the civilized or uncivilized identity is highlighted, when "Mandeville" refers to the customs of the island of Lamory, where

> þider gon merchauntes & bryngen with hein children to selle to hem of the contree & þei byȝen hem And ȝif þei eten hem anon, And ȝif þei ben fatte & þanne þei eten hem . . . And þei seyn þat it is the best flesch & the swettest of all the world (Hamelius 1919:119).

[Merchants bring children . . . to sell, and the people of the country buy them. Those that are plump they eat . . . And they say it is the best and sweetest meat of the world] (Moseley 1983:127).

The Orient is undoubtedly a place both fascinating and threatening, able to undergo the process of civilizing and dangerous in its uncivilized mores. Here, as in other oriental romances, what you eat may determine your identity, with a negative emphasis placed on the cannibalism of savages and the shockingly positive dimension of eating Saracen bodies if it is performed, as in *Richard*, by a Christian ruler.

According to Higgins, who analyzes the role of the traditional marvels, they are the text's "defining feature", since the identity of the narrator is constantly renegotiated in relation to those marvels (1997:143). The roster of monsters, however, is not as important as the relationship between "Mandeville" and the Orient (1997:144). Importantly, it often happens in *The travels* that "the ethnographic portrait of the other suddenly shifts to become a self-critical mirror" (Higgins 1997:117). The role of the self is constantly renegotiated and granted a different status, since the Western character does not appear fully Western if he voluntarily travels to the East, perhaps in search of some important part of his identity. *The travels* also briefly discusses Alexander in what Higgins terms the ruler's "heart changing encounters" with the people of Bragmey, Oxydrate, and Gysonophe (1997:229). Alexander's heart is changed upon coming to the East as he abandons his pride, comprehending the superiority of those tribes over the civilized world he comes from. The Bragmans (Brahmins) present themselves to the ruler in the letters they send to him, which touch Alexander to the heart:

And whan kyng ALISANDRE had rad þeise lettres he thoghte þat he scholde do gret synne for to trouble hem And þanne he sente hem surteez þat þei scholde not ben aferd of him & þat þei scholde kepen hire gode maneres & hire gode þees as þei hadden vsed before of custom & so he let hem allone (Hamelius 1919:196).

[And when King Alexander had seen their letters and read them, it seemed to him in his heart that it would be a great pity and great unmanliness to hurt or trouble such folk; and he granted them a guarantee of peace, and bade them to continue with their good living and follow their good customs without having any fear of him, for he would not harm them] (Moseley 1983:179).

The Oxidrace and the "Gynoscryphe" (generally known as Gymnosophists) follow the customs of the Brahmins as well, so "whan he saugh hire gret feyth & hire trouthe þat was among hem he seyde þat he wolde not greuen hem And bad hem aske of hym what þat þei wolde haue of him, richess or ony thing elles & þei scholde haue it with gode wille" (Hamelius 1919:196) [as soon as he saw their manner of life and their loyalty and love to each other, he said he would not harm them, but told them to ask of him what they would, and he would give it to them] (Moseley 1983:179). They ask for nothing, because they value neither riches nor political power, in which the authority of Alexander has been grounded. As a consequence, he realizes the extent of his pride upon contact with those "saintly" peoples of India, as Chism calls them, which changes his heart and perhaps allows him to peacefully ruminate on the brevity of life and inevitability of death when it comes later, once he realizes he has been poisoned (2002:127). Alexander features as a representative of the same here and the contrast that is created between him and the Brahmins and their like demonstrates the positive impact of the other on the same. The positivity of this image is highly striking, since the didactic function of this encounter is indubitable. Alexander was begotten by an Egyptian magician upon a Greek lady and he demonstrated his bodily difference already in his infant years, but the conquest of India evinced his Western-ness and the breach that separated him from the East.

As for Alexander's Western-ness, it was a category constantly confirmed by the text after the controversial scenes describing his biological father. The West and the East appear to be contrasted on the basis of the dichotomy between the natural and the supernatural. Despite the fact that Anactenabus is Alexander's begetter, Philip is consistently presented as his natural father, because he functions as his father in the social context after having accepted the infant as his own child. In contrast, Anactenabus became the father to Alexander only due to his supernatural tricks, the magic potions (or drugs) he administered to Olympias in *Kyng Alisaunder*, and the adoption of the shape of a revered deity. Alexander interrogates the bishop of Tripoli about the identity of his father:

> Kyng Alisaundre teris ganne stoppe
> And þus he saide to þe bishope
> Byshop he saide þer is asclaunder
> Y layd on me Kyng Alisaunder
> Y scholde beo byȝete amys
> Tel me who my fadir is
> Pryuely bytweone þe and me
> Þy trauaile schal Y ȝeilde þe
> Þe byschop graunteþ þe kynges talent
> And dude him on a vestement
> And made of a sarsynes wyse
> To Jubiter sacrifise
> After longe þe sacrefyeng
> He cam and saide to þe kyng
> How his fadir hette Felip
>   (*KA* 1545-1559)

This passage confirms the naturalness of Philip's fatherhood of Alexander, portraying Anactenabus's siring of him as unnatural and ultimately unimportant since Alexander was acknowledged by Philip, took over the throne after his death, and had earlier murdered the Egyptian magician by pushing him off a cliff and had found out about his parentage as Anactenabus was dying. Alexander's attachment to Philip was confirmed when Olympias participated in the intrigue planned by Pausanias, her Greek admirer, against Philip. "Kyng Felip was woundid verament/ Dely woundid" (*KA* 1340-1341) as a result of the plot which was to bring Pausanias and Olympias together. Alisaunder reacted at once against Pausanias: "his hed smot atwo" (*KA* 1352). Thus he reaffirmed his devotion to Philip, breaking all the associations between himself and the Eastern world to which Anactenabus belonged. The fully Westernized self may therefore encounter the creatures of the East from the point of view of someone entirely foreign to them in their marvellous nature.

Nevertheless, the peoples of India are not shown as uncultured, since their attitude to worldly power and riches becomes for Alexander a source of reflection on the values he pursues. As a result, those ethnic groups are neither monstrous nor need to be made more cultured. The conquest of India is not connected to the medieval idea of conquering and christening pagans, because Alexander acknowledges the superiority of Brahmins and their like despite their uncivilized way of life. No such reaction was possible in a bid to subject "heathens" to the will of Christian rulers, since the latter knew better what was necessary for the good of those who did not know Christian God. India becomes what Mary-Louise Pratt designated as the "contact zones", that is, "social spaces where disparate cultures meet, clash, and grapple with each other, often in highly asymmetrical relations of domination and subordination – such as colonialism and slavery" (2008:7).[118] The cultures of the Greek ruler of Macedon and other subdued places and the "exotic" cultures of India with their entire wealth and variety are presented as clashing against each other, but also influencing each other not only negatively, but also positively, as when the experience of the Brahmin way of life touches him deeply. Their values shape not only their own lives and the lives of the peoples living in the vicinity of them, but also affect Alexander and perhaps even give him the feeling of transitoriness of all fame, glory, and wealth. Theirs is a spiritual wealth that perhaps even he would like to learn from. The asymmetrical relations of domination and subordination metamorphose into another example of asymmetrical bonding: no values that Alexander represents are admired by the

---

118 If India was one of the literary "contact zones", there existed historical zones of the type in medieval Europe, such as Spain before the *Reconquista*, as Chism notes (2002:116).

Brahmins, while their beliefs and code of behaviour are respected by the ruler, who realizes how worldly his pursuits have been. "Mandeville" didactically adds a Christian perspective, preaching about the virtuous heathenism of the peoples Alexander encountered:

> And þerfore all be it þat þere ben many dyuerse lawes in the world, ȝit I trowe þat god loueth hem & þat god [taketh] hire seruyese to gree, right as he did of IOB þat was a peynem & held him for his trewe seruant (Hamelius 1919:197).
>
> [And even if there are many different religions and different beliefs in the world, still I believe God always loves those who love Him in truth and serve him meekly and truly, setting no store by the vainglory of the world – just like these folk and Job.] (Moseley 1983:180)

There appear here allusions to the existence of a medieval ecumenism, which could embrace the peoples of India. The main rationale behind it remains the conviction that even the barbarians in the East may teach us the truths otherwise known to us from the Bible, such as the story of Job.

It is open to question to what extent the same may be regenerated upon contact with the other. Naturally, the myth of Eastern innocence and purity as opposed to the Western degeneration that was propagated especially by Romantic thinkers cannot be employed here because neither is the Occident spoilt through and through nor is the Orient free from degeneration. Nevertheless, Alexander is given a chance to undergo some regeneration, even though the chance is lost once the ruler is poisoned and dies, realizing the futility of his pursuits, as Middle English writers have us believe. The East with its inhabitants becomes an object of fantasy and the fantasy does not focus on the material wealth only. The unusual nature of the Orient is demonstrated by the uncanny bodies of the monstrous races, which are believed to be sending a message for the Westerners to decipher. What Pratt termed the "imperial meaning making" is here transformed into the East that adds more more meaning to the life of Europeans and approaches the nineteenth-century conventions of writing about the journey to the Orient as enlightening and liberating (2008:4). To be sure, the medieval vision does not go as far as the nineteenth-century myth of the Orient as that which enriches the self, but it gestures in that direction. As a result, the Middle English oriental romances present a complex discourse on the issue of sameness and otherness, on the influence of the others and their exotic corporeality on what is marked as the same, and on the possible transformation of the same upon contact with the other. The material wealth observable in the Orient that was broached in the epigraph to this chapter could only be a point of departure for enrichment of the Western self, since the ultimate wealth of the East could be spiritual, as was argued several centuries later, in the late eighteenth and nineteenth centuries. Tellingly, in Gérard de Nerval's *Voyage en Orient*, first published in 1851, the East is thought to preserve the equal status that all humans once cherished; it is a status which Europeans should attempt to regain for their own countries, as Nerval postulates in a utopian manner. The myth of Eastern innocence and virtue is most readily recognized as belonging to Romanticism, but it needs to be remembered that traces of it could already be found in the medieval Alexander romances.

Conclusion

> On the basis of the assimilation of Aristotelian biology and Galenic medicine, the human body acquired a central place as the locus of individuality, as a source of significant influence on behavioral patterns, as a treasure-trove to be applied to a series of philosophical and theological questions.
> (Benjamin Isaac, Miriam Eliav-Feldon, and Joseph Ziegler *Introduction* to *The origins of racism in the West*) (2009:23).

The discourse on the human body considerably changed from the antiquity to the Middle Ages, despite medieval thinkers' frequent reliance on ancient theories. The scope of investigation on the question of corporeality broadened, since theology started to play a significant role in inspecting the actual nature of the body. Bodies were undoubtedly one of the chief philosophical concerns of the period and, importantly, the bodies of cultural others were also central to those divagations, because they materialized the exotic in all its perilous and enticing essence. In medieval literature the other tended to be represented as both the object of desiring and the desiring subject.

In the genre that we have loosely specified as oriental romances, cultural others are presented as characters whose corporeality matters a great deal. The corporeality becomes a subject of fantasy and is distorted into what is convenient for a given writer's message, be it the attraction and simultaneous inaccessibility of an Eastern princess, Muslim flesh that integrates the community, the hybrid body of a Muslim slave that needs to be converted, the black bodies that keep the Frankish community operating, or the others who turn Horn into the other by usurping his political power and leading him to abandon individual desire in favour of the communal kind. Ethnic difference and the identity of an enamoured princess situate Canace in *The Squire's tale* and Floripas in *Sir Ferumbras* on the side of simultaneous attraction and inaccessibility, while for Richard le Coer de Lyon racial others are merely flesh to be ingested and digested. In the narratives of slavery, *Aucassin et Nicolete* and *Floris and Blancheflour*, the bodies of Muslims do not need to alter upon conversion, since they are already pale-skinned before it, while Christianity does not protect the future king Horn against being "othered" in diverse locations, which occurs both in *King Horn* and its variant, *Horn Childe and Maiden Rimnild*. Relative negativity about others integrates those images, and out of the texts taken here for discussion only the Middle English Alexander romances, *Kyng Alisaunder* and *The wars of Alexander*, revolve around corporeality and alterity in a more positive manner, because they express a degree of infatuation with the outlandish bodies of the marvellous creatures of India. Furthermore, the cultured Alexander appreciates the values of at least some inhabitants of the oriental world and they make him realize the futility of his own pursuits.

The focus on the other's corporeality in these romances very likely stemmed from the conviction that the souls of cultural others were defective, or that they were not endowed with souls at all. The context is important for assessing the status of a given body marked by alterity and interpreting it correctly. The physicality of racialized others in these romances often complicates their contact with the Western world. The authors of the texts seem usually to have had specific ideological goals. The Deleuzian "what can a body do?" could be answered in a number of ways in these romances and one answer is that it can undergo metamorphosis. Significantly, the romances show that the same may metamorphose into the other or even undergo regeneration upon contact with those others. Paradoxically, some of the negativity inherent in presenting the other may stem from the chivalric tradition and not from such ignoble social institutions as slavery, in which a body functioned merely as chattel to be traded.

Corporeality, including that which is marked by alterity, ties in very closely with the social world. The body of the other may be an entity integrating a community, but it may also testify to its disintegration or remain on its margins, paradoxically perpetuating the community's existence. The bodies of medieval cultural others cannot be seen from one perspective only, since they functioned in their social environment in a number of ways. They were an important identity-making force, because Westerners often defined themselves in opposition to them, arguing that the practices of those exotic bodies testified to who those others were inside. This study has attempted to show how bodies are constructed in the Middle English oriental romances, recovering their history, but also to show the idea of how those bodies sustain communities. This question has hopefully been historicized adequately in the discussion, even though the texts themselves are mostly purely fictional.

Bodies marked by alterity were all too frequently treated instrumentally in medieval texts, as oriental romances show. I have attempted to break the relative silence which has enveloped the others in those texts. In oriental romance not only female corporeality but also, as has consistently been stressed here, all representations of corporeality marked by alterity in Middle English oriental romances were subjected to fantasy. Fantasy is the staple of oriental romance, which non-mimetically feeds on Western fears and fascinations rather than relies on the reality of the cultural others who lived near Christians in medieval Europe.

References

PRIMARY SOURCES:

Ali, Tariq
    1998   *The book of Saladin. A novel.* London – New York: Verso.

Benson, Larry D. (ed.)
    1987   *Riverside Chaucer.* 3rd edition. Oxford: Oxford University Press.

Brunner, Karl (ed.)
    1913   *Der mittelenglische roman über Richard Löwenherz.* Wien – Leipzig: Wilhelm Braumüller.

Bullett, Gerald (ed.)
    1992   John Keats. *The Poems.* London: Everyman's Library.

Burnley, David – Alison Wiggins (eds.)
    2003   *Roland and Vernagu.* http://auchinleck.nls.uk/mss/roland.html. Date of access: 2.01.2012.

Carpine, John of Plano
    1955   "History of the Mongols". In: Dawson, Christopher (ed.). 3-72.

Cobby, Anne Elizabeth – Glyn S. Burgess (eds. and trans.)
    1988   *The Pilgrimage of Charlemagne. Aucassin and Nicolette.* New York – London: Garland Publishing.

Correale, Robert M. – Mary Hamel (eds.)
    2009   *Sources and analogues of* The Canterbury Tales. Cambridge: D.S. Brewer.

Dawson, Christopher (ed.)
    1955   *The Mongol mission: narratives and letters of the Franciscan missionaries in Mongolia and China in the thirteenth and the fourteenth centuries.* London – New York: Sheedd and Ward.

DiMarco, Vincent J. (ed.)
    2009   "The Squire's tale". In: Correale, Robert M. – Mary Hamel (eds.). 169-209.

Hamelius, Paul (ed.)
    1919   *Mandeville's travels.* London: Early English Text Society.

Henry, Patrice (ed.)
    1935   *Les enfances Guillaume: chanson de geste du XIIIe siècle.* Paris: Société des anciens texts français.

Herrtage, Sidney J. (ed.)
    1879 [1966] *Sir Ferumbras. Edited from the unique manuscript Bodeleian Ms. Ashmole 33.* London – New York – Toronto: Oxford University Press.

Herrtage, Sidney J. (ed.)
    1880 [2008] *The Sege of Melayne, The Romance of Duke Rowland and Sir Otuell of Spayne.* Woodbridge, Suffolk: Boydell and Brewer.

Horace
1932 *Satires, epistles, and Ars Poetica with an English translation.* Cambridge: Harvard University Press.
Janes, Cecil (ed.)
1930 *The voyages of Christopher Columbus.* London: Argonaut Press.
John of Salisbury
2000 *Policraticus.* Ed. Cary J. Nederman. Cambridge: Cambridge University Press.
Lupack, Alan (ed.)
1990 *The sultan of Babylon.* Kalamazoo, Michigan: Medieval Institute Publications. http://www.lib.rochester.edu/camelot/Teams/sultfrm.htm. Date of access: 20.08.2011.
Lupack, Alan (ed.)
1990 *The tale of Ralph the collier.* http://www.lib.rochester.edu/camelot/teams/collfrm.htm. Date of access: 13.10.2012.
Map, Walter
1983 *De nugis curialium. Courtiers' trifles.* Ed. and trans. M.R. James. Oxford: Clarendon Press.
Mills, Maldwyn (ed.)
1988 *Horn Childe and Maiden Rimnild, ed. from the Auchinleck Ms, National Library of Scotland, Advocates Ms 19.2.1.* Heidelberg: Carl Winter, Universitätsverlag.
Mills, Maldwyn (ed.)
1992 *Six Middle English romances.* London – Rutland, Vermont: J.M. Dent – Charles E.Tutle.
Moseley, C.W.R.D. (trans.)
1983 *The travels of sir John Mandeville.* London: Penguin Books.
Mosès, François (ed.)
1991 *Lancelot du Lac. Roman français du XIIIe siècle.* Paris: Librarie Générale Française.
O'Sullivan, Mary Isabelle (ed.)
1935 [1987] *Firumbras.* Millwood, N.Y.: Kraus Reprint.
Painter, William (ed. and trans.)
1965 "The Tartar Relation". In: Skelton, R.A. – Thomas E. Marston – George D. Painter (eds.). 21-51.
Paris, Matthew
1877 *Chronica majora.* Ed. Henry Richards Luard. *Rerum Britannicarum Medii Aevi Scriptores 57/4.*
Plotinus
1917-1930 *The works.* Trans. Stephen MacKenna. London: Faber and Faber Limited.
Régnier, Claude (ed.)
1990 *Aliscans.* Vol. I and II. Paris: Librairie Honoré Champion.
Sands, Donald B. (ed.)
1986 *Middle English verse romances.* Exeter: University of Exeter Press.
Sewter, E.R.A. (ed.)
1969 *The Alexiad of Anna Comnena.* Harmondsworth: Penguin.

Sinclair, John (trans. and ed.)
  1961	*The divine comedy of Dante Alighieri. Inferno.* New York: Oxford University Press.
Skeat, Walter W. (ed.)
  1936 [2002]	*The wars of Alexander.* London: Early English Text Society.
Skelton, R.A. – Thomas E. Marston – George D. Painter (eds.)
  1965	*The Vinland map and the Tartar relation.* New Haven – London: Yale University Press.
Smithers, G.V. (ed.)
  1961a	*Kyng Alisaunder.* Vol. I. *Text.* London – New York – Toronto: Oxford University Press.
Smithers, G.V. (ed.)
  1961b	*Kyng Alisaunder.* Vol. II. *Introduction, commentary, and glossary.* London – New York – Toronto: Oxford University Press.
Vitruvius
  1985	*De architectura.* Trans. Frank Granger. Cambridge: Harvard University Press.

SECONDARY SOURCES:

Abaza, Mona – Georg Stauth
  1988	"Occidental reason, orientalism, and Islamic fundamentalism". *International Sociology* 3/4: 343-364.
Aers, David – Anabel Wharton
  1997	"Preface". *Desire, its subjects, objects, and historians. Special Issue of Journal of Medieval and Early Modern Studies* 27/1:1-2.
Akbari, Suzanne
  1998-99	"Imagining Islam: the role of images in medieval depictions of Muslims". *Scripta Mediterranea* XIX-XX: 9-27.
Akbari, Suzanne Conklin
  2000	"From due East to true North: orientalism and orientation". In: Cohen, Jeffrey Jerome (ed.). 19-34.
Akbari, Suzanne Conklin
  2005	"The hunger for national identity in *Richard Coer de Lion*". In: Stein, Robert M. – Sandra Pierson Prior (eds.). 198-227.
Akbari, Suzanne Conklin
  2009	*Idols in the East: European representations of Islam and the Orient, 1100-1450.* Ithaka – London: Cornell University Press.
Akbari,. Suzanne Conklin – Karla Mallette (eds.)
  (forthcoming) *A sea of languages: literature and culture in the medieval Mediterranean.* Toronto: University of Toronto Press.
Alcoff, Linda Martín
  2002	"Philosophy and racial identity". In: Osborne, Peter – Stella Sandford (eds.). 13-28.

Alexander, Edward
1989 "Professor of terror". *Commentary* 88/2:49-50.
Ambrisco, Alan S.
1999 "Cannibalism and cultural encounters in *Richard Coer de Lion*". *Journal of Medieval and Early Modern Studies* 29/ 3: 499-528.
Ambrisco, Alan S.
2004 "It lyth nat in my tonge": occupatio and otherness in *The Squire's tale*". *The Chaucer Review* 38/ 3: 205-228.
Appiah, Kwame Anthony
1990 "Racisms". In: Goldberg, David Theo (ed.). 3-17.
Appiah, Kwame Anthony
1995 "Race". In: Lentricchia, Frank – Thomas McLaughlin (eds.). 274-287.
Appiah, Kwame Anthony
2002 "History of hate. A review of *Racism: a short history* by George M. Fredericson". *New York Times Book Review*. August 4, 2002. http://www.nytimes.com/2002/08/04/books/history-of-hatred.html?ref=bookreviews. Date of access: 26.04.2012.
Archibald, Elizabeth
2004 "Ancient romance". In: Saunders, Corinne (ed). 10-25.
Arens, William
1979 *The man-eating myth: anthropology and anthropophagy*. New York: Oxford University Press.
Arens, William
1998 "Rethinking anthropophagy". In: Barker, Francis – Peter Hulme – Margaret Iversen (eds.). 39-62.
Ashcroft, Bill – Pal Ahluwalia
2009 *Edward Said. Routledge critical thinkers*. London – New York: Routledge.
Ashurst, David
2011 "Alexander literature in English and Scots". In: Zuwiyya, Z. David (ed.). 255-290.
Atkinson, Clarissa
1991 *The oldest vocation: Christian motherhood in the Middle Ages*. Ithaca – London: Cornell University Press.
Bakhtin, Mikhail
1984 *Rabelais and his world*. Trans. Helene Iswolsky. Bloomington – Indianapolis: Indiana University Press.
Barker, Francis – Peter Hulme – Margaret Iversen – Diana Loxley (eds.)
1985 *Europe and its others: proceedings of the Essex conference on the sociology of literature, July 1984*. Vol. I. Colchester: University of Essex.
Barker, Francis – Peter Hulme
1988 "Nymphs and reapers heavily vanish: the discursive con-texts of *The tempest*". In: Drakakis, John (ed.). 191-205.
Barker, Francis – Peter Hulme – Margaret Iversen (eds.)
1998 *Cannibalism and the colonial world*. Cambridge: Cambridge University Press.

Barnes, Geraldine
1984 "Cunning and ingenuity in the Middle English *Floris and Blancheflur*". *Medium Aevum* 53:10-25.
Bartlett, Robert
1993 *The making of Europe: conquest, colonization and cultural change 950-1350.* Princeton, New Jersey: Princeton University Press.
Bartlett, Robert
2009 "Illustrating ethnicity in the Middle Ages". In: Eliav-Feldon, Miriam – Benjamin Isaac – Joseph Ziegler (eds.). 132-156.
Beckett, Katharine Scarfe
2003 *Anglo-Saxon perceptions of the Islamic world.* Cambridge: Cambridge University Press.
Behdad, Ali
1994 "Orientalism after *Orientalism*". *L'Esprit Créateur* 34/2:1-11.
Bela, Teresa
1994 *The image of the Queen in Elizabethan poetry.* Kraków: Wydawnictwo Uniwersytetu Jagiellońskiego.
Benson, Larry D.
1987 "The Canterbury Tales". In: Benson, Lary D. (ed.). 3-22.
Benson, Larry D. (ed.)
1987 *Riverside Chaucer.* 3rd edition. Oxford: Oxford University Press.
Bernasconi, Robert – Simon Critchley (eds.)
1991 *Re-reading Levinas.* London: Athlone
Bernau, Anke – Ruth Evans – Sarah Salih (eds.)
2003 *Medieval virginities.* Cardiff: University of Wales Press.
Berrong, Richard M.
1986 Rabelais and Bakhtin: popular culture in Gargantua and Pantagruel.
Bhabha, Homi K.
1984 "Of mimicry and man: the ambivalence of colonial discourse". *October* 28:125-133.
Bhabha, Homi K.
1985 "Signs taken for wonders: questions of ambivalence and authority under a tree outside Delhi, May 1817". In: Barker, Francis – Peter Hulme – Margaret Iversen – Diana Loxley (eds.). 89-105.
Bhabha, Homi K.
2004 *The location of culture.* London – New York: Routledge.
Biddick, Kathleen
1993 *Genders, bodies, borders: technologies of the visible. Speculum* 68/2: 389-418.
Biddick, Kathleen
1998 "The ABC of Ptolemy: mapping the world with the alphabet". In Tomasch, Sylvia – Sealy Gilles (ed.). 268-294.
Biddick, Kathleen
2000 "Coming out of exile: Dante on the orient express". In: Cohen, Jeffrey Jerome (ed.). 35-52.

Blacking, John
1977 "Preface". In: Blacking, John (ed.). v-x.
Blacking, John
1977 *The anthropology of the body.* London – New York – San Francisco: Academic Press.
Blanks, David R. – Michael Frassetto (eds.)
1999 *Western views of Islam in medieval and early modern Europe: perception of the Other.* Houndmills, Basingstoke – London: Macmillan.
Blurton, Heather
2007 *Cannibalism in high medieval English literature.* Houndmills, Basingstoke – New York: Palgrave Macmillan.
Boose, Lynda E.
1994 "'The getting of a lawful race': racial discourse in early modern England and the unpresentable black woman". In: Hendricks, Margo – Patricia Parker (eds.). 35-54.
Bracken, Harry M.
1999 "René Decartes". In : Popkin, Richard H. (ed.). 336-345.
Braude, Benjamin
1996 "Mandeville's Jews among Others". In: Le Beau, Bryan F. – Menahem Mor (eds.). 133-158.
Brewer, D.S.
1955 "The ideal of feminine beauty in medieval literature, especially *Harley Lyrics*, Chaucer, and some Elizabethans". *Modern Language Review* L/ 3: 257-269.
Brewer, Derek
1988 "Introduction: escape from the mimetic fallacy". In: Brewer, Derek (ed.). 1-10.
Brewer, Derek (ed.)
1988 *Studies in medieval English romances: some new approaches.* Cambridge: D.S. Brewer.
Bristow, Joseph
1997 *Sexuality.* London – New York: Routledge.
Brown, Catherine
2000 "In the Middle". *Journal of Medieval and Early Modern Studies* 30:3: 547-574.
Brunner, Otto – Howard Kaminsky
1992 *Land and lordship: governance in medieval Austria.* Trans. James Van Horn Melton. Philadelphia: University of Pennsylvania Press.
Buschinger, Danielle
2011 "German Alexander romances". In: Zuwiyya, Z. David (ed.). 291-314.
Bynum, Caroline Walker
1987 *Holy feast and holy fast: the religious significance of food to medieval women.* Berkeley – Los Angeles – London: University of California Press.
Bynum, Caroline Walker
1995 "Why all the fuss about the body? A medievalist perspective". *Critical Inquiry* 22: 1-33.
Bynum, Caroline Walker
2001 *Metamorphosis and identity.* New York: Zone Books.

Calkin, Siobhain Bly
2004 "The anxieties of encounter and exchange: Saracens and Christian heroism in *Sir Beues of Hamtoun*". *Florilegium* 21:135-158.

Calkin, Siobhain Bly
2011 "Romance baptisms and theological contexts in *The king of Tars* and *Sir Ferumbras*. In: Purdie, Rhiannon – Michael Cichon (eds.). 105-119.

Camille, Michael
1994 "The image and the self: unwriting late medieval bodies". In: Kay, Sarah – Miri Rubin (eds.). 62-99.

Campbell, Mary Baine
1999 *Wonder and science: imagining worlds in early modern Europe.* Ithaca – London: Cornell University Press.

Cary, George
1956 *The medieval Alexander.* Cambridge: At the University Press.

Cassuto, Leonard
1997 *The inhuman race: the racial grotesque in American literature.* New York: Columbia University Press.

Chism, Christine
2002 *Alliterative revivals.* Philadelphia: University of Pennsylvania Press.

Clifford, James
1988 *The predicament of culture: twentieth century ethnography, literature, and art.* Cambridge, Massachusetts: Harvard University Press.

Coakley, Sarah (ed.)
1997 *Religion and the body.* Cambridge: Cambridge University Press.

Cawsy, Kathy
2009 "Disorienting orientalism: finding Saracens in strange places in medieval English manuscripts". *Exemplaria* 21/4: 380-397.

Cohen, Jeffrey Jerome
2003 *Medieval identity machines.* Minneapolis: University of Minnesota Press.

Cohen, Jeffrey Jerome
2006 *Hybridity, identity, and monstrosity in medieval Britain: on difficult middles.* Houndmills, Basingstoke: Palgrave Macmillan.

Cohen, Jeffrey Jerome (ed.)
1996 *Monster theory: reading culture.* Minneapolis and London: University of Minneapolis Press.

Cohen, Jeffrey Jerome (ed.)
2000 *The postcolonial Middle Ages.* New York – Houndmills, Basingstoke: Palgrave Macmillan.

Cohen, Jeffrey Jerome
2003 *Medieval identity machines.* Minneapolis: University of Minnesota Press.

Cohen, Jeffrey Jerome
2004 "'Kyte oute yugilment': an introduction to *Medieval noise*". *Exemplaria* 16/2: 1-8.

Cohen, Jeffrey Jerome – Gail Weiss
2009 "Introduction: bodies at the limit". In: Cohen, Jeffrey Jerome – Gail Weiss (eds.). 1-10.

Cohen, Jeffrey Jerome – Gail Weiss (eds.)
2009 *Thinking the limits of the body.* New York: SUNY.
Cohen, William A.
2009 "Deep skin". In: Cohen, Jeffrey Jerome – Gail Weiss (eds.). 63-82.
Colwell, Tania
2003 "Mélusine: ideal mother or inimitable monster?" In: Davis, Isabel – Miriam Müller – Sarah Reese Jones (eds.). 181-203.
Connelly, Frances S.
2003 "Introduction". In: Connelly, Frances S. (ed.). 1-19.
Connelly, Frances S. (ed.)
2003 *Modern art and the grotesque.* Cambridge: Cambridge University Press.
Copeland, Rita – David Lawton – Wendy Scase (eds.)
1998 *New medieval literatures 2.* Oxford: Clarendon Press.
Cowen, Janet M.
1996 "The English Charlemagne romances". In: Pratt, Karen (ed.). 149-168.
Crane, Susan
1986 *Insular romance: politics, faith, and culture in Anglo-Norman and Middle English literature.* Berkeley – Los Angeles – London: University of California Press.
Cruz, Jo Ann Hoeppner Moran
1999 "Popular attitudes towards Islam in medieval Europe". In: Blanks, David R. – Michael Frassetto (eds.). 55-82.
Curry, Walter Clyde
1916 *The Middle English ideal of personal beauty as found in the metrical romances, chronicles, and legends of the XIII, XIV, and XV centuries.* Baltimore: J.H. Furst Company.
Dagenais, John – Margaret R. Greer
2000 "Decolonizing the Middle Ages: introduction". *Journal of Medieval and Early Modern Studies* 30:3: 431-448.
Daniel, Norman
1984 *Heroes and Saracens: an interpretation of the* chansons de geste. Edinburgh: Edinburg University Press.
Danzig, Allan (ed.)
1971 *Twentieth century interpretations of* The eve of St. Agnes: a collection of critical essays. Englewood Cliffs, N.J.: Prentice Hall.
Davies, R.R.
2000 *The first English empire: power and identities in the British Isles 1093-1343.* Oxford: Oxford University Press.
Davis, Isabel – Miriam Müller – Sarah Reese Jones (eds.)
2003 *Love, marriage, and family ties in the later Middle Ages.* Turnhout: Brepols Publishers.
Degler, Carl N.
1972 "Prejudice and slavery". In: Winks, Robert W. (ed.). 70-80.
Delany, Sheila
1994 *The naked text: Chaucer's* Legend of good women. Berkeley – Los Angeles – Oxford: University of California Press.

Deleuze, Gilles
    1992   *Expressionism in philosophy: Spinoza*. New York: Zone Books.
Derrida, Jacques
    1991   "At the very moment in this work here I am". In: Bernasconi, Robert – Simon Critchley (eds.). 11-48.
De Weever, Jacqueline
    1994   "Nicolette's *blackness* – lost in translation". *Romance Notes* 34/3: 317-325.
De Weever, Jacqueline
    1998   *Sheba's daughters: whitening and demonizing the Saracen woman in medieval French epic*. New York – London: Garland Publishing.
Devisse, Jean
    1979   *The image of the black in Western art*. Vol. II. Part I. *From the early Christian era to the "Age of discovery"*. Trans. William Granger Ryan. Harvard: Office du Livre.
DiMarco, Vincent J.
    2002   "The historical basis of Chaucer's *Squire's tale*". In: Lynch, Kathryn L. (ed.). 56-75.
Dinshaw, Carolyn
    2001   "Pale faces: race, religion, and affect in Chaucer's texts and their readers". *Studies in the Age of Chaucer* 23: 19-41.
Dockès, Pierre
    1982   *Medieval slavery and liberation*. Trans. Arthur Goldhammer. London: Methuen.
Douglas, Mary
    2009   *Purity and danger: an analysis of concept of pollution and taboo*. London – New York: Routledge.
Drakakis, John (ed.)
    1988   *Alternative Shakespeares*. London – New York: Routledge.
Duby, George (ed.)
    1988   *A history of private life: revelations of the medieval world*. Trans. Arthur Goldhammer. Cambridge, Massachusetts and London: The Belknap Press of Harvard.
Dutton, Michael – Peter Williams
    1993   "Translating theories: Edward Said on Orientalism, imperialism and alterity". *Southern Review* 26/3: 314-357.
Eagleton, Terry
    1989   *Literary theory: an introduction*. Oxford: Basil Blackwell.
Edwards, A.S.G.
    1990   "The contexts of the Vernon romances". In: Pearsall, Derek (ed.). 159-170.
Elias, Nobert
    1939 [2000] *The civilizing process: sociogenetic and psychogenetic investigations*. Oxford: Blackwell Publishing.
Eliav-Feldon, Miriam – Benjamin Isaac – Joseph Ziegler (eds.)
    2009   *The origins of racism in the West*. Cambridge: Cambridge University Press.

Emelina, Jean
1994 "Les grandes orientations du rire". In: Faure, Alain (ed.). 55-72.
Esposito, Roberto
2004 *Immunitas: schutz und negation des lebens*. Trans. Sabine Schulz. Berlin: diaphanes.
Esposito, Roberto
2008 *Bios: biopolitics and philosophy*. Trans. Timothy Campbell. Minneapolis – London: University of Minnesota Press.
Esposito, Roberto
2010 *Communitas: the origin and destiny of community*. Trans. Timothy Campbell. Stanford: Stanford University Press.
Evans, Ruth
2003 "The Jew, the Host and the Virgin Mary: fantasies of the sentient body". In: Bernau, Anke – Ruth Evans – Sarah Salih (eds.). 167-186.
Everest, Kelvin
2002 *John Keats. Writers and their work*. Tavistock, Devon: Northcote House Publishers.
Faure, Alain (ed.)
1994 *Rires et sourires litteraires*. Nice: Université de Nice Sophia Antipolis.
Feher, Michael
1986 "Introduction". In: Feher, Michael – Ramona Naddaff – Nadia Tazzi (eds.). 10-17.
Feher, Michael – Ramona Naddaff – Nadia Tazzi (eds.)
1986 *Fragments for a history of a human body. Part one*. New York: Zone Books.
Fink, Bruce
1995 *The Lacanian subject: between language and jouissance*. Princeton: Princeton University Press.
Finlay, Moses I.
1972 "The extent of slavery". In: Winks, Robert W. (ed.). 3-15.
Finlayson, John
1980 "Definitions of the Middle English romance. Part II". *The Chaucer Review* 15/2: 168-181.
Finlayson, John
1990 "*Richard, Coer de Lyon*: romance, history or something in between?" *Studies in Philology* 87/2: 156-180.
Finlayson, John
1998 "Legendary ancestors and the expansion of romance in *Richard, Coer de Lyon*". *English Studies* 4: 299-308.
Finlayson, John
1999 "The marvellous in Middle English romance". *The Chaucer Review* 33/4. 363-408.
Fletcher, Richard
2003 *Bloodfeud: murder and revenge in Anglo-Saxon England*. Oxford: Oxford University Press.

Foucault, Michel
   1988   "Technologies of the self". In: Martin, Luther H. – Huck Gutman – Patrick H. Hutton (eds.). 16-49.
Fowler, Elizabeth
   2000   "The romance hypothetical: lordship and the Saracens in *Sir Isumbras*". In: Putter, Ad – Jane Gilbert (eds.). 97-121.
Fradenburg, Louise O.
   1998   "Analytical survey 2. We are not alone: psychoanalytic medievalism". In: Copeland, Rita – David Lawton – Wendy Scase (eds.). 249-276.
Fradenburg, L. O. Aranye
   2002   *Sacrifice your love: psychoanalysis, historicism, Chaucer*. Minneapolis – London: University of Minnesota Press.
Fradenburg, L. O. Aranye
   2004   "Simply marvelous". *Studies in the Age of Chaucer* 26: 29-63.
Frakes, Jerold C.
   2011   *Contextualizing the Muslim Other in medieval Christian discourse*. New York: Palgrave Macmillan.
Fredrickson, George M.
   2002   *Racism: a short history*. Princeton – Oxford: Princeton University Press.
Freedman, Paul H.
   2008   *Out of the East: spices and medieval imagination*. New Haven: Yale University Press.
Freedman, Paul H. – Gabrielle M. Spiegel
   1998   "Medievalisms old and new: the rediscovery of alterity in North American medieval studies". *The American Historical Review* 103:677-704.
French, Walter H.
   1940   *Essays on* King Horn. Ithaca – New York: Cornell University Press.
Freud, Sigmund
   1946   *Totem and taboo: resemblances between the psychic lives of savages and neurotics*. Trans. A.A. Brill. New York: Vintage Books.
Fyler, John M.
   1994   "Chaucerian romance and the world beyond Europe". In: Maddox, Donald – Sarah Sturm-Maddox (eds.). 256-263.
Ganim, John M.
   2005   *Medievalism and orientalism: three essays on literature, architecture and cultural identity*. New York – Houndmills, Basingstoke: Palgrave Macmillan.
Georgopoulou, Maria
   1999   "Orientalism and crusader art: constructing a new canon". *Medieval Encounters* 5: 289-321.
Gerritsen, Willem P. – Anthony G. van Melle (eds.)
   1998   *A dictionary of medieval heroes*. Trans. Tanis Guest. Woodbridge: The Boydell Press.
Gillingham, John
   2000a   *The English in the twelfth century: imperialism, national identity and political values*. Woodbridge, Suffolk: The Boydell Press.

Gillingham, John
- 2000b *Richard I.* New Haven – Lond on: Yale University Press.

Gittings, Robert
- 1971 "Rich antiquity". In: Danzig, Allan (ed.). 86-98.

Goldberg, David Theo (ed.)
- 1990 *Anatomy of racism.* Minneapolis – Oxford: University of Minnesota Press.

Gómez, E. García
- 1929 *Un texto arabe occidental de la leyenda de Alejandro.* Instituto de Valencia de Don Juan, Madrid.

Goodman, Jennifer R.
- 1983 "Chaucer's *Squire's tale* and the rise of chivalry". *Studies in the Age of Chaucer* 5: 127-136.

Goodman, Jennifer R.
- 1997 "Marriage and conversion in late medieval romance". In: Muldoon, James (ed.). 114-128.

Grady, Frank
- 2005 *Representing righteous heathens in late medieval England.* Houndmills, Basingstoke: Palgrave Macmillan.

Gray, Douglas (ed.)
- 2003 *The Oxford companion to Chaucer.* Oxford: Oxford University Press.

Grieve, Patricia E.
- 1997 *Floire and Blancheflor and the European romance.* Cambridge: Cambridge University Press.

Gurevich, Aron
- 1985 *Categories of medieval culture.* Trans. G.L. Campbell. New York: Routledge Kegan & Paul.

Guzman, Gregory G.
- 1991 "Reports of Mongol cannibalism in the thirteenth-century Latin sources: oriental fact or Western fiction?" In: Westrem, Scott D. (ed.). 31-68.

Hahn, Thomas
- 2001 "The difference the Middle Ages makes: color and race before the modern world". *Journal of Medieval and Early Modern Studies* 31:1: 1-37.

Hall, Kim F.
- 1998 "'These bastard signs of fair': literary whiteness in Shakespeare's sonnets". In: Loomba, Ania – Martin Orkin (eds.). 64-83.

Hamaguchi, Keiko
- 2006 *Non-European women in Chaucer: a postcolonial study.* Frankfurt am Main: Peter Lang.

Handlin, Oscar – Mary F. Handlin
- 1972 "The Southern labour system". In: Winks, Robert W. (ed.). 38-50.

Hannaford, Ivan
- 1996 *Race: the history of an idea in the West.* Baltimore: The John Hopkins University Press.

Harpham, Geoffrey Galt
1982   *On the grotesque: strategies of contradiction in art and literature.* Princeton, NJ: Princeton University Press.

Heffernan, Thomas J.
1986   *The popular literature of medieval Europe.* Knoxville: The University of Tennessee Press.

Heffernan, Carol F.
2003   *The Orient in Chaucer and the oriental romance.* Cambridge: D. S. Brewer.

Hendricks, Margo – Patricia Parker
1994   "Introduction". In: Hendricks, Margo – Patricia Parker (eds.), 1-14.

Hendricks, Margo – Patricia Parker (eds.)
1994   *Women, "race", and writing in the early modern period.* London – New York: Routledge.

Hendricks, Margo
1996   "'Obscured by dreams': race, empire, and Shakespeare's *A midsummer night's dream*". *Shakespeare Quarterly* 47: 37-60.

Heng, Geraldine
2003   *Empire of magic: medieval romance and the politics of cultural fantasy.* New York: Columbia University Press.

Higgins, Iain Macleod
1997   *Writing East: the Travels of sir John Mandeville.* Philadelphia: University of Pennsylvania Press.

Holsinger, Bruce
2002   "Medieval studies, postcolonial studies, and the genealogies of critique". *Speculum* 77: 1195-1227.

Hulme, Peter – Margaret Iversen – David Loxley (eds.)
1983   *The politics of theory.* Colchester: The University of Essex Press.

Hulme, Peter – Neil L. Whitehead (eds.)
1992   *Wild majesty: encounters with Caribs from Columbus to the present day.* Oxford: Clarendon Press.

Hulme, Peter
1998   "Introduction: the cannibal scene". In: Barker, Francis – Peter Hulme – Margaret Iversen (eds.). 1-38.

Huot, Sylvia
2007   "Love, race, and gender in medieval romance: Lancelot and the son of the giantess". *Journal of Medieval and Early Modern Studies* 37/2: 373-391.

Ingham, Patricia Clare
2001   *Sovereign fantasies: Arthurian romance and the making of Britain.* Philadelphia: University of Pennsylvania Press.

Isaac, Benjamin – Joseph Ziegler – Miriam Eliav-Feldon
2009   "Introduction". In: Eliav-Feldon, Miriam – Benjamin Isaac – Joseph Ziegler (eds.). 1-31.

Jameson, Fredric
1975   "Magical narratives: romance as a genre". *New Literary History* 7:1: 135-163.

Jameson, Fredric
1981 *Narrative as a socially symbolic act.* Ithaca, New York: Cornell University Press.
Janes, Cecil (ed.)
1930 *The voyages of Christopher Columbus.* London: Argonaut Press.
Jones, Terry
1994 *Chaucer's Knight: the portrait of a medieval mercenary.* London: Methuen.
Jordan, William Chester
2001 "Why 'race'?" *Journal of Medieval and Early Modern Studies* 31/1: 165-173.
Kahrl, Stanley J.
1973 "Chaucer's *Squire's tale* and the decline of chivalry". *Chaucer Review* 7: 194-209.
Kalaga, Wojciech – Tadeusz Rachwał (eds.)
2003 *Viands, wines and spirits: nourishment and (in)digestion in the culture of literacy. Essays in cultural practice.* Katowice: Wydawnictwo Uniwersytetu Śląskiego.
Kantorowicz, Ernst
1957 *The king's two bodies: a study in medieval political theology.* Princeton: Princeton University Press.
Kay, Sarah – Miri Rubin
1994 "Introduction". In: Kay, Sarah – Miri Rubin (eds.). 1-9.
Kay, Sarah – Miri Rubin (eds.)
1994 *Framing medieval bodies.* Manchester – New York: Manchester University Press.
Kay, Sarah
1995 *The chansons de geste in the age of romance: political fictions.* Oxford: Clarendon Press.
Kayser, Wolfgang
1981 *The grotesque in art and literature.* Trans. Ulrich Weisstein. New York: Columbia University Press.
Kelly, Kathleen Coyne
1994 "The bartering of Blancheflour in the Middle English *Floris and Blancheflur*". *Studies in Philology* XCI/2: 101-110.
Kilgour, Maggie
1990 *From communion to cannibalism: an anatomy of metaphors of incorporation.* Princeton, New Jersey: Princeton University Press.
Kilgour, Maggie
1998 "The function of cannibalism at the present time". In: Barker, Francis – Peter Hulme – Margaret Iversen (eds.). 238-259.
Klinck, Anne L.
2010 "Singing a song of sorrow". In: Tolmie, Jane – M.J. Toswell (eds.). 1-20.
Kowalik, Barbara
2010 *Betwixt* engelaunde *and* englene londe: *dialogic poetics in early English religious lyric.* Frankfurt am Main: Peter Lang.
Krueger, Roberta L.
1983 "*Floire et Blancheflor*'s literary subtext: the 'version aristocratique'". *Romance Notes* 24/1: 65-70.

Kruger, Steven F.
1995 "Medieval Christian (dis)idenifications : Muslims and Jews in Guilbert of Nogent". http.//www.geogetown.edu/labyrynth/conf/cs95/papers/kruger.html. Date of access: 2.09.2006.

Lacan, Jacques
1981 *Four fundamental concepts of psychoanalysis.* New York: W.W. Norton.

Lacan, Jacques
1992 *The ethics of psychoanalysis 1959-1960: the seminar of Jacques Lacan: ethics of psychoanalysis, 1959-60 Bk.7.* Ed. Jacques-Alain Miller. Trans. Dennis Porter. New York: Routledge.

Lampert, Lisa
1998 "'O my daughter!': 'Die schöne Jüdin' and 'Der neue Jude' in Hermann Sinsheimer's *Maria Nunnez*". *The German Quarterly.* 71/3: 254-270.

Lampert, Lisa
2004 "Race, periodity, and the (neo)Middle Ages'. *Modern Language Quarterly* 65/3: 391-421.

Lassner, Jacob
1993 *Demonizing the Queen of Sheba: boundaries of gender and culture in postbiblical Judaism and medieval Islam.* Chicago and London: The University of Chicago Press.

Le Beau, Bryan F. – Menahem Mor (eds.)
1996 *Pilgrims and travelers to the Holy Land.* Omaha, Nebraska: Creighton University Press.

Lees, Clare A.
2007 "Engendering religious desire: sex, knowledge, and Christian identity in Anglo-Saxon England". *Journal of Medieval and Early Modern Studies* 27/1: 17-45.

Le Goff, Jacques
1980 *Time, work, and culture in the Middle Ages.* Trans. Arthur Goldhammer. Chicago: The University of Chicago Press.

Le Goff, *Jacques – Nicholas Trouong*
2006 *Historia ciała w średniowieczu [Une histoire du corps au Moyen Âge].* Trans. Ireneusz Kania. Warszawa: Czytelnik.

Lentricchia, Frank – Thomas McLaughlin (eds.)
1995 *Critical terms for literary study.* Chicago – London: University of Chicago Press.

Lestringant, Frank
1997 *Cannibals: the discovery and representation of the cannibal from Columbus to Jules Verne.* Trans. Trans. Rosemary Morris. London: Polity Press.

Levinas, Emmanuel
1969 *Totality and infinity.* Trans. Alphonso Lingis. Pittsburg: Duquesne University Press.

Lewis, Bernard
1982a "Orientalism: an exchange". *New York Review of Books* 29/13: 46-8.

Lewis, Bernard
1982b "The question of Orientalism". *New York Review of Books* 29/11: 49-56.

Lewis, C.S.
1990   *Studies in words.* Cambridge: Cambridge University Press.
Lochrie, Karma – Peggy McCracken – James A. Schultz (eds.)
1997   *Constructing medieval sexuality.* Minneapolis – London: University of Minnesota Press.
Lomperis, Linda
1993   "Unruly bodies and ruling practices: Chaucer's *Physician's tale* as socially symbolic act". In: Lomperis, Linda – Sarah Stanbury (eds.). 21-37.
Lomperis, Linda – Sarah Stanbury (eds.)
1993   *Feminist approaches to the body in medieval literature.* Philadelphia: University of Pennsylvania Press.
Lomperis, Linda
2001   "Medieval travel writing and the question of race". *Journal of Medieval and Early Modern Studies* 31/1: 147-164.
Loomba, Ania
1994   "The color of patriarchy: critical difference, cultural difference, and Renaissance drama'. In: Hendricks, Margo – Patricia Parker (eds.). 17-34.
Loomba, Ania – Martin Orkin (eds.)
1998   *Post-colonial Shakespeares.* London – New York: Routledge.
Louth, Andrew
1997   "The body in Western Catholic Christianity". In: Coakley, Sarah (ed.). 111-130.
Lynch, Kathryn L.
2002   *Chaucer's cultural geography.* New York – London: Routledge.
McDonald, Nicola
2004   "Eating people and the alimentary logic of *Richard Coeur de Lion*". In: McDonald, Nicola (ed.). 124-149.
McDonald, Nicola (ed.)
2004   *Pulp fictions of medieval England: essays in popular romance.* Manchester: Manchester University Press.
Maalouf, Amin
1984   *The crusades through Arab eyes.* London: Al Saqi Books.
Madeyska, Danuta
2001   *Poetics of the sirah: a study of the Arabic chivalrous romance.* Warszawa: Academic Publishing House Dialog.
Maddox, Douglas – Sarah Sturm-Maddox (eds.)
1994   *Literary aspects of courtly culture: selected papers from the Seventh Triennial Congress of the International Courtly Literature Society. University of Massachusetts, Amherst, USA 27 July – 1 August 1992.* Cambridge: D.S. Brewer.
Maddox, Douglas – Sarah Sturm-Maddox (eds.)
1996   *Melusine of Lusignan: founding fiction in late medieval France.* Athens: University of Georgia Press.
Mani, Lata –Ruth Frankenberg
1985   "The challenge of *Orientalism*". *Economy and Society* 14: 174-192.

Martin, Luther H. – Huck Gutman – Patrick H. Hutton (eds.)
1988 *Technologies of the self: a seminar with Michel Foucault*. London: Tavistock Publications.

Meale, Carol M. (ed.)
1994 *Readings in medieval English romance*. Woodbridge, Suffolk: D.S.Brewer.

Mehan, Uppinder – David Townsend
2001 "'Nation' and the gaze of the other in eight-century Northumbria". *Comparative Literature* 53/1:1-26.

Mehl, Dieter
1968 *The Middle English romances of the thirteenth and fourteenth centuries*. London: Routledge and Kegan Paul.

Menocal, María Rosa
1987 *The Arabic role in medieval literary history: a forgotten heritage*. Philadelphia: University of Pennsylvania Press.

Menocal, María Rosa
1989 "Signs of the times: self, other and history in *Aucassin et Nicolette*". *Romanic Review* 80/4: 497-511.

Metlitzki, Dorothee
1977 *The matter of Araby in medieval England*. New Haven – London: Yale University Press.

Millar-Heggie, Bonnie
2004 "The performance of masculinity and femininity: gender transgression in *The sowdone of Babylone*". *Mirator Lokakuu* (October). At: <http://www.cc.jyu.fi/%7Emirator/index_en.html>. Date of access: 11.08.2008.

Mills, Maldwyn
1988 "General introduction". In: Mills, Maldwyn (ed.). 8-82.

Mills, Maldwyn (ed.)
1988 *Horn Childe and Maiden Rimnild, ed. from the Auchinleck Ms, National Library of Scotland, Advocates Ms 19.2.1*. Heidelberg: Carl Winter, Universitätsverlag.

Morrison, Susan Signe
2008 *Excrement in the late middle ages: sacred filth and Chaucer's fecopoetics*. Houndmills, Basingstoke: Palgrave Macmillan.

Moseley, CW.R.D.
1983 "Introduction". In: Moseley, C.W.R.D. (ed.). 9-39.

Moseley, C.W.R.D. (trans.)
1983 *The travels of sir John Mandeville*. London: Penguin Books.

Muldoon, James
1997 "Preface". In: Muldoon, James (ed.). vii-viii.

Mulddon, James (ed.)
1997 *Varieties of religious conversion in the Middle Ages*. Gainesville: University Press of 'Florida.

Mydla, Jacek
2003 "Akwinata, Kaliban i Piętaszek na wspólnym bankiecie? Ścieżki i bezdroża antykanibalizmu" [Aquinas, Caliban and Friday at a cannibalistic bonfire? The vagaries of the theology of anti-cannibalism]. *Errgo* 7/2: 9-16.

Nykl, Alois Richard
1929 *A compendium of Aljamiado literature.* New York: Protat.
Omi, Michael and Howard Winant
1994 *Racial formation in the United States from the 1960s to the 1980s.* New York – London: Routledge.
Orchard, Andy
1995 *Pride and prodigies: studies in the monsters of the* Beowulf-*Manuscript.* Cambridge: D.S. Brewer.
Osborne, Peter – Stella Sandford
2002 "Introduction". In: Osborne, Peter – Stella Sandford (eds.). 1-9.
Osborne, Peter – Stella Sandford (eds.)
2002 *Philosophies of race and ethnicity.* London – New York: Continuum.
Patterson, Orlando
1982 *Slavery and social death: a comparative study.* Cambridge, Massachusetts: Harvard University Press.
Patterson, Lee
1993 "Perpetual motion: alchemy and the technology of the self". *Studies in the Age of Chaucer* 15: 25-57.
Pearsall, Derek
1988 "The development of the Middle English romance". In: Brewer, Derek (ed.). 11-35.
Pearsall, Derek (ed.)
1990 *Studies in the Vernon Manuscript.* Cambridge: D.S. Brewer.
Pearsall, Derek
2011 "The pleasure of popular romance: a prefatory essay". In: Purdie, Rhiannon – Michael Cichon (eds.). 9-18.
Perryman, Judith
1980 "Introduction". In: Perryman, Judith (ed.). 1-69.
Perryman, Judith *(ed.)*
1980 The King of Tars. Edited from the Auchinleck MS, Advocates 19.2.1. Heidelberg: Carl Winter, Universitätsverlag.
Peterson, Joyce E.
1970 "The finished fragment: a reassessment of the Squire's tale". *The Chaucer Review* 5/ 1: 62-74.
Piwińska, Marta
2005 *Złe wychowanie [Bad upbringing].* Gdańsk: słowo/ obraz terytoria.
Plezia, Marian
1971 "Historia Tartarorum". *Studia źródłoznawcze* 15: 167-172.
Poole, Gaye
2003 "Reel meals: food and public dining, food and sex, food and revenge", in: Kalaga, Wojciech – Tadeusz Rachwał (eds.), 9-29.
Popkin, Richard H.
1999 *The Columbia history of Western philosophy.* New York: Columbia University Press.

Porter, Dennis
   1983   "Orientalism and its problems". In: Peter Hulme – Margaret Iversen – David Loxley (eds.). 179-193.
Pratt, Karen (ed.)
   1996   *Richard and Charlemagne in Europe: essays on the reception and transformation of a legend.* London: King's College London.
Pratt, Mary-Louise
   2008   *Imperial eyes: travel writing and transculturation.* 2nd edition. New York: Routledge.
Price, Jocelyn
   1982   "Floris and Blancheflour: the magic and mechanics of love". *Reading Medieval Studies* 8: 12-29.
Price, Merrall Llewelyn
   2003   *Consuming passions: the uses of cannibalism in late medieval and early modern Europe.* New York: Routledge.
Purdie, Rhiannon – Michael Cichon (eds.)
   2011   *Medieval romance, medieval contexts.* Cambridge: D.S. Brewer.
Putter, Ad
   2000   "A historical introduction". In: Putter, Ad – Jane Gilbert (eds.). 1-15.
Putter, Ad – Jane Gilbert (eds.)
   2000   *The spirit of medieval English popular romance.* Harlow: Longman.
Racheviltz, Igor de
   1971   *Papal envoys to the great khans.* London: Faber and Faber.
Radulescu, Raluca L.
   2009   "Genre and classification". In: Radulescu, Raluca L. – Cory James Rushton (eds.). 31-48.
Radulescu, Raluca L. – Cory James Rushton (eds.)
   2009   *A companion to medieval popular romance.* Cambridge: D.S. Brewer.
Ramey, Lynn Tarte
   2001   *Christian, Saracen, and genre in medieval French literature.* New York – London: Routledge.
Ramsey, Lee C.
   1983   *Chivalric romances: popular literature in medieval England.* Bloomington: Indiana University Press.
Régner-Bohler, Danielle
   1988   "Imagining the self". In: Duby, George (ed.). 311-394.
Reiss, Edmund
   1971   "Symbolic detail in medieval narrative: *Floris and Blancheflour*". *Papers on Language and Literature* 7/1: 339-350.
Reiss, Edmund
   1986   "Romance". In: Heffernan, Thomas J. (ed.). 108-129.
Rivkin, Julie – Michael Ryan (eds.)
   1998   *Literary theory: an anthology.* Oxford: Blackwell Publishing.
Roques, Mario
   1969   "Introduction". In: Roques, Mario (ed.). iii-xxxviii.

Roques, Mario (ed.)
1969 *Aucassin et Nicolette. Chantefable du XIIIe siècle*. Paris: Librairie Honoré Champion.
Rubin, Gayle
1998 "The traffic in women : notes on the 'political economy' of sex". In: Rivkin, Julie – Michael Ryan (eds.). 533-560.
Runciman, Stephen
1987 *A history of the crusades.* Vol. 3. *The kingdom of Acre and the later crusades.* Cambridge: Cambridge University Press.
Ryan, James D.
1997 "Conversion vs. baptism? European missionaries in Asia in the thirteenth and fourteenth centuries". In: Muldoon, James (ed.). 146-167.
Said, Edward W.
1994 *Orientalism.* New York: Vintage.
Said, Edward W.
2000 *Out of place: a memoir.* New York: Vintage Books.
Sands, Donald B.
1986 "Floris and Blancheflour". In: Sands, Donald B. (ed.). 279-282.
Sands, Donald B. (ed.)
1986 *Middle English verse romances.* Exeter: University of Exeter Press.
Saunders, Corinne
2004 *A companion to romance: from classical to contemporary.* Oxford: Blackwell Publishing.
Schildgen, Brenda Deen
2001 *Pagans, Tartars, Moslems, and Jews in Chaucer's* Canterbury Tales. Gainesville: University Press of Florida.
Schofield, William Henry
1903 "The story of Horn and Rimenhild". *PMLA* XVIII: 1-83.
Sénac, Philippe
1983 *L'image de l'autre: l'histoire de l'occident medieval face à Islam.* Paris: Flammarion.
Sewter, E.R.A.
1969 "Introduction". In: Sewter, E.R.A. (ed.). 11-16.
Sewter, E.R.A. (ed.)
1969 *The Alexiad of Anna Comnena.* Harmondsworth: Penguin.
Shahar, Shulamith
1994 "The old body in medieval culture". In: Kay, Sarah – Miri Rubin (eds.). 160-186.
Shimomura, Sachi
2006 *Odd bodies, visible ends.* Houndmills, Basingstoke: Palgrave Macmillan.
Shusterman, Richard
2008 *Body consciousness: a philosophy of mindfulness and somaesthetics.* Cambridge: Cambridge University Press.
Shusterman, Richard
2010 "Przemowa do wydania polskiego" [Preface to the Polish edition]. In: Shusterman, Richard. 7-10.

Shusterman, Richard
  2010   Świadomość ciała. Dociekania z zakresu somaestetyki [Body consciousness: a philosophy of mindfulness and somaesthetics]. Trans. Wojciech Małecki and Sebastian Stankiewicz. Kraków: Universitas.
Snowden, Frank M., Jr.
  1983   Before color prejudice: the ancient view of blacks. Cambridge, Massachusetts: Harvard University Press.
Sollors, Werner
  1995   "Ethnicity". In: Lentricchia, Frank – Thomas McLaughlin (eds.). 288-304.
Speed, Diane
  1990   "The Saracens of *King Horn*". *Speculum* 65: 564-595.
Speed, Diane
  1994   "The construction of the nation in medieval English romance". In: Meale, Carol M. (ed.). 135-157.
Spiegel, Gabrielle
  1996   "Maternity and monstrosity: reproductive biology in the *Roman de Mélusine*". In: Maddox, Douglas – Sarah Sturm-Maddox (eds.). 165-182.
Stallybrass, Peter – Allon White
  1986   *The politics and poetics of transgression*. London: Methuen.
Stein, Robert M. – Sandra Pierson Prior (eds.)
  2005   *Reading medieval culture: essays in honor of Robert W. Hanning*. Notre Dame, Indiana: University of Notre Dame Press.
Stoneman, Richard
  2011   "Primary sources from the classical and early medieval periods". In: Zuwiyya, Z. David (ed.). 1-20.
Strickland, Debra Higgs
  2003   *Saracens, demons, and Jews: making monsters in medieval art*. Princeton – Oxford: Princeton University Press.
Suleri, Sara
  1992   *The rhetoric of English India*. Chicago: Chicago University Press.
Tarn, W.W.
  1956   *Alexander the Great*. Boston: Beacon Press.
Taylor, Andrew
  1993   "Chaucer our Derridean contemporary?" *Exemplaria* 5: 471-86.
Taylor, Astra
  2008   *Examined life* [Film]. Sphinx Productions and the National Filmboard of Canada.
Taylor, Jane H.M.
  1996   "Melusine's progeny: patterns and perplexities". In: Maddox, Douglas – Sarah Sturm-Maddox (eds.). 165-182.
Todorova, Maria
  1997   *Imagining the Balkans*. New York: Oxford University Press.
Tolan, John V.
  2002   *Saracens: Islam in the European medieval imagination*. New York: Columbia University Press.

Tolmie, Jane – M.J. Toswell (eds.)
2010   *Laments for the lost in medieval literature.* Turnhout: Brepols Publishers.
Tomasch, Sylvia – Sealy Gilles (eds.)
1998   *Text and territory: European imagination in the European Middle Ages.* Philadelphia: University of Pennsylvania Press.
Turner, Bryan
1984   *The body and society: explorations in social theory.* Oxford: Basil Blackwell.
Turner, Bryan S.
2006   "Body". *Theory, culture & society* 23: 223-229.
Turner, Victor – Edith Turner
1995   *Image and pilgrimage in Christian culture.* New York: Columbia University Press.
Uebel, Michel
1996   "Unthinking the monster: twelfth-century responses to Saracen alterity". In: Cohen, Jeffrey Jerome (ed.). 264-291.
Veldhoen, N.H.G.E.
1988   "*Floris and Blancheflour*: to indulge the fancy and to hear of love". In: Veldhoen, N.H.G.E. – H. Aertsen (eds.). 53-68.
Veldhoen, N.H.G.E. – *H. Aertsen (eds.)*
1988   *Companion to early Middle English literature.* Amsterdam: Free University Press.
Verkerk, Dorothy Hoogland
2001   "Black servant, black demon: color ideology in the Ashburnham Pentateuch". *Journal of Medieval and Early Modern Studies* 31/1: 57-77.
Wallace, David
2004   *Pre-modern places: Calais to Surinam, Chaucer to Alphra Behn.* Malden, Massachusetts: Blackwell.
Warren, Michelle R.
2000   *History on the edge: Excalibur and the borders of Britain, 1100-1300.* Minneapolis: University of Minnesota Press.
Warton, Thomas
1824   *The history of English poetry.* Ed. Richard Price. London: Printed for T. Tegg.
Weiss, Timothy
2004   *Translating Orients: between ideology and utopia.* Toronto – Buffalo – London: University of Toronto Press.
Wentersdorf, Karl P.
1981   "Iconographic elements in *Floris and Blancheflour*". *Annuale Mediaevale* 20: 76-96.
Westrem, Scott D.
1997   "Introduction: 'From worlde into worlde'". In: Westrem, Scott D. (ed.). viii-xxxiii.
Westrem, Scott D. (ed.)
1991   *Discovering new worlds: essays on medieval exploration and imagination.* New York – London: Garland Publishing.

Wieczorkiewicz, Anna
2000   *Muzeum ludzkich ciał [The museum of human bodies]*. Gdańsk: słowo/obraz terytoria.
Wilcox, Rebecca
2004   "Greeks and Saracens in *Guy of Warwick*". In: McDonald, Nicola (ed.). 217-240.
Williams, Eric
1972   "Slavery in the West Indies". In: Winks, Robert W. (ed.). 25-37.
Windeatt, Barry
1988   "*Troilus* and the disenchantment of romance". In: Brewer, Derek (ed.). 129-147.
Winks, Robert W.
1972   "Introduction". In: Winks, Robert W. (ed.). xi-xvi.
Winks, Robert W. (ed.)
1972   *Slavery: a comparative perspective. Readings on slavery from ancient times to the present*. New York: New York University Press.
Yeager, Suzanne M.
2008   *Jerusalem in medieval narrative*. Cambridge: Cambridge University Press.
Young, Robert J.C.
1990   *White mythologies: writing history and the West*. London – New York: Routledge.
Zamperini, Alessandra
2008   *Ornament and the grotesque*. Trans. Peter Spring. London: Thames and Hudson.
Žižek, Slavoj
1992   *Looking awry: an introduction to Lacan through popular culture*. Cambridge, Massachusetts: MIT Press.
Žižek, Slavoj
2005   *The metastases of enjoyment: on women and causality*. London – New York: Verso.
Žižek, Slavoj
2008a   *The plague of fantasies*. London – New York: Verso.
Žižek, Slavoj
2008b   *The sublime object of ideology*. 2nd edition. London – New York: Verso.
Zuwiyya, Z. David
2011   "The Alexander romance in the Arabic tradition". In: Zuwiyya, Z. David (ed.). 73-112.
Zuwiyya, Z. David (ed.)
2011   *A companion to Alexander literature in the Middle Ages*. Leiden – Boston: Brill.

Studies in English Medieval Language and Literature

Edited by Jacek Fisiak

Vol. 1 Dieter Kastovsky / Arthur Mettinger (eds.): Language Contact in the History of English. 2nd, revised edition. 2003.

Vol. 2 Studies in English Historical Linguistics and Philology. A Festschrift for Akio Oizumi. Edited by Jacek Fisiak. 2002.

Vol. 3 Liliana Sikorska: *In a Manner of Morall Playe*: Social Ideologies in English Moralities and Interludes (1350-1517). 2002.

Vol. 4 Peter J. Lucas / Angela M. Lucas (eds.): Middle English from Tongue to Text. Selected Papers from the Third International Conference on Middle English: Language and Text, held at Dublin, Ireland, 1-4 July 1999. 2002.

Vol. 5 Chaucer and the Challenges of Medievalism. Studies in Honor of H. A. Kelly. Edited by Donka Minkova and Theresa Tinkle. 2003.

Vol. 6 Hanna Rutkowska: Graphemics and Morphosyntax in the *Cely Letters* (1472-88). 2003.

Vol. 7 The *Ancrene Wisse*. A Four-Manuscript Parallel Text. Preface and Parts 1-4. Edited by Tadao Kubouchi and Keiko Ikegami with John Scahill, Shoko Ono, Harumi Tanabe, Yoshiko Ota, Ayako Kobayashi and Koichi Nakamura. 2003.

Vol. 8 Joanna Bugaj: Middle Scots Inflectional System in the South-west of Scotland. 2004.

Vol. 9 Rafal Boryslawski: The Old English Riddles and the Riddlic Elements of Old English Poetry. 2004.

Vol. 10 Nikolaus Ritt / Herbert Schendl (eds.): Rethinking Middle English. Linguistic and Literary Approaches. 2005.

Vol. 11 The *Ancrene Wisse*. A Four-Manuscript Parallel Text. Parts 5–8 with Wordlists. Edited by Tadao Kubouchi and Keiko Ikegami with John Scahill, Shoko Ono, Harumi Tanabe, Yoshiko Ota, Ayako Kobayashi, Koichi Nakamura. 2005.

Vol. 12 Text and Language in Medieval English Prose. A Festschrift for Tadao Kubouchi. Edited by Akio Oizumi, Jacek Fisiak and John Scahill. 2005.

Vol. 13 Michiko Ogura (ed.): Textual and Contextual Studies in Medieval English. Towards the Reunion of Linguistics and Philology. 2006.

Vol. 14 Keiko Hamaguchi: Non-European Women in Chaucer. A Postcolonial Study. 2006.

Vol. 15 Ursula Schaefer (ed.): The Beginnings of Standardization. Language and Culture in Fourteenth-Century England. 2006.

Vol. 16 Nikolaus Ritt / Herbert Schendl / Christiane Dalton-Puffer / Dieter Kastovsky (eds): Medieval English and its Heritage. Structure, Meaning and Mechanisms of Change. 2006.

Vol. 17 Matylda Włodarczyk: Pragmatic Aspects of Reported Speech. The Case of Early Modern English Courtroom Discourse. 2007.

Vol. 18 Hans Sauer / Renate Bauer (eds.): *Beowulf* and Beyond. 2007.

Vol. 19 Gabriella Mazzon (ed.): Studies in Middle English Forms and Meanings. 2007.

Vol. 20 Alexander Bergs / Janne Skaffari (eds.): The Language of the Peterborough Chronicle. 2007.

Vol. 21 Liliana Sikorska (ed.). With the assistance of Joanna Maciulewicz: Medievalisms. The Poetics of Literary Re-Reading. 2008.

- Vol. 22 Masachiyo Amano / Michiko Ogura / Masayuki Ohkado (eds.): Historical Englishes in Varieties of Texts and Contexts. The Global COE Program, International Conference 2007. 2008.
- Vol. 23 Ewa Ciszek: Word Derivation in Early Middle English. 2008.
- Vol. 24 Andrzej M. Łęcki: Grammaticalisation Paths of *Have* in English. 2010.
- Vol. 25 Osamu Imahayashi / Yoshiyuki Nakao / Michiko Ogura (eds.): Aspects of the History of English Language and Literature. Selected Papers Read at SHELL 2009, Hiroshima. 2010.
- Vol. 26 Magdalena Bator: Obsolete Scandinavian Loanwords in English. 2010.
- Vol. 27 Anna Cichosz: The Influence of Text Type on Word Order of Old Germanic Languages. A Corpus-Based Contrastive Study of Old English and Old High German. 2010.
- Vol. 28 Jacek Fisiak / Magdalena Bator (eds.): Foreign Influences on Medieval English. 2011.
- Vol. 29 Władysław Witalisz: The Trojan Mirror. Middle English Narratives of Troy as Books of Princely Advice. 2011.
- Vol. 30 Luis Iglesias-Rábade: Semantic Erosion of Middle English Prepositions. 2011.
- Vol. 31 Barbara Kowalik: Betwixt *engelaunde* and *englene londe*. Dialogic Poetics in Early English Religious Lyric. 2010.
- Vol. 32 The Katherine Group. A Three-Manuscript Parallel Text. Seinte Katerine, Seinte Marherete, Seinte Iuliene, and Hali Meiðhad, with Wordlists. Edited by Shoko Ono and John Scahill with Keiko Ikegami, Tadao Kubouchi, Harumi Tanabe, Koichi Nakamura, Satoko Shimazaki and Koichi Kano. 2011.
- Vol. 33 Jacob Thaisen / Hanna Rutkowska (eds.): Scribes, Printers, and the Accidentals of their Texts. 2011.
- Vol. 34 Isabel Moskowich: Language Contact and Vocabulary Enrichment. Scandinavian Elements in Middle English. 2012.
- Vol. 35 Joanna Esquibel / Anna Wojtyś (eds.): Explorations in the English Language: Middle Ages and Beyond. Festschrift for Professor Jerzy Wełna on the Occasion of his 70th Birthday. 2012.
- Vol. 36 Yoshiyuki Nakao: The Structure of Chaucer´s Ambiguity. 2013.
- Vol. 37 Begoña Crespo: Change in Life, Change in Language. A Semantic Approach to the History of English. 2013.
- Vol. 38 Richard Dance / Laura Wright (eds.): The Use and Development of Middle English. Proceedings of the Sixth International Conference on Middle English, Cambridge 2008. 2012.
- Vol. 39 Michiko Ogura: Words and Expressions of Emotion in Medieval English. 2013.
- Vol. 40 Anna Czarnowus: Fantasies of the Other´s Body in Middle English Oriental Romance. 2013.

www.peterlang.de